Out of the Darkness

Coping With and Recovering From the Death of a Child

Hope, Help, and Healing Resources
For Bereaved Parents and
Anyone Touched by the Loss of a Child

Kimberly Amato

The information in this book is not meant to be a substitute for professional counseling, medical, or psychological care. The author of this book does not prescribe the use of any particular technique or treatment for medical conditions or for physical, emotional, or psychological problems. The reader is strongly encouraged to seek the advice and treatment of a physician for any of the above noted conditions.

The intent of the author is to offer general information for those searching for information, resources, support, understanding, and healing after the death of a child.

The goal of the author is to help the reader on their grief journey to spiritual, mental, emotional, and physical well-being after the loss of a child. Should you, the reader, choose to use any of the information in this book for yourself, as is your right to do, the author and publisher assume no responsibility for your actions.

ISBN-10: 1505441315
ISBN-13: 978-1505441314

you for your help in raising awareness, saving lives, and your encouragement to write this book.

- Fellow bereaved parents. None of us want to belong to this club. We are joined together by a common experience. We want to understand why. We want others to stop saying stupid things that don't help. We want others to give us what we really need. We need to help our friends and families understand not only the depths of our pain, but also their own. We need to talk about it. We need to talk about our children. We need them to talk about our children. This is for you and your families, friends, and caregivers. Thank you for sharing your stories and experiences with me and others. Let there be transparency, understanding, hope, peace, and most of all, love. This book is for you *and* for them.

- My editor, Lea Sullivan. Editing is a challenging and time consuming job. To edit a book that is of a difficult and emotional subject matter must be an exquisite challenge. I am grateful for her support, encouragement, and of course, her keen editing skills!

- My friend and cover designer extraordinaire, Steve Owen. He knew Meggie personally and was able to bring the vision I had in my head for the cover design to what it is today. He's a tremendously gifted photographer, too. Check him out on Flickr, search for sdowen.

- I would not be here today were it not for the most unlikely of a life partner. I want to thank my husband and soul mate Joe. I couldn't have done this without his support and encouragement. Joe, for all the times you have listened to me rant, tell the same stories over and over, held me when I cried, and patiently helped me edit this book, this is for you. To have you by my side, walking this path together has felt so right. It is as it should be. Accepting me for who I am, as I am, is such a gift. Thank you for saying her name and crying with me. For being an amazing step-father to all my children. For dancing with me and so beautifully expressing the song and love I have in my heart for her. I am eternally grateful. You are amazing and I love you.

- Most importantly, I want to thank my daughter, Meghan. She is my inspiration, my guide, and my heroine. My heart is broken, yet full of love and gratitude for the gifts she gave me, both in her life and in her death. I miss you terribly my beautiful little girl but I will forever hold you in my heart. I love you, Meggie Moo.

For My Meggie Moo

Because Love Never Dies

Table of Contents

o   Preface

o   Introduction

o   Advice for the Reader

o   Chapter One: Be With Me, Just for Today

o   Chapter Two: No! I Don't Want to Join This Club!

o   Chapter Three: Memories, Keepsakes, and the Importance of Grief Keeping

o   Chapter Four: Preparing to Say Goodbye and the Rituals Associated With Death

o   Chapter Five: Understanding Grief: A Survival Guide

o   Chapter Six: Supporting the Bereaved: How You Can Help

o   Chapter Seven: Expecting the Unexpected: Triggers, Holidays, and Anniversaries

o   Chapter Eight: Out of the Darkness: Finding Your way to Hope and Healing

o   Chapter Nine: The Gifts of Grief

o   Chapter Ten: Signs and Spirituality

- Chapter Eleven: The "New" You. Weaving Your Child's Memory into the Fabric of Your Life

- A Letter to Meggie

- Resources for Bereaved Parents and Those Who Support Them

- About the Author

Preface

There is a tremendous population of bereaved parents in the world and hundreds more join them every day. It's not a place they are in for a little while. It's a club they are in for the rest of their lives. You don't "get over" the death of your child. How could you? You hopefully learn to integrate their life and their death into yours. It's a lifelong journey, a roller coaster you can't ever get off of. So many bereaved parents ride it alone.

The statistics are sobering. The World Health Organization reports that in 2013, 6.3 million children under the age of five died globally, nearly half within the first month of life. The Kids Count Data Center reports that in 2011, the child and teen death (age 1-19) rate in the United States was 20,241 and the infant mortality rate (newborn to 1 year) was 23,985. In 2011, the most recent statistics available, a total of 44,226 parents lost a child. *That's at least 44,226 parents that could use the information in this book every single year in the United States alone.* Furthermore, according to the Children's Defense Fund, every day in the United States, 4 children die as a result of abuse or neglect, 5 are lost to suicide, 7 are killed by guns, 24 children die from accidents, and 66 babies die before their first birthday.

Every single day, over one hundred and twenty parents suffer the death of their child under the age of 19 in the U.S. alone! This does not count babies not yet born or adult children over the age of 19, nor does it account for those lost outside the U.S. There number of newly bereaved parents every single day is staggering.

These parents are all thrown into a world they never expected to be in and certainly don't want to be a part of. Yet they have no choice. No frame of reference. No idea how to navigate the storm. They are deeply in pain and often feel very alone and lost in their experience.

Just as a lighthouse is a beacon, shedding light and guiding ships through the darkness, so is this book. It is a guide, a companion, a source of help and hope, to assist you and them in the most difficult journey of their life.

This book is your lighthouse. It is for the parents who have had to say goodbye to their children, those who love them and support them, and those who work with them in a professional capacity. It is a source of truth, support, experience, explanation, validation, reassurance, and hope that they can and will get through this most difficult of experiences without ever forgetting about their child or the love they shared.

Introduction

I'm so very sorry that you are holding this book in your hands. If you are reading this, I presume it's because you have suffered the most horrible of losses, the death of a child you love.

If you are a bereaved parent, first, please let me extend my deepest condolences to you and your family on the loss of your precious and beautiful child. No parent should ever have to say goodbye to their child. Ever. I am so, so, sorry for your loss.

Perhaps you are reading this because you have or know of a child who is critically or terminally ill, and you are being proactive in looking for support, resources, and guidance. I applaud you for your insight and strength. I do hope this book will help you and those you care for.

If you are a grandparent or sibling, your grief is unique and just as real and deep as that of a parent. Extended family and friends can also be deeply impacted by the loss of a child they know. This book is just as much for you as it is for a bereaved parent.

Perhaps you work with families in your job who have lost a child, or, have a child who is critically or terminally ill. You might be a medical professional, EMT, or first responder, family counselor, hospital social worker, member of clergy, teacher, or another paraprofessional. Your job demands you detach from emotion in order to effectively do your job, yet it's impossible not to be impacted by the emotions that swirl around you when a family loses a child. Especially if the loss was tragic, violent, or involved more than one child. Understanding what the bereaved parents truly feel and experience will help you to more effectively help and guide them at a critical time in their grief. Allowing you to acknowledge the impact of grief on yourself and to debrief, process, and grieve is important for your own healing. You must take care of yourself, so you can effectively take care of others. No one is immune.

Perhaps your loss is very recent, or, maybe, it was many years ago. Wherever you are in your grief journey, this book holds something for you.

No matter what your reason for reading this, I thank you. You should be applauded for your courage and strength in doing so. I know it's not easy, as this book is never something you would choose to read unless you had to. Understanding you don't need to walk this road alone and the tremendous value in seeking support and guidance along the way is an important part of your healing. I'm so glad you are taking care of you.

Please, know I write this resource guide as a parent who has stood in your shoes. I, too, lost a child... a precious and beautiful 3-year-old little girl, suddenly and tragically, the Saturday before Christmas in 2004. She was my youngest of three, my only daughter, and a twin. Her name was Meghan Agnes Beck. I was devastated and felt so alone and lost... for a really long time. It was difficult to find resources and support, especially in that first week, when all sorts of decisions had to be made quickly.

The things people said and did, or sometimes, and more importantly (and unintentionally hurtful), the things they did not say or do, later made me realize they had no frame of reference. Neither did I. Even those who were supposed to have experience in guiding parents through this most awful of experiences, from some hospital employees to the religious community, gave me little comfort, and at times, a whole lot of anger and frustration. Others, though, were absolutely amazing. I don't know how I could have done it without them.

I want you to have those amazing people in and around you in your time of need. I want to teach others how to *be* one of those amazing people.

I chose to write this for *you* and for the young person you love that has left this earth too soon. I hope for it to be a guide for you. One that offers information, resources, love, light, and hope for healing as your walk this path as, or beside a bereaved parent. It's your path and yours alone to walk, but you need not walk it alone.

I know you don't know me, but consider me a friend and your personal grief mentor. I am someone who cares about you and your child... the bond you had... the pain of your loss. One who knows in many ways what you are going through and also knows it is now part of my life purpose to help you get through your journey, too.

I want to help you down this road, hand in hand, up the hills and into the valleys. I will do so with a loving energy, to help you process, understand, and recover from this most profound of losses. Together, we will get through it. You will see the light. You will find laughter and happiness again. You will come to know an existence where your child lives in your heart forever, integrated into every fabric of your being. You will gain new perspective. No, it won't ever be "normal", but it will be new and different. Full of light, love, hope, and a depth of understanding and appreciation for life you might not have otherwise had.

No, it is not an easy road to walk. No, it will never be the same, but it will be different. You will integrate the loss of this precious child into your life and learn to weave their love and light into your future. They will always live in your heart. *Always*. I know right now you can't fathom much, if any, of that, so I humbly ask your trust. From grief comes grace.

Whether you have suffered a pregnancy loss, stillbirth, the death of an infant, toddler, school aged child, or an adult child, I hope this is a helpful resource for you and for those who love you to help you walk this hard, difficult, painful, and at times, very lonely road into, through, and out of grief. I hope this will serve as the book and guide I couldn't find, but desperately looked for and wanted. The book someone should have handed to hand me when I walked out of the emergency room that sunny December morning, without my beautiful little girl. Forever changed.

Yes, I said a resource for your journey into, through, and *out* of the pain and grief. I know if your loss is recent, that right

8

now you can't imagine how it can or will get better or easier. I know the pain you feel is visceral. I know you are probably on a roller coaster of emotion from shock and disbelief to depression and profound sadness, and then suddenly angry. Really angry. Maybe you even smile or laugh once in a while and then feel guilty for it. Then you find the entire cycle begins again. I know you don't want to get out of bed, can't sleep, and feel restless, at least some of the time. Or maybe you want to sleep all the time or have kept yourself busy with work or mundane activities to distract yourself. You might be forgetful, you don't want to eat, or, maybe eat all the time, and you may not want to talk to anyone.

Or, you could want the opposite of all of those things. Maybe you wish you could either die right now to be with your child or somehow broker a deal with someone, anyone, to get them back. But you can't. It's not fair. It's not right. It sucks. I know. And I'm so, so sorry.

I can also tell you, I've been there. It's all considered a normal part of grief. It's a life-long journey, and the only way out is through. I also know, right now, none of this is probably very comforting because it just plain hurts. A lot.

No, you'll never "get over" the death of your child, even that of an adult child. They will live forever in your heart, your mind, and hopefully always around your home in the form of mementos and memories. Grieving is a life-long process, and we all grieve differently, at our own pace, in our own way, and in our own time. It can be difficult to manage any other aspect of our life, our relationships, and even any other children we might have because the work of grieving is so profound, so necessary, and so time consuming for some of us.

The most important thing is that you honor the process. Allow yourself to grieve. Nurture your soul. Nurture the love.

Let me be your guide... your bereavement doula. Historically, doulas are women who provide emotional, informational, and physical support to the parents during the childbearing year. They "mother the mother", using their inherently nurturing manner and experience to facilitate the journey for the parents. They honor and hold the space; they don't tell the parents what to do. They support and guide them, present options, and facilitate the process. I am a certified birth doula. I also have experience as a "death doula." I have had the bittersweet honor of supporting parents through the loss of their child. I have also had the honor of supporting families through the loss of an adult loved one. I know that part of my life path is to be a bereavement doula. Today, allow me to be yours.

So begin by taking a deep breath... in and out... slowly. Close your eyes and envision a loving energy around you, a bubble of light that is the love and light of your child. Feel their love. Feel your love. Feel your love mix with theirs. Isn't it beautiful? It's okay if a smile dances across your lips or if tears fall from your eyes. That's the love.

Take my hand, and let's walk together.

Advice for the Reader

Discussing death, dying, and grief are, by virtue of the subject matter, emotional. This book, of course, will evoke a variety of emotions for the reader, all of them instrumental to healing. The book contains practical, useful, and insightful information for anyone touched by the loss of a child. It also contains powerful and emotional real life examples of the experiences of bereaved parents.

Although this book was written primarily for the bereaved parent, there are chapters and sections of chapters specifically for those who support the bereaved parents in their journey. It is my belief that the entire book will provide insight, information, and support for *anyone* touched by the death of a child in any capacity.

Furthermore, much of the information presented applies to the loss of *any* loved one, not just to the death of a child. As we all will face the death of someone we love in our lifetimes, the information in this book has the potential to benefit everyone.

The chapters do not need to be read in any particular order. Although written in the typical order one might need them immediately following the loss of a child, I realize not everyone is picking up this book at the very beginning of their journey. Each chapter can stand alone as information on a particular topic related to recovering from grief. For that reason, there is some redundancy in information that is important and relative to several different chapters. I have attempted to arrange the chapters to allow for quick reference and access to information by subject matter. Subheadings within the chapters will allow for further quick identification of topics that may be of particular interest or importance.

Throughout the book, there are places I have included some of my own personal experiences. For some, real experiences, by real people are more powerful ways to convey information than simply explaining things in general terms. I have attempted to put all of these personal stories in italics. While I believe they are illustrative and helpful to understanding the journey, they are not necessary to benefit from what each chapter has to offer. If you, as the bereaved parent, are not interested in, or, ready to read my personal experiences, feel free to skip the italicized portions. I do recommend when you are ready, that you revisit them. I included them so you will know you are not alone in what you think, feel, say, or do. Many have found it resonates with what they felt or experienced and they found comfort in the similarities.

For anyone who is supporting a bereaved parent or who works with bereaved parents, siblings, and grandparents in a professional capacity, I strongly recommend you do read them. You will gain valuable insight into what really goes on inside a bereaved parent's mind, body, and soul throughout the process and be better able to support them.

Most of all take what resonates with you and leave the rest. It is my deepest hope you find whatever you need for *your* very personal journey.

Chapter One

Be with me, Just for Today

They say the best place to start is at the beginning…

In this chapter, I share my physical and emotional experience of the day my daughter Meghan died and how I choose to remember and cope with it every year on her Angelversary, as I originally wrote on the eight anniversary of her death. It took me eight years to feel comfortable sharing it on my blog with what I thought were just close family and friends. It turned out; it was shared around the world, with over a million people reading it in a matter of two weeks. What I wrote resonated with parents everywhere.

It's my hope something in it will resonate with you on some level. As a bereaved parent, perhaps, it may help you to know you are not alone in what you thought, felt, said, or did after learning your child had died. You may be able to identify with some of the emotions I describe and perhaps find comfort in knowing you shared a similar experience. You may also have had an entirely different experience, and that's okay.

I know, right now, you may not be in a place where you care to read about another parent's experience of the death of their child. You may not care what happened to Meggie right now. That's okay, too. I understand and respect that. I remember feeling that way when my grief was so fresh and raw.

You may find it difficult to read, a trigger for your own unresolved grief, and if it becomes overwhelming, stop, save it, and come back and read it later, when you feel better able to. You can still benefit greatly from the rest of this book even if you don't read this chapter first.

Many who have heard or read this story have found it immensely helpful in their journey, for various and very different and very personal reasons. They've thanked me for sharing and encouraged me to do so in this format. It's why you are reading this now. Perhaps it will bring comfort in knowing you are not alone in your experience.

It is my hope that this book will be particularly helpful for those of you who are friends and family members of bereaved parents, as well as those who support bereaved parents in a professional capacity. It is my hope that I can help you to better understand what goes on in the minds and hearts of the parents as they live through the pain and learn to cope with their loss. Day by day, and step by step, so that you have insight and tools to better understand and support them in the future.

It's not an easy story to read – Meggie's story. Death stories never are. Whether you are a health care provider, member of clergy, grief counselor, friend, or close family member, it can be very difficult to understand a parent's grief, especially while struggling with your own.

We, as a culture, don't deal with dying, death, or grief very well. Especially when the death is of a young child. I'm hoping Meggie can help change some of that. Thank you for being with me.

Adapted from my personal blog, <u>Love, Light, Laughter and Chocolate</u>.

December 18, 2012

.

Be With me. Just for Today.

Eight years ago this morning, I woke to a nightmare. One that will really never end. My beautiful 3-year old daughter, Meghan, was found lifeless under her dresser. Somehow, she managed to tip it over on herself while we slept. We did not hear it fall, for it fell onto her. She was unable to cry. She died in minutes while the rest of our family slept, her airway compressed by a drawer under the weight of the dresser. When most people see a picture of it, they are flabbergasted, expecting it to have been a much larger piece.

Every year on her the anniversary of her death, her Angelversary as we call it, I allow myself to participate in my own ritual of remembrance. It has become an essential part of my healing and coping. I eagerly wait for the rest of the family to go off to work and school, so I can have time alone with Meggie. It's difficult to go back to that day, yet it's important for me. Important that I allow myself one day to deeply grieve, to really grieve, to honor my feelings from that day to this day, to reflect on my life and how it's changed as a result of her life and of her death. It's the one day I allow myself to really *be* with the pain, to remember, and relive

15

the details of that day. For in the pain of it all, I am also reminded that there were absolute angels who helped us through.

It always starts with an overpowering sense of guilt. I am, by nature, an early riser. That day, I wanted to sleep in. In fact, our entire family did. Every year on the anniversary, I wake early and get up. My heart heavy. I desperately wish I had that day, too. Had I gotten up earlier, when she first woke up, she'd still be here with us. Instead, I told her it wasn't time to get up yet, and it was still time for sleep, and I went back to bed. That was about 4 am. She was apparently playing in her room instead of sleeping, as she often did before it was "get up time." Add to that, the fact that if we had secured her dresser to the wall, like we had taller and heavier pieces of furniture in our home, she would not have died.

The fact that I failed as a parent to keep my child safe, partially because of my own selfishness in wanting to sleep, and that resulted in her very preventable death is something I have to live with for the rest of my life. I'm sure I don't need to tell you how much that hurts. IT COULD HAVE BEEN PREVENTED! *I* could have prevented it. Yet, I did not. And now my daughter is dead.

Then, I read some of the letter I began to her on December 28th, 2004. Less than 2 weeks after she died. It's now over 400 pages long. It is a painful reminder of what I felt during those days, weeks, and months after her death. It's also a reminder of how Meghan's Hope began and grew and of the love and support we received from so many. I'm so glad I wrote it, for I've forgotten many of the details of those days,

16

and had I not recorded it in my letter to her, I'd likely not remember it now.

It always moves me to tears. I'm always surprised by what I've forgotten. Yes, they are my own words, but it brings everything back. I actually need that. There was a lot of goodness in there that came out of the pain. The acts of kindness of friends, family, neighbors, and complete strangers, who walked with us through the pain, were gifts that helped us endure the hell. The depth of my gratitude for them is difficult to convey.

I, of course, add to the letter each anniversary and periodically during the year. With the social media tools available today, I also write about it here and on her Facebook page. I vow to somehow turn the letter into a book. I don't know when I will find the time to do it, or what exactly I will write, but it is inching ever closer.

My hope in sharing all of this today is that it will touch someone, somehow, that will be compelled to DO something to prevent what happened to Meggie from happening to another child and to share the information with everyone they know. I don't want any other parent to ever know my pain.

My ritual then turns to time in her room. Some of her toys are still in a basket. Some of her clothes still hang in her closet. Her dresser is still there. It has many Meggie items on top of it. Some made by her, some given to me in memory of her. It is now secured to the wall. The irony kills me.

Her room is still her room in many ways, but it also a room for me. For us. It's the place where I scrapbook and do my bead work. A place where I go to connect with her and her memory. My scrapbook table is actually in the place her dresser was when it fell. Sometimes I simply sit and meditate. I find her room peaceful and sacred. Artwork by Meg and her twin hang on the wall. Her twin brother actually will go in there once in a while to read or listen to his iPod. He needs to be near her energy, too.

I stand in the doorway to her room and pause. I close my eyes. I allow myself to remember my husband screaming my name "Kim, oh God, KIIIIIMMMMM" and being woken from a deep sleep knowing instantly something horrible had happened from the tone of his voice. I remember running into her room, seeing her tiny, beautiful body, pale and blue, lifeless on the floor. He had thrown the dresser off of her and placed her on the floor. At that point, I still did not know what happened. I remember my older son, then 6, literally freaking out by her head, crying and yelling, "What happened to Meggie... is she okay... Mommy make her wake up, MAKE HER WAKE UP!"

I remember doing CPR, simultaneously begging her to come back to us and yet knowing in my heart it was already too late. I remember her twin, also just three, kneeling at her feet, quietly saying, "Mommy, Meggie not wake up." It was not a question. It was a statement of spiritual fact. He knew she was gone on a different level. He was not upset. It was as if he just... was privilege to a knowledge we did not have.

I remember my husband falling down the stairs trying to get the door for what he thought were the EMT's, but was actually a young neighbor who was an EMT, who heard the call on the police scanner. I remember him walking into the room behind me and audibly gasping. I remember the EMTs arriving and taking over CPR. I remember running frantically into my room to change my clothes, (I still have the sweatshirt I last held her in. I can't bear to part with it) and then running outside in bare feet in the cold December morning to yell to ambulance to ask which hospital they were taking her to. I remember flying to the car in a panic and nearly running over neighbors who were already flocking to our house to help and support us as I backed out of the driveway. I was in such a panic; I almost left without my husband or my purse!

I have no idea how I drove. I shouldn't have. I had no idea how to get to the hospital, yet I managed to get there. It was a Saturday. All I could think was "it's been more than six minutes." Although none of us knew how long she had been under the dresser or not breathing, I knew on a soul level she was gone. We hoped with all that we were that they would bring her back. Miracles happen, right? What I would have given for a Christmas miracle that morning...

I remember, very vividly, walking into the ER at the local community hospital. By then, I was having chest pain. Like really serious chest pain. I was pretty sure I was having a heart attack from the stress. My heart was breaking... literally. I felt it. It hurt. Like hell. I can actually still feel the visceral pain of it when I allow myself to fully go back to that day. I felt like I'd pass out... my head was spinning, my vision was fuzzy, and my legs were as heavy as cement. I could barely breathe. Walking was such an effort and so very slow and unsteady. I have no idea how I managed to put

19

one foot in front of the other. I really thought I was dying myself right then. I remember the girl at the check in desk, telling her I was here and my daughter was just brought in by ambulance. She told me they'd be right with me and not to worry, she was sure it would be okay. I literally almost slapped her across the face. I wanted to scream at her, "She's dead! What the hell do you mean it will be f*cking okay?!" Instead, I just walked away.

I remember the little room, the kind woman (a nurse or chaplain maybe) who sat with us. Who brought me ginger ale and tissues, which I asked for in the hopes it would quell the nausea and keep me from passing out, because it is nothing short of a miracle I did not hit the floor. She prayed with us, because clearly, we needed it, and there was little else we could do. I remember talking to our neighbor, also an ER doctor, who was part of the team caring for her. The look on his face said everything, but they were opting to Life Flight her to a trauma hospital. He said it didn't look good, but they were not giving up yet.

We were allowed to see her before they took her. I was vaguely aware of the many people around her, yet all I saw was her beautiful face. I ducked under someone's arm and kissed her, stroked her silky blonde hair, and told her I loved her. That I would see her at the next hospital. I remember thinking she'd have loved the helicopter ride. She always wanted to fly. There were tears in the eyes of the staff tending to her. A few later posted on the guest book of the Meghan's Hope website and their words were so sweet and kind. I remember one nurse saying she promised me Meggie was well loved and deeply cared for by everyone who tended to her that morning in the ER. I was so touched she had reached out like that for it brought me comfort.

One of the EMT's drove us to the next hospital. I remember trying to sit in the car seat in the back seat, unable to process that I should remove it and sit in the regular seat, or even figure out how to remove the car seat. I just stood there and stared at it. The EMT did it for us. He was a wonderful man. We tried to call at least one family member to let them know what was happening, so they could share with others. I called to see how the boys were doing since we left in chaos, essentially leaving them with people they barely knew. I was told our babysitter, who knew them well, was already with them, and the entire neighborhood was in our house holding vigil. It gave me some peace of mind that I needn't worry about them. I called my sister who let everyone else know. Thank goodness for cell phone contacts. I couldn't remember anyone's phone number.

When we arrived at the trauma hospital, we were led to the God-awful room. You know the one. Where the priest is waiting with you and your family to hear the words you don't want to hear. Thankfully, there was no one else there yet that morning in the ER. It wasn't long before a very uneasy looking resident and the trauma chief, who had on a lovely Christmas tie (odd what you remember), said something to the effect of "blah, blah, blah... I'm very sorry, but Meghan had died." It was like the Charlie Brown voice... slow and distant and mumbly. They really didn't tell me anything I didn't already know, but now it was official. There was no more hope. It was over. My baby girl was gone forever. I couldn't have hurt any more than I already did. So I bowed my head, took a deep breath, and asked to see her. I wanted

21

to cry but I don't remember if I did or could. I don't remember who else was in that room with us. All I wanted to do at that moment was to see her. It was a few minutes before the nurse came back and said we were able to see her.

Let me say, the pediatric trauma nurses rock. How they do it, I'll never know. The priest accompanied us. Quite frankly, I found him irritating. I'm not sure if it was just my reaction to her death or if he was really annoying. He did not comfort me at all. He read the 23rd Psalm. It took every ounce of my being not to tell him to shut up. It did NOT help. He left. Rather, I dismissed him, thanking him, but not sure what for.

Meggie looked so peaceful... a true sleeping beauty. If only a kiss could really bring her back to us! I actually wish we had a picture of her then. She was SO beautiful and so at peace. Her color was better thanks to an hour or more of CPR.

The nurses asked if they could call anyone for us. I couldn't remember phone numbers. I couldn't even dial a phone. One of the nurses got me a chair, so I could sit by the phone while they looked up numbers. They dialed for me. They held the phone to my ear because I was shaking so badly I couldn't even hold it. How do you tell your parents their granddaughter is dead? They stood behind me with their hands on my shoulders and rubbed my back while I told my parents. I think they also talked to them since I was likely incoherent. I don't remember what I said. The nurses also called my uncle, the deacon, who baptized Meghan, almost three years earlier, and asked him to come for me. All I could tell them was his name and what town he lived in, they did the rest. When he came, I sobbed into his belly. It was the first good cry I had. He was my spiritual comfort. Then I looked up at him and smiled through the tears, a comforting thought and connection coming to me. "She's with Gram!" I said. We knew Gram would take care of her.

The nurses asked if I'd like to hold her. Of course, I said yes. I'd have held her forever if I could have. One nurse brought me a rocking chair, placed my beautiful daughter in my arms, and covered us both with a warm blanket. I rocked her and held her little hand. So delicate and tiny... so sweet. I stared and stared and stared at her face. It was surreal. How could she really be gone? I kissed her. Often. I talked to her. I cried. But mostly, I stared at her and loved her. The nurses gave us our space but checked on us often.

The nurses asked if we'd like to make hand/foot prints for us and the boys. They helped us paint a hand and a foot pink and purple and stamp several pieces of paper with them. The "Meggie prints" hang to this day in her brothers' rooms. The nurses also made a little soft plaster heart, and together we imprinted her hand and a foot on it. They added a little pink bow. It sits on our mantle now.

Eventually, the nurses placed her back on the bed. Other family members were invited to see her and say goodbye. Then, we had a bit more time with her. After about an hour and a half, they gently encouraged us to say goodbye. This was as much from a practical physiological standpoint as it was psychological for us in need. We were blessed to have all that time alone in the trauma room with her, with no one else in the ER that morning. For that, I am grateful.

I left the hospital with a cardboard box that had the painted hand and foot prints, a lock of her hair, and the plaster heart. My own heart shattered into a zillion pieces. The social worker handed me a brochure on grief. I just stared at it in disbelief. As if this little piece of paper was going to help at all.

I remember it was a beautiful day for December. The sky was blue; it was in the 40's. I glanced at the sky. Were you up there, Meg? I wondered where our car was as we waited for my brother-in-law to get his car. The EMT had driven it home for us. I stood there in complete shock. Getting irritated at the smiles on other people's faces. I hated that their child wasn't dead and mine was. It was surreal. How was I going to tell the boys? How was I going to do this? MY DAUGHTER IS DEAD! How could I be living this nightmare? OMG, I have to plan a funeral. For my daughter! This couldn't be real. Yet, I knew it was. So painfully real. I wanted to run away. I wanted to die. I wanted to get the hell home to my boys.

I had to go home and tell my boys. I ended up telling them sitting on the kitchen floor of a neighbor's house. When I arrived, they immediately clamored into my lap and asked if Meggie was okay. They were clearly hoping for good news. Everyone was. I gently told them the truth, which was Meggie had died. She was never coming home with us again. The pain on their faces exponentially deepened my own pain. How could a 3 and 6-year old comprehend the death of their sister when their parents could not? We walked home, without our Meggie... and our lives have never, ever been the same.

I sat on the couch and stared at the Christmas tree, snuggled with her twin. I sat. I stared. That's all I did... for hours... for days. I couldn't function. I didn't want to function. My family wisely left me alone. They gathered downstairs and did their own grieving. I think there was pizza.

Not long after returning home, we went into Meggie's room. Her twin gently and methodically cleaned up all the clothes she had thrown all over the room and put her toys away. All on his own. When he was done, he quietly said, "There," and sat in my lap. It was as if he was comforting us. He continued to talk to her and play with her. It was comforting to know that just maybe, he *could* still see her. My husband turned the dresser to the wall, so the drawers could not open. It could never tip again.

I was starting to get pissed. When darkness fell, I went outside and swung on her favorite swing under the stars. I wondered what they looked like from the other side. I thought about how she always wanted to "fly in the sky!" I started to cry. Sob. Loud, uncontrollable sobs. Finally. I was able to release that pain, the grief, the sadness of the day. I've never cried so hard and so long in my life. God and the Universe got a loud what for that night, directed toward the sky. I screamed, I cried, I threw myself on the ground in complete and utter despair and sobbed. Neighborhood dogs barked like crazy at my outburst. I didn't care. My daughter was dead. It was wrong. It was unfair. It was my fault. It hurt. So. Damn. Much.

I come back/return to the present now, and sit on her floor. I take out her jammies. The ones she was wearing that day. Cut off by the EMT's. I lay them out on the floor. They look so small now. I lay next to them. I imagine she's with me. Can you see her? I can. I touch them. I smell them. I cry. Because although she may be with me in spirit, she is not here physically. I miss her.

I open the purple bin. The one that holds all the cards and little gifts we received, the trinkets left for her, the guest book from her wake. I go through them. Bolstered by the outpouring of love and support we received.

I go through her clothes. Remembering what she loved about each thing. What I loved about each thing. I smell them, trying to smell her. Of course, I can't. It's been too long. But I try. Every year, I try. I hold the little red velvet skirt with white embroidery and the black turtleneck sweater I bought for her to wear for Christmas that year. It still has the tags, for she died before she could ever wear it. She'd have been so pretty in it! I hold the Marie, the cat from the Aristocats, one of her favorite movies. A Christmas gift she never saw either, but would have been SO excited to have. I slept with one of her stuffed kitties last night.

I wrap myself in the quilt made of her clothes, I snuggle one of her stuffed kitties. I smell it, hoping to smell her again. Of course, now it's been too long, but I still try. I look at her windows, still smeared with her finger prints, now dusty and even a wee bit moldy in spots, yet I cannot bear to clean them. I close my eyes, and I quietly try to be with her. Her memory, her spirit, her essence. There are tears. There are smiles.

There are more tears. I open her dresser drawers and wonder how the hell she managed to tip it over. What was she doing? Why was she doing it? What did she think? What did she feel? Was she scared? How a zillion other things could have happened and she'd have survived, but the pure physics of the situation instead led to a tragic outcome. I ask an unanswered, why? Why her? Why me? Why this way? Why at all? The whys get more angry and insistent. Why, why, why, why WHY?!

Then, I write.

That was only the beginning of a long and painful road, eight years long today. One I will walk for the rest of my life. Without my daughter. One that *I* could have prevented.

So, when people ask me why they should secure their furniture, I'd like to tell them this story. I'd like for them to feel what it's like to live with the pain, the guilt, the hole in your heart that will never ever be "fixed." Maybe, if the words don't compel you to do something, perhaps raw, visceral emotion will. Perhaps, knowing what your life might be like if you don't take action, will motivate you.

I don't, of course, tell the whole story every time someone asks why. Who would listen? Besides, it takes too long and is too painful to relive that often. Feel free to direct anyone to Meghan's story if you think it will help motivate them to act.

Here is my rant: What really pisses me off is knowing that people who know us, who knew her, who came to her wake and funeral, who have heard her story, who have children or children who visit their home and still, they choose to do nothing. The people who I ask to share the links to her website and Facebook page, especially on this day, and don't. That hurts me. Deeply.

I don't get it. I just don't. I'd be lying to say there are not times where I wonder WTF? Why not their kid? (I immediately hate myself for that thought) Why mine? Why not try to help someone else even if you don't believe it's a risk for you or your children? Everyone has furniture. Nearly everyone has a TV. Every child is at risk. Even adults are at risk! Why the hell do so many people think "it" can't happen to them? Ignorance is not bliss! It's stupid! If it can happen to me, it can happen to you. It doesn't matter who you are or what "it" is!

I'll never know all the answers. The simple answer to why Meghan died is because her dresser was not secured. Five dollars and fifteen minutes would have saved her life. It's that simple. Why she died when dressers have fallen on so many other children who were luckier and were not injured is not for me to answer. I'm glad for them that they were so fortunate. I hate that it was my daughter and our family who suffered this tragedy with deadly consequences.

All I can do now is try to educate as many people as I can about these dangers, so it never happens to another child again. So no other mother ever feels the pain I do. So no one need bury their child because of something that could have easily been prevented.

No one should have to experience what I did eight years ago today. No one. If everyone secured their furniture and TV's, no one would ever know the pain of this tragedy again. So please. Just do it.

So, I ask you. Have you shared Meghan's story with everyone you can? Have you secured ALL of your furniture and your TV's? Even if your children are older, do younger children visit your home? You must consider them, too. Have you "liked" the Meghan's Hope Facebook page, so you can be informed of all manner of child safety information? Have you been to The Meghan's Hope website? What about those at the homes of friends and family where your child visits? Have the furniture and TV's been secured there?

Yes? Thank you, thank you, thank you!

No? I'm sorry, but WTF is wrong with you? Most days, I don't judge. Today, I do. Today, when I'm so deep in the pain I just can't fathom why anyone wouldn't do everything they can to avoid ever knowing this horror. I just don't get it.

Current statistics are that 71 children are injured every single day in the U.S. from a falling piece of furniture or TV. More than 30 people every year lose their lives. Most of them are children. Even one death or injury is too many. They can ALL be prevented. Every single one of them. I am not the only parent who has lost a child this way, none of us knew of the dangers or thought it could happen to us. This is why I want you to help me raise awareness. These numbers are likely underestimated due to reporting methods; not all of these injuries and deaths are reported as the result of tip-over accidents.

Thank you for listening and for being with me. Now, "You listen to Meggie!" Go share her story and secure your furniture and TV's.

Addendum December 18, 2013:

It is with tremendous gratitude and a humble heart that Meghan's Hope has literally touched people around the world. I spent eight years trying as best I could to mother Meghan the only way I could after she died. By sharing her message in the hopes no other parent would ever have to experience what I did and have. Meghan's death was preventable. It's as simple as that. $5 and 15 minutes of our time would have saved her life. We didn't believe she could die from her small dresser falling on her. We were wrong. No parent should ever suffer the pain of this loss. No child should ever die from something that could have been prevented but wasn't because of a parent's lack of knowledge, or worse, blatant ignorance of the risk.

Meghan's Hope was born just hours after her death and became a non-profit. It eventually changed into just an educational and informational organization. Out of my beautiful daughter's death was born a life-saving campaign. A mission. Advocacy is not for everyone, but it is how I continue to mother her.

I began to specialize in teaching home and child safety classes and became certified as a CPR and First Aid Instructor. I spoke to moms' groups and local organizations and at conferences. I attended safety fairs and exhibited. I wrote to members of Congress, furniture retailers, and manufacturers. We had two bills in the US House of Representatives. My pleas for help from the industry and our government fell on deaf, ignorant and fearful ears. My ability to devote time to it decreased as my need to go back to work full time became imperative. I was frustrated; I could not accomplish what I wanted. It seemed simple enough.

Educate parents and help them understand the risks and teach them what to do to prevent this from happening to their child. So why was it not working?

Fear? Ignorance? Politics? Parents never believe "it" will happen to them. Did you ever think your child would be the one who would die? Of course not. None of us ever do. These horrible things only happen to other people. To "bad" or unfortunate parents. We are all too good at parenting to ever let anything happen to our children.

Those of us in need of this book now know all too well that's simply not true. We can't possibly protect our children from everything. We can be the best, most attentive parent in the world, but we are still not there 24/7. We must be pro-active. We must educate and save lives…

With the advent of social media, it became easier to share information. I started a blog, because, well, you might have noticed, I like to write. I started a Facebook Page for Meghan's Hope. I had about 500 likes before Meghan's Angelversary day in December of 2012.

On Meghan's Angelversary day 2012, I wrote the blog post you just read as this chapter on my personal blog Love, Light, Laughter, and Chocolate. My intent was to express for the first time to my close friends and family (really, the small handful of people who actually ever read anything I ever blogged about) what I really went through both the day Meghan died and every year since. I was frustrated. I wanted to compel them to share her story, her website, and her Facebook page and help me spread Meghan's Hope.

Help me save a life and honor hers. Please, for the love of God, help me!

Much to my shock and amazement, it was not only read, but shared. Someone shared it on a new moms' message board, and it went viral. In a matter of days it had been read a million times, and I received thousands of messages from all over the world thanking me for sharing in such a raw, real way. For compelling them to take this issue seriously. For saving their child's life. Many a tearful father wrote to me saying they were leaving work in the middle of the day to go buy furniture straps and install them as soon as they got home. I couldn't keep up with all the messages. I was absolutely blown away. Finally! Finally, they were listening to Meggie! I was so thankful. I wondered why I hadn't thought of it before. The reason was simple. I wasn't ready to put it out there yet. I was not at a point in my grief where I was ready.

Meggie is the reason you are holding this book in your hands. The part death story, part love story between a mother and daughter that was originally written as a blog post is how this book was born. You might have already read the blog post before picking up this book. The feedback I received from other bereaved parents, health care professionals, and the family members of other bereaved parents was tremendous. They were thankful for the insight. Bereaved parents wrote and said they, too, felt much the same way I did, and thought they were alone. They were afraid to share how they felt, until they read our story and felt comfortable sharing with me.

If our story helps just one person, this labor of love is worth it. I hope beyond hope, that person is you.

Thank you for being with me. Now please, let me be with you. Join me, and let's journey through grief to gratitude and grace, together.

Chapter Two

No! I Don't Want to Join This Club!

It's likely you are reading this book as a bereaved parent. Perhaps you are a grandparent, sibling, aunt, or uncle who has lost a child near and dear to your heart. Maybe you are a friend or a teacher. You may even be a health care professional or a mental health professional. You are all holding this book for the same reason. You have been touched by the death of a child. I am so very sorry for your loss.

None of us ever thought we'd be here... in *this* place... a lifetime member of *this* club. Holding *this* book. It may have been our worst fear, but it was never a place any of us expected we'd actually be. Certainly not a place we could ever have imagined being... never a place anyone should have to be.

Yet, we are here. We've been indoctrinated into a club no one wants to belong to. It wasn't by choice. It's not a nightmare we will wake from. It's our new reality. It's not fair. It's not right. It hurts like hell. It's dark and heavy like a lead blanket upon our shattered hearts.

It hurts... to think... to breathe... to remember. To not remember. To hear their name. To not hear their name. To laugh. To cry. To move. To live.

But not to love. No… it doesn't hurt to love. Love is what brought them here. Love is what brought them to us. Love is what keeps them alive in our hearts and in our memory. Love is powerful. More powerful than the pain.

It hurts *because* we love. Not because we loved them. Because we love them. LOVE. Present tense. Always. *It hurts because we love.* We still love them. We will always love them. They will always love us. The heart will and does go on. Because of love.

I know you don't want to walk this road. Neither do I. We have but two choices. To stand still in this mind-numbing place forever, or to follow the path before us to healing. I know right now it may seem impossible. Perhaps your loss is very recent. Perhaps it was less recent but you are wondering why it's still hard sometimes or maybe all of the time.

Don't worry. You can do this. It won't be easy, but you will get through it. *I promise you, right now, you are not alone.* You have at the very least, me. Your very own bereavement doula. A guide. Take my hand and let's walk together.

Understanding the Impact of Learning your Child has Died
There is so much to say about grief that it's hard to know where to begin. Conventional wisdom suggests one start at the beginning. In this case, that would be the experience of finding out your child is going to die or has died.

You would think the first day is the worst. It often is. More appropriately, it is the first of many worst days. There is no quantifying them. Your child has died. You cannot know any greater pain.

How you find out about the death of a child, especially if it is your own, can impact how you grieve. Not that it makes it truly any easier, for there is nothing easy about it. Certainly, the circumstances around how your child died can impact your experience in significant ways. Everyone will process their experience differently, even in similar circumstances. There is no right or wrong way.

Anticipatory Grief: Knowing a Child is Going to Die

Having a child who is terminally ill, or who has an unexpected critical illness from an injury or accident, or, perhaps a child who you are choosing to remove from life support affords a bittersweet opportunity many parents don't have. The opportunity to prepare, both emotionally and practically, for your child's passing.

There is often time to prepare for the post-death rituals of your culture, such as a funeral or memorial service. These parents have the opportunity to get support from loved ones and the guidance and support of professionals *before* their child dies. The opportunity to ask questions. To begin letting go in a way that is meaningful for them. They often have more control over the situation, because it wasn't completely unexpected. They have the opportunity to notify and gather family and friends before and after the child passes. *They get the chance for everyone to say goodbye.*

It doesn't lessen the pain of their death, but it does make the experience a bit different from parents who didn't have those opportunities. Many have had the gift of being able to hold their child in their arms or hold their hands when they took their last breath. To be surrounded and supported by those who love them. This can be incredibly important to some parents, although not everyone feels that way.

I have heard some absolutely amazing and beautiful death stories about how families have prepared and gathered to surround the child with love and loved ones, often with their child's favorite things or favorite music playing as they transitioned from their earthly life. Some singing favorite songs or reading favorite books to the child. The strength and love of these families is inspiring.

I will always wish I had that opportunity. One of the hardest aspects for me to process and accept with regard to my own daughter's death is that she died alone. She was one room away from me, but she died alone. Her death was tragic and unexpected, but as her mother, I still struggle with the guilt I wasn't there when she left this world. The fact it was just over three years since I had brought her into the world, along with the tragic and sudden circumstances of her death, further complicated the guilt, and thus, the pain.

Sometimes you just don't know if you will want to be present when your child dies, if given the opportunity. Sometimes, the child decides for you. They will transition when you are not with them, sometimes, right after you leave their room. This is not unusual or uncommon, but it can be difficult for parents who wanted to be there and a blessing to those who could not bear to see their child take their last breath.

Not Being Able to say Goodbye

For parents who didn't get a choice about saying goodbye, their grief can be compounded. The death of a child is hard enough. Waking up to find your child has died, getting that awful phone call about a freak accident and rushing to the hospital hoping beyond hope everything would be okay, only to learn your child has died, is traumatic to say the least. If your child's death was the result of violence, suicide, drug overdose, or one that involved another child or family member, it can further complicate grief. Having the experience of being there and bearing witness to an accident that took the life of your child is also tremendously difficult for parents. It all impacts your experience of that first day and the entire grieving process. For some, it can lead to the added complication of posttraumatic stress.

The common denominator in these situations, no matter how the child died, was that you had no time to prepare. You were literally blindsided. You had no idea your child was going to die. You were a happy normal family one minute and literally shattered as your world came crashing down around you the next. You didn't get to say goodbye when they were alive. You may be racked with guilt for a gazillion reasons, like things you said or didn't say that day or the day before, yet it's over. Just like that. You thought your day, your life, would be like any other, and literally, in an instant, it and your child, was snatched from you.

Those Dreaded Words

Nothing is worse than being told your child has died. *Nothing.* Whether you expected it or not. Nothing can really prepare you for the experience. It doesn't matter whether that child was not yet born or a grandparent themselves. The loss of a child at any age is devastating to a parent. Once a parent, always a parent.

Unless you've been through it before, no one can ever really know or ever imagine what it's like. It's not the same as losing a pet, a grandparent, or even another close family member or spouse. Although people will try to tell you they "know what it is like" because they lost so-and-so, they don't know. They have no idea. Even if they have lost a child, their experience, the age of their child when they died, the circumstances of the child's death, and their beliefs around death and dying may be very different from yours and, therefore, you can, and often do, feel very much alone and lost in the fog. Your experience of loss is yours and yours alone.

If you are a spouse, friend, family member or loved one, co-worker, member of clergy, teacher, health care worker or counselor who works with bereaved families; this is a very important thing to remember. You don't know how they feel, so don't say you do or that you can "imagine" how they feel. Just don't. Please don't tell them how they should or shouldn't feel, either. They feel what they feel, and it's real. They cannot help how they feel. They cannot control it. They cannot choose it. It is what it is to them in that moment and it may change... frequently and frustratingly. You have to respect that and be with them where they are and not try to convince them how they *should* feel instead.

I am so grateful that you are reading this book, because it will give you a glimpse into what it's like to live that hell as a bereaved parent and it will make you a better friend, a better counselor, a better health care provider, and a better support

40

to anyone who is grieving. I have gotten feedback from many people who read my blog post about the day Meghan died. Many thanked me for giving them a glimpse into what it's like from the parent's perspective, saying it helped them to be more empathetic because they had no idea what bereaved parents truly experienced. Especially nurses and doctors who often are the ones to first tell parents their child has died and provide the initial support. I am so grateful that you care enough to read this book in order to better understand and help those you serve.

The First Day - Learning Your Child has Died

That first day is often a mix of panic, disbelief, and fear until you are officially told your child has died. There is often an agonizing trip to and wait at a hospital. Even if you had a long time to prepare for the death of your child, it's never enough. Even if you are there with them, when it's actually about to happen, you are often frozen in disbelief and experiencing a roller coaster of emotion. You play the bargaining game. You want them to be at peace, but you also desperately want them to stay present with you and somehow be okay. It's an agonizing dance of love and loss.

Then, once you are told your child has died, the world collapses around you. It often feels as if it has collapsed right on top of you. The color drains from the world around you. You go into shock... physically and emotionally... perhaps, even spiritually. It's unfathomable until you live it. Even then, it's surreal.

Common Physical and Emotional Reactions

Many people experience physical symptoms. You may have chest pain and feel as if you are having a heart attack. You may feel as if you can't breathe; you might (or do) pass out. You may feel sick to your stomach or throw up. You may feel dizzy or lightheaded. Your legs may feel heavy, like they are made of cement. You may feel shaky and weak, so much so that you cannot stand or walk. You may want to say something, but be unable to make the words come out. You may behave as if nothing has happened at all and keep talking and functioning as if your day would be like any other. Denial is powerful.

As you would expect, strong reactions are common. You may scream, cry hysterically and uncontrollably, lash out in anger, fall to your knees, or sit completely still and emotionless and say and do nothing. You may want to cry or express how you feel and be unable to. You may simply refuse to believe it and say so. You may shut down and be unable to process any of it. You may withdraw and become instantly and profoundly depressed. You might hope the doctors are wrong; that a miracle will happen. You may direct your anger toward the medical staff or another person by physically or verbally lashing out. You may even be angry with your child and lash out at them verbally. Some people just want to die themselves, so they can be with their child. You probably can't think straight. Your memory may be completely non-functional and you may find that you can't remember anything at all... even the simplest things like your phone number or address.

In some cases, you or another family member may have to identify your child. This is often the case in abduction, a criminal or violent death, or any death where your child was taken to the hospital and died before you arrived. Needless to say, this can be tremendously traumatic. It's recommended you not go alone to identify your child. Ideally, someone else in the family or a good friend should accompany you along with a member of clergy and/or a social worker from the hospital in order to prepare and support you during and after this most difficult of circumstances. In some cases, another family member can be the one to identify your child, especially if it is too hard for the parents to do.

You may desperately want to see or be with your child and never, ever leave them, or you may be unable to bring yourself to see them or spend time with them after they have died. Either way, it's okay. You may run out of the room and have to leave wherever you are. Your spouse and other family members and friends may have completely different reactions. I wrote about my experience of learning how my daughter had died in Chapter One. If you have not read it yet, you may find it helpful to read or reread it.

Everyone is in the experience of this tragedy together, but yet so alone in their personal experience of the moment they find out. This is true of the journey of grief in general. It's a lonely and intensely personal and individual road, despite the company we have along the way.

The good news is these are all common and normal ways to react to the news a child you love has died. It's common to ride the roller coaster of physical and emotional symptoms of grief for a long time following the death of a child, but those first few days and weeks are by far, the worst. One of the greatest sources of comfort to a bereaved parent is to realize that what they are feeling, thinking, and experiencing is normal. That they are not "crazy." That they are not the only ones to feel this way. That others have been through it and have found their way out of the darkness. That was a significant reason why I wanted to write this book. For you.

How we learn about a child's death and what we do with that information is incredibly important to our experience of death and healing. How we are informed about the death of our own child or one we know and care for is a significant part of the journey.

Especially for Those who Deliver the News
If you are the one who must deliver the news to the parents that a child has died, chances are you are a health care provider, first responder, or para-professional. Knowing the different ways parents may react to the news their child has died, no matter how old that child was, and understanding they are all normal reactions, is essential. Being able to reassure them of that is very important to their processing.

When parents do want to see and spend time with their deceased child, there are some very important things that must be taken into consideration.

- Preparing the parents for what the child and room will look like is very important. This is especially important if there are machines around or tubes and wires still attached from medical procedures.
- Finding as quiet and as secluded place as possible for the parents to have uninterrupted time to spend with their child is important. If there is a way to turn down a hospital intercom or paging system, it should be done.
- Tending to them and supporting them is also very important. A nurse or other representative should remain present with them at all times. You don't

need to hover, but make your availability known and check on how the parents are handling this most difficult task frequently.

- Helping parents call loved ones or summoning a member of their religious preference is often needed.
- Helping parents create memories in the form of hand or foot prints, saving a lock of hair, even taking photographs, can be a wonderful gift for them.
- Offering food and water and making sure they are physically stable themselves is another aspect of the health care provider's role.
- Realizing they will need ample warning and time to prepare to leave their child is also important. Separation is the most difficult thing for parents who just want to hold and look at their child forever. They will also need to know what will happen with their child after they leave them. Where will they go? How will they get there? When can they see them again?

If the parents are unable or don't want to see their deceased child, it's not because they love them any less. They are just not in a place where they feel they are ready or able to see their deceased child, and that's okay.

Helping Parents Create Keepsakes

In this case, creating memories for them to look at when they are ready is often very much appreciated. Even if the parents do not ask for them. Many hospitals and even police officers will hold on to these items, or other personal effects, until the parents ask for them or, they will reach out to the parents to ask if they'd like them months after the child's death. This is especially true of perinatal loss, stillbirth, and infant loss. Photographs, often black and white, can be done beautifully and tastefully. Organizations, like Now I Lay Me Down to Sleep, have professional bereavement photographers who will photograph children and families before or at/after the time of their death for free. Their photographs are so amazingly touching and a truly beautiful keepsake.

Other things done around the time of death that can be a keepsake and mean a lot to parents are:

- Creating hand and foot prints or plaster molds.
- Saving a lock of hair.
- Saving the clothes the child was wearing or the hospital hat, blanket, and T-shirt in the case of an infant.
- Saving any jewelry they may have been wearing.
- Some hospitals have bereavement kits especially for premature and stillborn babies that include all of these things plus a little outfit and hat and naming certificate.
- Writing down any information that the older or adult child might have said prior to their death, or observations made by staff that the parents might find comforting is also a tremendous gift.

Any and all of these things can be placed in a box or envelope and given to the parents to open when they are ready.

Who Gives the Parents the News Their Child has Died and Why it Matters How the Parents are Told

If you are the parent, you are most likely told by a physician or a police officer that your child has died. If you are a family member or friend, you may find out from the parents, another family member or friend, a co-worker, or perhaps even on the news. Whether you knew it was going to happen for years because of a progressive or terminal illness, or the death was sudden and unexpected, the pain is no different.

How you are told and what support comes along with that information can make a big difference in the experience.

The experience of the moment you first find out a child you love has died and the days that follow will be as individual as that precious child. There are things, however, that can help or, potentially add salt to the wound so to speak. We will explore these in greater depth in later chapters.

There are so many ways that parents, family members, and friends can first learn of the death of a child. One would hope that this news is delivered as gently and lovingly as possible and respect given to the parents and siblings to absorb and adjust before the news is spread.

This is not always possible due to the news media or even well-meaning, but inadvertently disrespectful friends and family, who share information with others before hearing it directly from you. Never thinking a close relative or friend might hear it from someone other than their family member. Sometimes this is how grandparents or siblings hear of a death, and it makes it all that much more traumatic!

It's important to realize how the parents and loved ones are told the child has died makes a difference. It's also important to realize that it's not your place as a member of health care, school community, an extended family member, friend, or acquaintance to share the news of that child's death publicly without the family's permission. Until it is truly public knowledge, (a media story or obituary), and even then, you should be very careful what information you share and with whom. You can't be sure that person you told in confidence will understand or honor that.

Words of Caution about Social Media and News Media

It's also very important that you are very careful with social media. On Facebook, Twitter, and other social media platforms, news travels quickly. Often, opinions are misconstrued as fact. People can post wonderfully supportive comments or infuriatingly insensitive ones. It can be very hurtful to the family at a time when they are in tremendous crisis and pain to also have no control over how the news of their child's death is spread.

This is especially true if the death was in a public place or particularly tragic and "newsworthy" and you, as a family member, friend, or member of the community, happened to be there or have "inside" knowledge. Violent deaths, murders, abductions, and those that include suspected family involvement in the circumstances of the child's death are highly volatile and particularly complicated situations. They may involve immediate and persistent media coverage and legal action down the road, and what you say could impact that process for good or bad.

As someone with information about the family or situation, you may be the target of news media. Don't give names, addresses, and personal information to media sources without the family's permission. The media can find that information out on their own. Be very careful with disclosure of details. The parents will likely eventually hear about what you said. How will they feel? The media will find out details soon enough. Resist the urge for your fifteen minutes of "fame" when asked for an on-camera or print interview. Think of the family and their needs first. If you do grant an interview, choose your words carefully, as they can easily be taken out of context in editing. Imagine how you would feel if you learned of your sibling's, niece's or nephew's, or grandchild's death from the newspaper or TV news before the child's parents had told you! It happens.

Tips for Dealing with the Media

I hate having to put this topic here. I hate having to address it at all. Unfortunately, dealing with the media is a painful reality for many parents who lose their children. It can be a wonderful thing or a very stressful and painful thing, depending on the circumstances. The way the media approaches the story and you makes all the difference.

Sometimes, you will approach them, requesting an article or news story. Most of the time, they will approach you. Hopefully, they will do so gently and respectfully. Sometimes, though, it is forceful, intrusive, and not at all respectful of your need to grieve. Especially if the child's death was tragic, violent, or in a public place. For the media, it's about getting the "scoop", and being the first to report on it.

Important Information for Reporters and News Media

While I understand the need to report "newsworthy" events, the tragic death of a child is a story that needs to be handled delicately. Getting the "scoop" should be secondary to consideration for the family's grief. You can report the story and get information with respect and compassion. In particular, on the day of the death and through the day of the funeral or memorial service, families need privacy. They need to grieve. They need to be with family and friends. They are devastated. In pain so deep you cannot even imagine it.

They do not need media calling them persistently, knocking on their door endlessly, and camping out on their front lawn or on their street. It compounds the trauma they are experiencing and makes the all-important work of grieving much harder than it already is. They do not need to feel as if they can't be in their own homes, where their child lived, where they need to grieve, because the media won't leave them alone. They can't think as it is. Give them time. If it's truly important information, it will still be important in a few days. If not, why are you reporting about it in the first place?

Please. Be respectful. For one moment, imagine if it were YOUR child. I know it's impossible, for you can't possibly fathom what it's like unless you've been there. But imagine. Of the many reporters that interviewed me, the ones who were parents themselves had a very different approach with me than those who were not parents. It was because they could put themselves in my shoes and identify with my pain.

Give grieving parents respect and distance. If they want to speak, they will. Offer your condolences. Send them a card. It may make them more likely to give you the story when they are ready. Low pressure "sales" often work much more effectively. Thank them if they do share information with you. Do not hound their family, friends, or neighbors. Do not be rude if they don't understand what is a matter of public record and what is not. Their child just died! They don't even know how they will take their next breath!

We need to create a culture of respect around death and grieving, and the media could be such a powerful force in modeling respect for and understanding the pain of loss. How the media chooses to report and gather the information that they do publish a story about can make a tremendous difference in that family's healing and in society's understanding of grief.

Media Tips for Parents, Family Members, and Community Members

The media may contact you for a statement or to get a "scoop" on what happened, how the family is coping, or any other information they feel newsworthy. They often take advantage of catching you "off guard" to glean information they can't get elsewhere. If the child's death was tragic, at a public place, or occurred at home, it's likely to be reported. If the child's death was from an illness like cancer, media coverage is usually not an issue for parents unless they are in the public eye because of their jobs, or if they pursue the media.

The media is a very competitive field... both print and TV media. There is a rush to get the story first and get it in the paper or on air first and with the most intimate and detailed information. Hopefully, it's accurate, but that is not always the case.

An accidental or tragic death may be reported only in the local paper or on a local TV station as a quick fifteen second clip or a one paragraph story and then dropped. It may initially simply be reported as a parent's name and/or the child's name, address, and that the death is being "investigated." It could be a longer piece and have a very sympathetic tone and be in support of your family or in an attempt to raise awareness. Or, it could be a "sensational" piece of news or there are some unanswered questions about the cause of death. Especially if it's a slow news day. It may play out for days and on national TV if it was a particularly tragic, violent, or public accidental death.

As difficult as it is, you often must decide in the midst of your pain, and sometimes within mere hours of learning your child has died, if you will talk to the media, or if you will designate a representative to speak on behalf of you or your family and what will be shared.

Here are a few tips for dealing with media
1. You don't have to say, "Yes." You don't have to say anything! You can refuse to answer the phone or the door. You can refuse to comment if someone shoves a microphone in front of you. However, you may be shown on video doing so.
2. The release of the child's name (or anyone who has died) is usually withheld until notification of next of kin: the parents of a minor child or the spouse or parents of an adult child. It's often not enough time for you to inform extended family because you are doing your own grieving as a parent, before it's made public by the authorities. After the next of kin is notified, the news is released as public record and is accessible to the media. You could ask the authorities to wait a certain period of time, so you can notify others. However, they may not grant it to you. The

media likely won't respect your wishes and can also get your child's name and other information they want from other people (usually friends, family, or community members who just don't think about repercussions) before this happens, and it can be a nightmare.

3. You can choose which media outlets you want to share with. If you have a favorite reporter or news station and you trust them, reach out to them to share the story. If they aren't interested and their competition is, tell them. That may be enough to perk their interest, too.

4. Realize you can't control what other people say. Nor can you take back what you've said. Once it's out there, it's out there. A quick email blast to family and friends requesting they not speak to media if that is your wish (and you have the presence of mind to do so) may prevent unnecessary hurt feelings and additional pain. When an accident happens at a school or other large public place, it's more likely information will get shared before you are ready for it to be public.

5. It's best to choose a representative that can speak to the media on your behalf who can stick to the facts and only share what you wish to be shared, without being swayed by the media's questions, lights, microphones, and "in your face" attempts at getting information. This person should ideally read prepared statements or express only what the parents have approved.

6. If you choose to speak to the media, *be very careful what you say*.

a. Know anything you say or do can be used from the moment you say, "Hello" to the moment you say, "Goodbye." This is true even for a phone or TV interview when you are not on camera. Be careful with small talk!

b. Know that your interview will probably be boiled down to a 10-30 second piece or a story that may be completely taken out of the context in which you spoke or meant it in order to fit the "angle" of the story. Your intention and that of the media may be completely different. Ask what their focus is before you speak to them. Try to speak in sound bites (short phrases or sentences) that only convey the message *you* want to send.

c. If you don't want it to be public knowledge, don't say it.

d. If the camera is on, it can be used; this includes any footage before/after the official interview is over. Cameramen can simply video you coming and going from your home from across the street without you even realizing you are being videotaped.

e. Be careful what is posted on social media sites like Facebook and Twitter and sent in e-mails by your family and friends. They can easily be forwarded to the media and become part of public domain. Anything that is on a blog, website, or other public site that you, your spouse, or that child had is often quickly found, pictures lifted, and information gleaned to be used in stories.

f. If media is hounding you or on your property, contact the local police and ask for their assistance.

g. You might want to alert family and friends if you don't want anyone to discuss the circumstances of your child's death with the media. You can't control what others do or say, but you can ask.

h. Realize that police reports, including your child's name or 911 calls are usually public record. Once a news story is published with your child's name, it's out there, and they have the right to share it. It's upsetting to see or hear sometimes, but there is nothing you can do about it.

i. Often, the initial reports, especially if a child died at home, might indicate it was "under investigation." This can be upsetting as it implies you as a parent were somehow at fault. Try not to take it personally. The police must investigate injuries and deaths to children that die following an accident in the home. This is a good thing, for it is meant to protect children.

j. You can contact the media when and if you want to share something about your story. They may or may not decide to do the story, but keep trying. When you do want to get the word out, persistence can pay off.

News media is fickle. How much, if any, attention your particular story gets depends on many variables. The attention of the media is also very fleeting. It may seem overwhelming on one day because everyone wants to talk to you and your story is "news." Then, the next day your story (and your child) is forgotten, and *that*, as annoying as the media attention can be, can be even more upsetting. This can be especially frustrating when your attempts to follow up the story about their death with informative stories about prevention are ignored and not considered newsworthy.

Your Relationship to the Child and the Impact of Grief
Our relationship to the child who has died obviously impacts our experience of grief. The parent-child relationship, the sibling relationships, the grandparent-child, and all other relationships people had with that child are unique. It stands to reason then, that everyone's experience of grief will vary, and be impacted by the nature of the relationship each person had with that child.

What we do and say in the minutes, days, hours, weeks, months, and years that follow the death of a child can have a profound impact on the grief journey and recovery of the parents and those who love and support them. Everyone also has their own unique grief to cope with.

This is vitally important for everyone to be aware of. We will all eventually experience the death of a loved one. We will probably all eventually meet someone who has lost a child. Chances are you already know someone who has lost a child; they just may not share that information freely. I am constantly amazed by the sheer number of people I've met in my work as a physical therapist who share with me that they, too, have lost a child or children. Often before they realize I lost Meghan. Many of them are older or elderly and still grieve their stillbirths, infant deaths, and the deaths of their adult children. You never know who else around you is also a member of this group.

There is a sense of relief in discovering you share that bond. A sense of safety in being able to talk about your deceased child to someone who gets it, because they've walked the same road you are now on.

A Grandparent's Grief
The grandparent's grief is a unique and complex one. They not only feel the pain of the loss of their grandchild... but also the compounded grief because they hurt for their own child's pain, too. This is especially true of mothers.

It can be difficult, because as the child's grandparent, you want to be close to your own son or daughter... to comfort them. You can identify with the pain because you can't imagine losing your own child, and now your "baby" has lost their baby, your grandbaby. It doesn't matter how old that "baby" is, they could be newborn or elderly themselves. Because of the parents' pain and coping mechanisms, they may not be aware of the depth of your pain as a grandparent, because their own pain is so very deep and raw.

I remember being so numb and detached from everything by the time my parents arrived at our home several hours after Meghan died that I barely acknowledged their arrival or their pain. In fact, I really don't remember it. All I remember is sitting on the couch and staring at the Christmas tree for hours. I wanted to be alone. My parents were devastated at the loss of their granddaughter and not being there for us, not being able to see her at the hospital. Then, when they finally arrived from Florida, they were unable to reach me emotionally. It compounded their grief. It can make an already impossibly painful and difficult situation even more emotionally painful when you can't reach your own child in their greatest moment of pain.

You also are reeling from the loss of your grandchild. You may feel judgmental toward your own child or their partner/spouse, depending on the circumstances of their child's death. Resist the urge to say anything beyond you are sorry for their loss and that you love them. Now is not the time to point out what could have prevented the child's death or how you told them such and such and now look what happened. Yes, it has happened. Don't be that person. Now is not the time for your opinions. Now is not the time to bring up "issues" you had about your child's partner or spouse or their relationship. Now is the time for love and only love.

You may want to see your grandchild, at the hospital or funeral home, or you may be emotionally or physically unable to. If you live a distance away or had not seen your grandchild in some time, you may also be racked with guilt on many levels. You also may live or be far away and not able to get to your family fast enough. If you must fly, airlines often offer bereavement fares and services.

My own parents lived in Florida and we, in Massachusetts. They immediately called Southwest Airlines and explained the situation. They were given a seat on the first flight they could get to the airport for. They were able to board early and were seated in the bulkhead row. The flight attendant was aware of the situation and lovingly tended to them during the flight, checking on them frequently to make sure they were doing okay. They deplaned first, so they could get their rental car and drive to our home. They were unable to see Meggie at the hospital as some of our other family members had. It's one of the reasons I wish we had taken a photo of Meggie there. She looked so very beautiful and peaceful. This was upsetting to them, that they missed that opportunity. They had to wait for the next day to go to the funeral home to see her. It wasn't the same.

As grandparents, you often want to help somehow. This may include trying to shop or clean or help prepare for services. You try to mother your children and take care of the everyday tasks they normally would and probably can't manage right now. Sometimes, as the grandparent, your focus is on your own child, and often inadvertently, you devalue the spouse or potentially interfere with their grieving needs, both alone and together with their spouse/partner.

If you are a parent-in-law, you can find yourself in a challenging place. Sometimes, simply being present or available, and staying out of the way to allow the parents to grieve in whatever way they need to, is the priority. Even if it goes against every instinct you have. How involved you are may largely depend on your relationship with the child's parents. It's a very difficult place to be and a very challenging role to play.

A word of advice: don't touch, move, or do anything without the permission of the child's parents. It may seem simple to wash the dishes, but maybe that parent wanted that last cup the child drank out of left dirty because it's suddenly sacred to them. By washing it, you erase a memory of their child. The same is true of "cleaning" a space, putting toys or clothes away, dusting, or vacuuming. Everything that now deceased child touched is now potentially quite sacred and important to that parent. You must be aware of and respect it. We discuss the do's and don'ts of supporting bereaved parents in greater depth Chapter six.

A Sibling's Grief

The loss of a sibling is an entirely different and unique experience. It varies of course, with the age of the siblings and what their relationship to the deceased child was like. It may also depend somewhat on how the parents and extended family reacts, for young children often take their cues from the important adults in their lives.

Very young siblings and infants may not understand or "miss" their older sibling. You may not even be able to tell them as an infant will not comprehend your words. They will know it's different though, because the parents are different.

Toddlers and older children will all process it differently and often take their cues from you. They may withdraw or perhaps be clingier. Some will continue to play with, talk to, and even tell you they see their deceased sibling. Let them! You don't know what their experience is; let them experience it their way.

Older children and teens may start to spend more time with friends and may do poorly in school or be tempted to experiment with drugs and alcohol or engage in other risky behaviors. Adult children are still brothers and sisters and may all cope very differently.

Oftentimes, children, even very young children, will blame themselves, feeling a sense of responsibility or a failure to protect their sibling. They may or may not express this. Even if asked directly. Imagine, if you, as a parent, feel a sense of guilt, why can't your kids? Grief does not always make sense or involve rational thought processes.

Kids often process their emotions through play and art so be attentive to what they say and do. I remember Meghan's twin finger painting a few days after she died. He painted a sky. I asked him, "What is that?" He said, "Meggie in the sky!" Then he pointed to where she was. It hangs in her room to this day and inspired a poem by a friend of mine, who has also now since passed, far too young herself.

Older children and adult children may be willing to talk about their feelings, either with you or with a counselor. Perhaps they talk with friends or write or express their feelings with music or dance or some other creative outlet.

Others may not want to talk about it at all. They may be angry and lash out or avoid any family events that remind them of their sibling. They may also "stuff" their feelings and not deal with them until much, much later in their lives.

Children, especially younger ones, also have a wonderful ability to self-regulate what they can cope with. Although they are often resilient, they also simply absorb and process only what they are capable of. It's a tremendous gift.

Siblings, especially young children, often suffer collateral losses. Most notably, that of their parents. Not literally, but in the way in which they were used to, because their parents are so deep in grief that they are often emotionally "not there" for their other children. Routines may fall apart. Other people may suddenly be in their house, taking them places, doing the things their parents had usually done for them. It can be confusing and upsetting. The changes in caregivers and routines may be unavoidable for a time, but trying to maintain a traditional routine for other children helps to provide a sense of comfort, structure and normalcy in their lives. As difficult as it may be, try to stay connected to at least one routine with your other children every day. Perhaps, it's as simple as a bedtime story or watching a TV show together.

Adult siblings may have a different experience. They may be weighed down with guilt over a rocky relationship or distance that prevented them from being closer. They may mourn the future more so than a younger child, simply because of their life experience. They may have not only lost a sibling but a best friend, if they were close friends, too.

Oftentimes we forget that adults who lose a sibling have suffered a profound loss, too. They are often the forgotten bereaved and there is little encouragement to seek support, counseling, or information to help them heal.

It's important to remember siblings have suffered a tremendous loss as well, no matter how old they are when their sibling dies. It's a loss that will impact them for the rest of their lives, just like their parents. The opportunity they have to learn about death, the rituals around it, and your own personal and cultural beliefs around death and bereavement, will shape how they cope, process, and ultimately deal with death in the future.

Memories of the Day Your Child Died

While some people remember their experiences very vividly, others do not. It may be by choice or they simply may have been in too much distress to remember what happened, how, when, or what their reactions were at the time. They may be able to remember at a later time, if they are willing to allow themselves to, or they may choose to forget it or just not think about it because it's just too painful to go back to that day.

I remember vividly and viscerally the three distinct "stages" of my experience the day Meghan died that happened in a matter of a few hours: discovering she had been injured and was not breathing, the hospital experiences, and coming home without her and explaining her death to family and friends. As you might imagine, it was the longest, most painful and difficult day of my life.

A journal written to Meghan, started just days after her death, became part of my therapy. It felt like an ongoing conversation with her. I'm so glad I did, for I'd have forgotten so many of my thoughts, feelings, experiences, and the amazing and meaningful gifts we received from both Meghan and others. After a few months, I began to consider writing a book from my journal entries. The working title was called "Letters to Meggie." It has evolved to this book.

Meggie's "Angel" Day

This story is similar to the one told in Chapter one; however the focus of that story was on how I choose to remember and honor Meggie on her Angel day.

This story focuses more on the very specific physical and emotional feelings I had and the things I remember doing and feeling the day she died. It captures the emotional roller coaster many parents experience on the day their child dies. While a valuable read for anyone, the friends, family members, and professionals who work with bereaved parents may find this especially helpful and insightful. This day is not just a "bad" day. It's a day that has changed the course of their life.

I remember waking to the sound of my husband screaming in a voice that left no doubt in my mind something horrible had happened. I practically flew out of bed and to our daughter's room where I found her lying in the middle of her floor, mottled and blue, not breathing. Her father had found her under her dresser, lifeless. It had fallen on her. I am a healthcare professional. I have known CPR since I was in high school. I knew she was long gone just by looking at her, but I also knew what I had to do.

As I continued CPR, I also remember my older son, then six, standing by her head, pacing, very upset, and begging me to wake his beloved baby sister up. He was asking nervously if she was going to be okay.

In contrast, her twin brother knelt calmly by her feet. He said very softly, very lovingly and very matter of factly, "Mommy, Meggie not wake up." It was less a question and more a statement of pure, loving, spiritual fact. I knew she was gone, flying with the Angels. He did, too. He was not upset. He radiated love. Twinship is an amazing thing...

The EMT's arrived, the first one was a young neighbor who had heard the 911 call on the scanner, and she was taken by ambulance to the nearest hospital. We are blessed to have an ER doctor in our neighborhood, who came to her aid. A neighbor heard the 911 call on the scanner and called to tell him. He ran to our house that cold December morning and cared for our daughter in the ambulance and at the hospital. How blessed we were.

I ran to the car and nearly ran over neighbors who were already coming to the house to support us as I backed out of the driveway. Our neighborhood is amazing. Our babysitter's father is a police officer. He heard the 911 call and sent his daughter to our house immediately, to care for our other children because she knew Meghan's twin had severe food allergies, and she understood his restrictions. More importantly, the boys knew and felt comfortable with her, which was so very important in crisis.

In retrospect, I should not have driven. I couldn't remember where the hospital was. I barely remembered how to operate a vehicle. The shock and horror of the day was beginning to hit me. I knew she was dead, yet I held out every hope she was not. My husband kept asking me if I thought there was a chance, if I thought she'd be okay. One thought kept running through my mind: "It was more than 6 minutes. It had to have been more than 6 minutes. Maybe it wasn't that long, maybe there is a chance!" I was so afraid to say out loud what I really thought. What I knew in my soul. I didn't want it to be real. At this point, I still didn't even really know what happened. I certainly couldn't fathom how we didn't hear the dresser fall or her cry.

I remember walking into the emergency room. Now reality and the shock of what was happening was beginning to set in. It was surreal and I didn't want to do it. I felt panicked. I felt so disconnected. From my body. From the experience. I had chest pain... severe chest pain... I thought I was having a heart attack crushing, heavy, chest pain. It was hard to take a deep breath. I was dizzy. There was a buzzing in my ears. Everything was fuzzy and gray and threatened to close in around me. My legs were so heavy, and I was so shaky I could barely put one foot in front of the other. The walk to the check in desk was excruciatingly long and slow, at least it seemed that way. I knew I had to remain upright, or I'd never get to see my little girl. So I said nothing and fought my body as hard as I could.

We gave our names to the young girl at the desk. We must have looked like zombies. We threw on sweat pants and sweatshirts, literally right out of bed. She said they'd be right with us. Then, she made a grave error, unbeknownst to her. She said, "I'm sure it will be okay." I damn near lost it on her. My mind reeled. My anger rose. She had no idea my baby girl was dead. I might have leapt across the desk, grabbed her by the shoulders, and shaken her senseless screaming at her for saying such horrible words to me, if I were not so numb and convinced I might by dying myself right then.

A nurse/chaplain came to get us right away and brought us to a private waiting room. She offered us tissues, drinks or a snack, and prayer. I forced down some ginger ale, hoping it would keep me from passing out. We just stood there and stared. Numb. Anxious. Nervous. Scared. Hopeful. Despondent. Everything. The nurse stood and sat with us and just held the space. She didn't try to speak. She was a grounding presence. She sent us love. I wish I knew who she was.

After what seemed like an eternity, but was probably only 10-15 minutes, our neighbor, friend, and ER physician emerged from the room Meghan was in. He walked slowly toward us. His face and body language told the story. He said it didn't look good, but they were doing everything they could. They wanted to send her by helicopter to the trauma hospital because they had pediatric equipment and staff the smaller hospital did not. They were not giving up, yet. He asked if we wanted to see her before they took her. Yes, absolutely, we did. He prepared us for what she would look like, what machines were attached to her and why. I was familiar with it all due to my work experience, but I think it helped my husband to be better prepared for all the tubes, lines, and machines around and attached to her.

I stepped in the room. It was probably a mess. I know there was equipment everywhere, though I saw none of it. I heard nothing. I know there were lots of people around her, caring for her, breathing for her, keeping her heart artificially beating. I saw none of them. I know their hearts ached for us and for her. I felt the love… the reverence.

The room was silent except for the sounds of medicine at work. I could feel the compassion of those tending to her care. I was grateful. All I saw was my daughter. I ducked under someone's arm and went to her head. She looked beautiful. Pale, sweet, angelic. I touched her hair, I kissed her. I told her we loved her. I again asked her to come back to us, but only if she could as our Meggie. I kissed her again, holding her tiny little hand. I told her to enjoy her helicopter ride. She always wanted to fly…

One of the EMT's who brought her in the ambulance was waiting for us. He offered to drive us, in our car, to the trauma hospital about a half hour away. Not that he would have let either of us drive if we insisted. We were both numb, silent, and deeply in shock. I remember trying to sit in the back seat, in one of the car seats. When he realized I couldn't remove the seat, he did it for us. I also remember it was a beautiful day for December 18th. We were supposed to be baking Christmas cookies together, not rushing to a trauma hospital with our daughter's life in the balance.

On the way to the next hospital, he asked if we needed to call anyone. I called the house to be sure my other children were okay. Thank goodness for speed dial. I didn't know my own phone number! I had forgotten so many neighbors had gone to our house and I was absolutely petrified something would happen to one of them, especially her twin with all the food allergies. I was assured they were safe and well cared for by their babysitter, who knew them well. Then, we each called one family member to spread the word. Thank God for cell phone contacts. I couldn't remember anyone's phone number. Dialing was near impossible, fingers didn't work. Nothing worked. Nothing.

When we arrived at the next hospital, the EMT guided us to a small, private waiting room with tissue boxes and comfy chairs, the room no one ever wants to have to enter. Everything was worked out before we got there, we didn't have to check in, and we were led down a back hall. Mercifully, we saw no one else.

I think some of our family joined us there to wait. I don't remember who was there and when. My sister and her husband. My grandmother and aunt. I can't remember if it was before or after we were officially told. A priest joined us, because Meghan was baptized Catholic. He sat quietly. He offered prayer. I was damn pissed off at God right then and found the priest's presence both comforting and annoying. We sat. Tears threatened to flow. We stared. I was still having chest pain. The wait was agonizing. I just wanted to be with her... Now.

It was not long before a doctor and a resident, who looked very nervous, joined us. Their faces said it all. I remember thinking the doctor had a very cool Christmas tie on. Meggie would have liked it. I heard them say, in a Charlie Brown voice, slow and thick and distantly "Blah, blah, blah blah blah... Meghan had died. I'm so very sorry."

Bam. Just like that. Our worst fears confirmed. Right there in that awful little room with no windows, no escape. Our daughter was dead. I felt the walls closing in, and the pain surge in my chest. Part of me wanted to give in to the darkness that was threatening to protect me from this horrible reality. I was so close to passing right out. The other part of me desperately wanted to see my daughter, so I fought it with all that I had. I asked, "Can I see her?" They answered, "Yes, in a few minutes." Then they left us to collapse into despair and the horror of the fact our gorgeous little girl was gone forever.

Everyone in that little room tried to comfort each other and cried, except me... I sat there... numb. Trying to make sense of it all. I wanted to cry. I wanted to scream. I wanted to throw things. I wanted to kick the priest out of the room. I think he offered a prayer. I couldn't summon the ability to do any of it. I just closed my eyes and tried to stay present and conscious.

After what seemed like forever, they allowed her father and I to see Meghan. She was on the stretcher in the ER bay, covered with a warm blanket. She still had the breathing tube in her throat but everything else was disconnected and gone. She looked so peaceful... so absolutely beautiful. I actually wish I had a picture of her then.

We stood by her side. We touched her. We talked to her. The priest stood across from us. He said a prayer. He read the 23rd Psalm. I hated it. I hated him. I wanted to tell him to shut the f*ck up. I was in a love/hate relationship with God right then. I just wanted him to leave. I found nothing he said or did comforting at all. I wanted to be with my daughter.

The social worker seemed just as annoying. She really said nothing. She looked uncomfortable. I asked her why I couldn't cry, even though I wanted to. She assured me I would, and it was okay. I felt like a horrible mother. My daughter was dead and I couldn't even cry. WTF? I had to ask her for resources. What do we do now? She handed me a standard brochure on when a loved one dies. Great. Thanks. As if a brochure was going to help me through this awful experience. I hated her, too.

I was beginning to struggle with standing up. I'm sure I was as pale as Meghan was. The nurses noticed and encouraged us to sit. They brought me ginger ale. They asked if there was anyone they could call. I suddenly thought of my Uncle Bud. He was a deacon. He baptized Meghan. I only knew his name and what town he lived in. I couldn't remember his phone number. Somehow, they found him, and he was on his way. It seemed like he arrived in just a few minutes but I know it was at least a half hour or more. Time was so warped for me.

A short time later, a nurse asked if I'd like to hold Meghan. YES! Yes, please, forever. Thank you! There was a rocking chair. I sat. She placed my delicate three-year-old baby girl in my arms. It was almost like the day she was born when they handed her to me. Except it was so, so different. She was pale and warm, still in her jammies, which had been cut, wrapped in a warm blanket. I stared at her face. I told her I loved her. I touched her hair over and over. I held her tiny hand. My husband sat next to me and did much of the same.

The nurses gave us space but cared for us, too. Offering us juice and ginger ale and encouraging us to eat/drink a bit. After a bit they helped us make hand and foot prints in a plaster mold and with paint on paper as a keepsake for us and her brothers. Then, they placed her back on the stretcher and invited family and friends that had gathered to have a chance to say their goodbyes.

The first in was my Uncle Bud. He came and stood by my side. When he hugged me, I had the sudden realization Meggie was with my grandmother... his mother Agnes. We had given Meggie her middle name in honor of Agnes. Then it occurred to me. They were together! She was safe! My gram would surely take good care of her! Then, I lost it. I sobbed into his belly after sinking back into the chair for

71

what seemed like forever. I was finally able to release some of the pain of this day. I'm sure he said a prayer. I don't remember it. I know it was not the 23rd Psalm! My sister, grandmother, and aunts also had a chance to visit with Meggie and say goodbye.

At some point the police detectives came to talk to us. It was an accident at home that led to a child's death. It was standard practice that the police had to interview the parents. Still, it was horrible. I don't remember much about it. They were as kind as they could be considering they had a job to do. I later learned they were at the house for a while too, while we were at the hospital.

After everyone had a chance to see her, we got to spend some more time with her. At some point, the nurses helped me to call my parents in Florida. They had planned to fly up to celebrate Christmas with us. How do you tell your parents that they'd now be getting on a plane to come to their granddaughter's funeral? My sister had told them Meggie was hurt, but we had to tell them she had died. I don't remember how or what I said. I do remember the nurse behind me (I was sitting), holding my shoulders, dialing the phone, rubbing my back and helping me hold the phone.

I think we were there close to two hours before the nurses guided us to separate and say our final goodbyes. I didn't want to leave my beautiful daughter... ever.

Because Meggie had been injured at home, the authorities needed to know the actual cause of death, so Meggie had to have an autopsy. We had no choice. I hated the thought of it, but I was in shock. I just chose simply not to think about it.

The nurses told us to call the funeral home in our town the next day, and they'd arrange to bring her there from the medical examiner and to arrange for her services. The nurses hugged us and presented us with a box of keepsakes. Those painted hand and foot prints, one for each of her brothers and for us. The plaster heart we had made of her hand and foot print with a pink ribbon. A long lock of her silky blonde hair, tied with a pink ribbon in a tiny baggie. A brochure on grief. The nurses said how sorry they were and guided us outside, where we waited on the sidewalk, for my brother-in-law to return with the car. The EMT had driven ours home for us so we didn't have to worry about it.

As I stood there, I gazed at the blue sky. Were you up there, Megs? I felt the warm sun on my face. I looked at the box I held in my hands.

I saw people walking by. Smiling. Laughing. Carrying gifts for those they were visiting in the hospital. I became angry. How dare they smile? Didn't they know my daughter just died? Christmas? Who the hell cares about Christmas? I have to figure out how to plan a funeral and bury my little girl! Oh my God. Is this real? This can't be real.

It was so hard to leave her. I knew we'd get to see her again at the funeral home, but she'd never look that peaceful, that beautiful. I could have held her forever. We were so blessed to have the time we did. The pain returned to my chest. What the hell were we going to tell her brothers?

Chapter Three

Memories, Keepsakes, and the Importance of Grief Keeping

After a loved one dies, no matter how old they were, all we are left with are things and memories. We fiercely protect these because it's all we have left.

Memories can be happy or sometimes, especially initially, difficult for the newly bereaved. The most vivid memories are often the ones of the last interaction the parents had with their child before their death. When that last interaction was negative or, perhaps, missed, "I was going to call him back, but I got busy…" or spoken with an, "I wish I had…" or, "I should have…," it can compound the grief and pain that parent feels. What if's and if only's are very common sentiments.

Guilt is a powerful emotion and we, as humans, especially bereaved ones, excel at it. We can't help how we feel, but know you are not alone if you feel guilty about something with regard to your child's death. It's not wrong to feel guilt. It's human. The important thing is that you process it and get the help you need to heal. This is something we will explore more later in the book in several different chapters.

A Search for Answers
In the days after the loss of a child, the parents are often lost themselves. Deep in their own grief, many search for the

answer to the often unanswerable question, "Why?" They may be on an endless search for answers. They may try to relive their child's last day. They may need to tell their death story, not unlike their birth story, as a way to process. They may search for information and details on the circumstances of their child's death or what led to it, especially if the death was sudden, unexpected, or due to an accident of some kind. They may even seem hyper focused on this. It's just a way of coping for some.

Sometimes, parents may find that others want to know the same thing and ask them repeatedly, "What happened?" For the parent who needs to talk about it, this can provide for therapeutic dialogue and an outlet for emotion. For the parent who cannot talk about it, it can be met with anger, silence, or tears.

There may be no answer. Or, perhaps, no good or acceptable answer. How could there be? Children are not supposed to die before their parents. It's so hard to accept and understand... for everyone.

Others may turn to their faith, going to religious services, praying, or seeking out books about coping with death and bereavement that are spiritually or religiously based. This can bring comfort and healing to many. The support of one's spiritual or religious community can be vital to coping and healing.

While these strategies can be helpful for the parent who is comfortable with talking about their child's recent death and needs to tell the story as a way of processing, coping and healing, or has a strong faith, for the parent who finds it too painful to address themselves, these questions are often met with anger, tears, or maybe even ignorance or withdrawal.

It's all normal.

We will explore different ways of coping with grief in more depth in Chapter five and throughout the book.

What to do With a Child's Possessions and When?
After a child dies, some parents do everything they can to connect with their child's energy. We no longer have our children's physical presence in our lives, so we desperately cling to their things or things that remind us of them. Parents often do this by wanting to be in their child's room, touching their toys, smelling their clothes, looking at photos and videos, or sleeping in their bed or sleeping with something that belonged to their child. Sometimes, they do this for a few days, others, for years, even if just on and off. Sometimes, I still sleep with one of my daughter's stuffed kitties. It's been nearly 10 years.

Others simply cannot cope with seeing their child's things and close the door to their room, refuse to look at photos or videos, and can't even say the child's name. Some cannot even bring themselves to attend their own child's services.

These are all ways of cherishing and protecting a child's memory. They are just different... different ways of coping with a broken heart.

It's not unusual, that at some point, parents feel compelled to share their child's possessions with those that loved them or they may wish to donate toys or clothes because they no longer need them. Often, they gift articles of clothing, toys, or art work the child made as a keepsake to friends or family members, while still deep in their own grief. Parents may do this because they feel it will help that friend or family member cope with their own grief, or maybe because that person asked for something of the child's to keep as a memento.

Bereaved parents are cautioned not to make decisions about their child's possessions immediately. When in the early stages of grief, when shock, numbness, and anger are swirling around them like a tornado, it's difficult to make a rational and balanced decision. It's best if parents wait at least 6-12 months before deciding what to do with their child's possessions... especially if it involves giving items away. Decisions made in the early stages of grieving may lead to regret later.

One thing is very important for loved ones to realize though, especially when a young child dies. *No one but the parents should touch the child's stuff without getting the parent's permission first.* You will read this line more than once in this book. It's because it's vitally important. Whether it's a toy on the floor, a dirty dish in the sink, or an article of dirty clothing, you must resist the urge to move or touch anything. I can't stress this enough. It may seem like nothing to you, but it could be everything to that parent. They may not even realize how important it is to them until someone does move or touch something and they find themselves angry or saddened by it.

Family and friends have no idea what those parents want or need. Hell, most of the time, the parents don't either. They have never done this before. They don't want to do it now. Their world is in complete emotional chaos. It is up to them, and only them, to decide what to do with their child's possessions and when. Don't touch and don't suggest what you think they should and should not do unless they ask you specifically for your opinion. They are so vulnerable and overwhelmed as it is. When they are ready and able, they will make the right decision for them.

How much and what of their child's possessions a parent has in their home or has access to will depend on the age of the child and if that child still lived with them. The challenge of deciding who gets what and why can be overwhelming, especially if the child did not live at home, the parents are not together, the adult child that died is married or in a committed relationship, or there is only one of something and more than one person wants it.

Age-specific Considerations
There are some age-specific challenges that parents may face that present unique situations to consider. Awareness of these considerations can help you preserve that child's memory and provide meaningful keepsakes for the parents even if they don't think of it themselves.

Pregnancy Loss, Stillbirth, and Infant Death
For parents who have suffered a pregnancy loss or stillbirth, they may only have ultrasound photos, photos taken at the hospital by the staff or family or, perhaps, professional bereavement photography services like Now I Lay Me Down to Sleep (NILMDTS), and any other keepsakes the hospital gave them such as a lock of hair, a hat or receiving blanket, or hand/foot prints. Some parents may not even have those

things if the pregnancy loss was before 20 weeks. Some states will not issue birth certificates or allow parents to take the baby out of the hospital for burial or cremation if they were born before viability or a certain gestational age. This can further complicate their grief and deepen their pain. It's as if their baby wasn't acknowledged as being their child!

Many people, especially friends, family members, and coworkers feel these pregnancy or stillborn losses are not "real" losses since the parents didn't "get to know" the child. There is a somewhat universal belief that these parents need to "get over it" because they can "always have another baby."

Nothing is more upsetting to these parents! To the parents they most certainly are real losses! They have lost a child *and* the dream of what they wanted for that child and their family. Their loss is just like that of any other parent who loses a child of any age. They deserve the same respect and often experience the same roller coaster of emotions any other parent does when their child dies. Naming their child and having a memorial service or funeral for them may be very important and necessary to their healing, no matter how small their baby might have been. Birth and death announcements are often still sent and are a beautiful way to honor this very special child to them and to their family.

There are wonderful bereavement organizations specifically for parents who have suffered these early losses. They offer information, support, and keepsakes that these parents can cherish for a lifetime. Many offer gifts that would be appropriate for friends and family to give for the holidays or the baby's birth or death anniversary. You can find links in the resource list to these and others, but they include: SHARE, the MISS (Mother's in Sympathy and Support) Foundation, A Place to Remember, AMEND (Aiding Mothers and Fathers Experiencing Neonatal Death), the March of Dimes Pregnancy and Newborn Loss Resources, Angel Babies Forever Loved, Hygeia, MEND (Mommies Enduring Neonatal Death), The Stillbirth Alliance, and Remembering Our Babies.

Babies, Toddlers and Young children

For babies, toddlers, and young children, parents often have more to think about, especially when it comes to their child's possessions. They have to decide about clothing, toys, furniture, mementos, and keepsakes their child made over the years. The older the child was, often the more there is to sort through.

Deciding if or when to deal with their bedroom or play space is an important tenet of grieving that many family members and friends don't understand. Some keep their child's room exactly the way it was left the day they died for a long time. Some... forever. I've met parents who simply closed the door to their child's room the day they died and did not open it for years. Other parents feel a need to spend time in their child's room and with their things as a way to connect, remember, and grieve. They may sleep in their child's bed, wear their clothes or simply sit and just be.

Other parents keep only certain things that belonged to their child and may incorporate them around the house or into their room, but in a different way or for a different purpose. Still others pack items up and store them or give things away to charities or other friends and family.

It's possible the child that has died shared a room with a sibling, which can further complicate grieving for both the parents and the sibling, because that room is still an active part of the household, and they have to continue to go in that room and be reminded of what is missing. It can also facilitate a beautiful way of remembering.

This age group is the one where extended family members, especially grandparents, often want or need something of that child's as a keepsake. It may be a creative project done by the child, an article of clothing, or a toy that has significance to that person. Siblings may want to choose an item to "take care of" or inherit to allow them a tangible way to connect with their sibling. There are many creative keepsakes available that can be purchased or specially made, and are appropriate for any loss, such as quilts or pillows. They are discussed in greater depth later in this chapter.

Teens and Adult Children

When teens or adult children die, especially those who have moved out of the family home, their friends, roommates, significant other, or spouse and family of their own, may feel they also have rights to their loved one's "stuff." It may not be a problem unless there is a dispute about who should have it.

Kids, even young adults and those with young children, rarely contemplate their own mortality. As a result, they have likely not thought about, nor shared with loved ones who they'd like their possessions to go to should they die. This can make for an already emotional need for parents, especially mothers, to connect with their child, more complicated. Especially when well-meaning friends or family fail to realize the need to discuss with the parents what they'd like to have of their child's things first.

This can also be complicated if the parent's relationship with the deceased child's spouse or friends is not a good one. The deceased child's parent may need to ask for the items you want very soon after their death and explain why it's important to you, before it is given away. It's usually not top of mind when in the initial stages of grief, however.

Honest communication and allowing some time to pass and for grief to take its course before making permanent decisions of any kind is wise. There is no right or wrong time frame for making these decisions.

It's imperative that well-meaning friends and family allow the parents to make their own decisions and respect the time it takes them to do so, as well as to respect the decisions the parents ultimately make. If the parents ask for your advice or opinion, by all means, share it, but reiterate that they need to take their time and not make decisions they may later regret. Open, honest communication and patience are gifts.

I remember my mom tried to help in the days after Meghan died, processing in her characteristic way by cleaning. When mom vacuumed Meghan's room a few days after her death, I damn near lost it. I used to lie on Meghan's carpet and try to connect with her. Her bedroom floor was the last place she touched. The last place she was alive. Her hair was on that carpet. Her skin cells were on that carpet. Her energy was in that carpet. Her smell was in that carpet. SHE was in that carpet and I desperately needed to connect with her. My mom sucked all that up in a few minutes, completely oblivious to the fact it would bother me.

How could my mom have known how I felt? That I used to lie on her floor and try to connect with Meg in that way? Of course she didn't. I certainly didn't share that's what I did. I never thought to ask anyone not to vacuum her room. It didn't occur to me anyone would. I didn't even realize how upset it would make me. Rational thinking or not, it really added salt to my emotional wounds at that time.

Along the same lines, Meghan's little smudgy fingerprints were on her bedroom windows. As of this very moment, it's been nearly 10 years, and I still have not washed those windows. We had the windows replaced, and I saved the sashes, complete with her fingerprints. I have no idea what I will do with them, but I still cannot bear to wash them away or part with them. It's as if cleaning the windows would somehow wipe away... her. Weird? Maybe. Maybe not. I just know I'm not ready yet. I know I am not alone in how I feel about certain items that belonged to my now deceased child.

I also remember giving away some of the things I had bought her for Christmas. I donated some of them to Toys for Tots a day or two after she died. At the time, it seemed like the right thing to do. To give the things intended for her to someone who otherwise might not have any toys for Christmas. I also sold many of her toys at a fundraising yard sale at my son's school in the spring, just a few months after she died. I gave items of her clothing away as Christmas gifts, just a week after she died to family, as keepsakes for them. In retrospect, it was too soon, even though it felt like the right thing to do at the time. I was responding to the grief of my family while not paying attention to my own needs in that moment. I did have some regrets, months, even years later. Even though I kept many things, or they are still "in the family", others I gave away, sooner than I should have. I wish I had kept some of them.

I have only one piece of advice for parents who may want to get rid of their child's possessions immediately, you may want to consider temporary storage. It's easy to make rash emotional decisions that seem like the right thing to do when overwhelmed with grief. Once things are given away, it's all but impossible to get them back.

Once the initial pain of the loss subsides and the fog clears, you may have regrets about getting rid of things. I definitely regret giving away some of the things I did. Even though in the moment, it seemed the right thing to do. Had I waited a few weeks or months, I might have realized how much I treasured, wanted, or needed those things. Ultimately, though, the choice is yours and yours alone.

The Importance of Keepsakes and Memorial Gifts

Keepsakes are another way to connect with the memory of a child who has died. Often, it's something directly related to the child, such as an actual item that belonged to their child or an item their child made. Most things in a child's room fall into this category, as do toys, art projects, awards, and photos.

Parents long to smell their child's scent, hear their voice, and touch things that touched them. It may be how they connect to their child, through memories. They may relive their last interaction over and over in their mind. They may wish to watch videos or look at pictures. They may want to hear and tell stories about their child. Really, any way they can connect with the energy of their child, they try. It validates the existence of their child. The love they shared. Their connection to each other.

Other parents are just not able to do that, especially in those early days after the death. The pain of their loss is too much to bear and they don't want to, or simply cannot, connect with those memories. The parents may refuse to talk about their child to or with others. They may not want to hear stories or memories others have about their child. They may not want to look at pictures. They won't read the cards that are sent in sympathy. They won't participate in planning memorial services or a funeral. They may not even be able to attend them. They may want to get rid of everything that reminds them of their child, thinking it will somehow make the pain less. While this can seem odd or even downright wrong to some people, it's not. This, too, is a normal grief reaction for some parents.

What can I bring to a bereaved family to support them?
Those who wish to support the bereaved family, such as friends, family, and community members, often bring gifts. Some gifts are more useful and meaningful to the parents than others. While it's true, it's the thought that counts, some of the best keepsakes are the most unique and personal.

The better you know the child and the parents, the easier it is to choose a gift or keepsake. That said, some of the most thoughtful and touching gifts I received were from those who did not know us well at all. Some were from complete strangers and yet I was so touched by them all. When I look at them now, I remember the love and compassion showed to us by so many. It was instrumental in our healing, to know we were being thought of, prayed for, and loved.

Some of the unique things people gifted to us after Meghan died included a tree planted in the Children's Forest in Israel in her honor, lots of angel themed gifts such as ornaments, Willow Tree Angel figurines, sun catchers, a music box, a collector's plate, and angel jewelry for me, memorial masses in her honor, a little pine tree that magically appeared at the cemetery on Christmas Eve day with some ornaments on it, donations to our local animal shelter in her memory (as we requested in her obituary), a glass plate with a replica of her hand and foot prints, a flag flown over the US Capitol in her memory complete with a certificate and the flag as keepsakes, cat themed gifts left for her at the cemetery or gifted to us (she loved kitties), and photos and a poem in a scrapbook frame suitable for framing.

One of my favorite gifts is a silver pin designed from one of Meghan's drawings of our cat, Duncan, which she had drawn a few weeks before her death. It's an amazing likeness and a wonderful conversation piece that allows me to tell people about Meghan when I wear it because they always ask, "Why are you wearing a potato pin?" I get to explain it's a drawing of our cat my 3-year old daughter made just a few weeks before she died. In fact, our oldest son wanted it on her headstone, so the "potato Duncan" is now etched into her stone, too.

Here are some ideas for meaningful and unique keepsakes and gifts for the bereaved parent:

- Angels: figurines, sun catchers, pins or jewelry, ornaments, garden statues, or stepping stones.
- Have a photo of their child put in a special frame with their name engraved on it.
- Purchase a digital frame and load your (or the parent's) favorite photos of the child onto it for the family.
- If you scrapbook, make a page or an entire album about their child.
- Write the parents a letter about what you loved best about their child and how they parented them.
- If you are crafty with beading or jewelry making, make a mother's bracelet or necklace with the child's name, birthstone, or beads that capture the essence of their child.
- Donate to a charity that is meaningful to them in memory of their child and have a note or card sent.
- Buy the child a star from the International Star Registry.
- Have a flag flown over the US Capitol in memory of them and have it sent to the family. Purchase a flag presentation case or shadow box so they can display it in their home properly folded in a triangle shape. It typically arrives folded square in a box with a certificate including the honoree's name and the date the flag was flown. You can request a special date to have the flag flown if you wish when you place the order.
- Have a pin or likeness made of a drawing or piece of artwork from the child.

- Offer to make or have a quilt or pillow made of the child's clothing, blankets, crib sheets, etc.
- Offer to help create a shadow box of the child's keepsake items like locks of hair, hand and/or foot prints, photos, art work, medals of honor, or awards.
- Press flowers from funeral or memorial service arrangements or those sent to the family home into a frame, perhaps with a meaningful picture, poem, prayer, or piece of scripture, or make potpourri from dried flowers in a beautiful bowl or vase.
- Plant a tree in honor of the child at a local park, their school, playground, cemetery, or at the parent's home. Place a plaque in dedication.
- Purchase a memorial brick or stepping stone for the family to incorporate into their home or garden or at a memorial such as an Angel of Hope Garden.
- Create or purchase ornaments that honor their child's memory.
- Create or purchase a beautiful candle centerpiece and a framed copy of "We Light These Five Candles."
- A music box.
- A keepsake box.
- Arrange memorial masses or enter the child's name for an eternal prayer.
- Wind chimes.
- Plants or flowers for a memorial garden at the parent's home or cemetery.
- Merry Christmas from Heaven ornament or wind chimes.
- Purchase a memorial stone at the Children's Lighthouse Memorial in Edgartown, MA.
- Participate in a memorial walk or run in memory and in honor of their child. Create a team in memory of

that child with T-shirts, buttons, or some other way to honor them.
- Inspirational garden stones or stepping stones or plaques for the home.
- Memorial jewelry like a locket or mother and child pendant.

I've been pleasantly surprised to visit Meggie's special place (the cemetery) to find someone has left her a little trinket. Sometimes, I never do find out who left it, but it's so comforting to know others think about her and visit her.

Keepsakes are ways to preserve our memories and to honor and incorporate our child's memory into our everyday lives. I am deeply grateful for the kindness and generosity shown to our family and the many gifts we received from others who wanted to do something to show us they were thinking of us and our Meggie. Each gift brought comfort at the time and whenever I look at those gifts now, it reminds me of the love and compassion we were blessed to have, then and now.

What Bereaved Parents Really Want and Need

Gifts are nice, but not necessary. The most powerful gifts are not things, but genuine words and actions. A hug. An, "I'm so sorry." A meal. Someone who will sit with you and listen, cry with you and laugh with you. These are often the most powerful gifts you can give a bereaved parent.

Most of all, we want to know our child has not been forgotten. Not just in those first few weeks, but forever. We will always remember them. We want you to, too. Cards, words, gestures and gifts are just ways that others can say, "We remember them and we love you."

The most wonderful gift I could ever receive? Anyone who says her name to me! Because that means they remember her, how much I love her and how much I miss her. There is no greater gift. Say their names. Over and over. Remember our children. Today. On their birthday. On the anniversary of their death. On Mother's and Father's Day. At holidays. On a random day. If you think of them, tell us!

I remember my sister once posted on my Facebook wall on Meggie's Angel day "Meggie, Meggie, Meggie, Meggie, Meggie…" She got it. I love seeing and hearing her name.

Nothing says love like hearing my child's name being spoken. Remembering them tells us you remember them, too. It's powerful medicine to heal a broken heart.

Chapter Four

Preparing to Say Goodbye and the Rituals Associated with Death

Since our culture as a whole does not "do" death, most of us are completely unaware of what is involved in preparing to publicly say goodbye to a loved one who has died. If we have any experience at all, it's usually in attending a wake, funeral, or memorial service for a grandparent or older person. Precious few of us, thankfully, have ever had the experience of attending the services for a child. Fewer still, have any idea what is involved in planning these services, how difficult they are, how costly they can be, and what choices they have.

This chapter is a guide to help you understand the process as a parent or as a family member or friend of a bereaved parent and lend some insight into what is involved. My hope is that it can help to demystify the process and give you resources and suggestions to help you through this most difficult part of the journey.

Even if you do not need this information right now, it is valuable for everyone to read because we will all eventually need to make these decisions for someone we love.

Preparing for the Rituals Associated with Death

No one wants to talk about what happens after we die. Most people are not even comfortable contemplating their own mortality, let alone that of someone they love. Especially when that loved one is a child. Unfortunately, ignorance and avoidance are not bliss, especially when you suddenly find yourself having to plan for or attend services for a loved one.

It's one thing to have to plan or attend the wake, funeral, or memorial service of an older person. The natural order of things is that children outlive their parents, and certainly, their grandparents. Many older people have made their wishes known, because they had the gift of time. Both they and their families often have time to prepare for their eventual death and talk about what kind of services they want. They may have a will and a health care proxy. They may even have planned and pre-paid for their own services to lessen the emotional and financial burden on their family.

When a child dies, the world is turned upside down for nearly everyone. The logical, natural, order of the cycle of life is broken, right along with the hearts of everyone who loves and cares for that child and their family. This is often even more difficult to cope with when the death is tragic or unexpected. It can make the difficult decisions that must be made nearly impossible.

If you are the parent of a child who has died, you are often completely unprepared for the many deeply personal and meaningful, decisions that must be made quickly after your child dies. If you are fortunate, those around you will guide you lovingly and gently through the process.

The decision making process has to begin with those who inform you of your child's death or impending death. They are the ones who need to tell you what the first step is and give you some recommendations and guidance as to what to expect and how to prepare. It's so difficult to think of a child's service as being a celebration of their life when you cannot even believe they have died.

The Purpose of Rituals

The rituals around death are an important part of the grieving process. They help us process our child's death. They help us heal. They facilitate a gathering of support for the bereaved family. They are very important to us for closure. It's not closure in the sense they are gone and forgotten, because we will never forget them. It's closure with regard to their physical presence here on earth with us.

The rituals and ceremonies we participate in after the death of a loved one validate and honor the life of that person and their significance in our lives, and allow those of us who are left behind a place and time to pay our respects to the family and to honor the tremendous loss in our lives. We celebrate their lives and what they brought to others through their living.

The process is, however, largely shrouded in mystery. We often have no idea what is involved, how quickly decisions need to be made, and how many decisions in such a short period of time. Most of us have little or no experience with these rituals of death, especially what's involved in planning for them.

We, as a culture, are largely uncomfortable with death. We don't know what to say, what to do, or perhaps, more importantly, what not to say or do. Our natural tendency is to avoid dealing with the process because we don't want to and we don't know how.

Until we are forced to… when someone in your family dies, you suddenly *have* to go there. For far too many people, especially younger ones, this first encounter with the rituals of death is through the death of a child. I don't need to tell you how incredibly difficult this is. Not only for the families and friends, but for the people in the industry who provide these services. Having to assist families in planning funeral services or the other rituals and ceremonies related to death for a child, especially a very young child, must be the most difficult situation they ever have to face.

Timing and Planning of Rituals
The rituals and ceremonies that are associated with death, and the time frames in which they happen, depend on many variables. There can be medical delays, for instance, in the case of organ donation, or if an autopsy is required or requested. There are certain religious requirements regarding how the deceased are to be cared for and the timing and treatment of their body as well.

Many factors could interfere with your plans and should be considered: the time of the year, holidays, religious holidays, other events at your local church or synagogue such as a wedding or baptism, or even other families' calling hours and funeral plans. Weather can also cause changes in plans or delays, especially in the winter months in areas prone to snow and ice. Allowing time for distant relatives to travel can also impact planning.

There are also your personal preferences, which are very important considerations. It can be difficult to know what these are when you are not expecting to be planning ceremonies of goodbye for a child, but they make the experience more personal and meaningful both to the parents and to those attending. With the right guidance, this can be a healing part of the process.

Difficult Decisions That Must be Made Quickly
From a practical and very realistic standpoint, there are many options that need to be considered for planning purposes and decisions that need to be made quickly, often much more quickly than parents are often ready for, when planning the rituals and ceremonies after the death of a loved one. No easy feat in the depths of emotional crisis you have just been thrown into. Parents are often still very deep in shock, pain, numbness, and sometimes denial when they are forced to make these decisions.

Typically the first decision you must make is where you want your child's body to go. When asked, many parents reflexively say, "With me." Although possible in some places, it's highly unlikely that it's practical or even legal, depending on where you live. So, unless the child needs to have an autopsy (typically only for an unexpected death or per request), a funeral home must be chosen immediately. The funeral directors will ultimately be the ones to guide you through the many seemingly impossible decisions you must make in the coming days as you prepare to lay your child's body to rest. For this reason, taking the time to choose the "right" funeral home has its merits.

Questions that need to be addressed, usually within 24-48 hours of someone's death include:

- The first question is what funeral home do you want to handle all the arrangements or will you be planning a "do it yourself" funeral? DIY funerals are more common in other countries but are gaining popularity in the U.S. Refer to the resource list for more information on DIY funeral planning if you are interested in this option. Most people just choose the closest funeral home to where they live, but you might want to ask for references on those who have experience or expertise in planning funerals for children. The compassion shown by these homes makes a difference.

- Do you want to have the body embalmed and the child ultimately buried or would you prefer cremation?

- Are there religious or cultural time frames or rituals that you wish to honor and follow?

- If you choose burial, you must choose the cemetery. You must also consider if you want to purchase a single plot for the child or a family burial plot at the same time so you can ultimately be laid to rest with your child. Cemetery spots are not held so if you don't purchase a space for yourselves when you purchase your child's, it may be sold to someone else and you will not be able to lay in rest beside your child. Cost can also be a factor, as fees are associated with the plot and services related to the burial.

- Do you want to have a wake or calling hours, and, if so, with an open or closed casket? Some people choose an open casket for immediate family in a private viewing and a closed casket for the public calling hours. It's really up to you and how "viewable" your child is. In the event of cremation or a closed casket, some opt to place a large photo of the child on top of the casket instead.
- For a wake or calling hours, what do you want your child to wear? You will have to bring in clothes, and, perhaps, a blanket or other personal item for them to have in their casket or "special box."
- Do you want to have the body cremated? If so, do you want it done after or in lieu of a formal wake or calling hours? What type of urn do you wish to place their ashes in and where do you want to place it? Ashes typically are returned in a plastic bag inside of a box unless an urn is chosen prior to cremation and given to the funeral home. Urns can be found online and are quite varied and beautiful and probably less expensive than the ones your funeral home or cremation society has. The resource list at the end of this book has some websites where you can find beautiful urns.
- If you choose cremation and an urn, do you wish to keep the urn and your child's remains in your home or bury it at a local cemetery? Or do you want to choose a natural, biodegradable urn and simply bury it near a tree at your home or other meaningful place if your state allows it? Do you wish to have small vials or bags of the ashes so family members can all have some of the remains, or do you want the ashes spread or released at a special place? They do sell

special pieces of jewelry for keepsake ashes. Check with your local area about restrictions on spreading of ashes.

- Do you want to have a memorial service or a religious mass or formal service? Perhaps, both? If so, will it be private or public? Will there be more than one? Where will it be? Sometimes, others will hold vigils or memorials, especially if the child was school-aged, the circumstances of their death was tragic, or if the child or their family was well-known in the community.

- If you choose burial, will it be private or public? If it is winter, does your chosen cemetery actually bury the deceased when the ground is frozen or is it a ceremonial graveside service, or, perhaps, no graveside service, and then will the body be stored until spring when a formal burial service can be held?

- Where and when do you want these events to take place? There may be scheduling conflicts with other planned services, holidays, and other circumstances. You may not be able to get your first choice of days and times.

- Will you publish an obituary? If so, what do you want it to say and which newspapers do you wish to publish it in? Aside from your local newspaper, consider the papers in the towns where the grandparents, adult siblings or in-laws of a married child live as well. The funeral directors will assist you with this process. There is sometimes a cost associated, and it varies by paper. Some are free, some charge a flat fee. Still others charge by the word! This can add up quickly. When do you want it to run and for how many days? Do you want to include a photo? Photos usually cost extra for obituaries.

- Many funeral homes allow for a web page like Legacy.com where you can have a guest book, a photo of your child, and a story about them, and the ability for mourners to light a virtual candle for your child. It is often referenced in the obituary and can be easily shared via a hyperlink on social media and through email. Often, these web pages are prepared and organized by the funeral home and copies of the guest book comments sent to the family after the funeral, but you can also set up your own memorial page at any time. There are several options listed in the resource list at the end of the book.

- Will you request that instead of flowers, donations be made to a charity or fund? If so, that must be determined and established prior to publishing the obituary. It's nice to notify the charity if you are requesting memorial donations. The charities often send a notice to you that donation was made in honor of your child. Many parents have funds set up at a local bank, so people can donate to offset funeral costs or to establish a scholarship fund. Go Fund Me or other crowdfunding sites are becoming popular as well, but using a local bank is advised.

- If you choose a funeral, memorial service, or burial, the details of these rituals must be determined. Who will speak? Will there be formal readings or eulogies and by whom, or an "open mic" for people to share their memories and thoughts? What music will be chosen if any? Who will perform the music and singing or will you use recorded music? Are there restrictions on the type of music allowed? Many churches will only allow non-secular music for masses. Will you display photos or a slideshow or video? Who will gather or prepare these things? Will you have some of the child's favorite personal items around? Keep in mind you won't have much time to prepare, so you may need to ask for help. Sometimes, preparing photos and videos and selecting items to display is tremendously healing and therapeutic for the parents, but for others it's too difficult. Be sure someone is assigned the task of ensuring all items used or displayed are returned to the parents.

The Post-Memorial or Funeral Reception
There is a strong tradition in many cultures and religions of returning to the home of the deceased, where there is food and sharing of memories and an opportunity to pay respects to the family once again.

While the intent is to provide support and make things easier on the bereaved family, it is not always the case. This can place a tremendous burden on the family, especially when a child has died. The stress of cleaning the house before and after, and preparing or arranging for food could be overwhelming. While the thought of people touching your child's stuff and the fact you might just be too exhausted and emotionally wrung out to deal with people can put you right over the edge.

Often, others think it will be easier for the family to be in their own home. However, it's important that you, as the child's parent, consider what you want and not be afraid to state how you feel. I thought it would be fine to return home, mourn together, and serve food at our house; it seemed to make the most sense. It's the only thing I'd ever seen done after a funeral. I didn't want to go anywhere else. I let others plan it. When it actually happened, I was overwhelmed and angry that there were people in my house when I just wanted to be alone. I did not anticipate this but I do wish someone had given me the option or suggested that I might feel that way.

Perhaps, a reception at the home of another family member, neighbor, or church hall may be more appropriate. Sometimes a local country club or function facility will provide a room and catering as well.

It's important to also consider costs. Our neighbors actually took up a collection and catered the reception, so no one had to worry about cooking or cleaning. This was a kind and generous gift and it was deeply appreciated, however, my friends wanted to help and they were not invited to do so. I later learned they felt the neighbor "took over" without consulting those who knew me best. Their feelings were hurt and they were denied an avenue for their own grief as a result. Everyone was just doing what they thought was best for us, but they were also blinded in some ways by their own grief.

If the parents do not wish to be there, or need to leave, they should feel free to do so. This still means someone needs to be in charge, but that someone should not be the parents or an immediate family member. Delegating this planning to extended family or good friends might be wise. Someone should be designated to clean up. You may want to donate flowers to a local nursing home or extra food to a local shelter or first responders.

Choosing a Headstone or Memorial Marker

If your child is going to be buried or interred, you will have to decide if you want a headstone or a memorial marker for their burial site. Headstones can be expensive, but do not need to be an immediate decision as they often take months to be created and placed.

Because it is an eternal marker of your child's life and death, you should take as much time as you need to find just the right one. The artists that etch them are often quite talented, so don't be afraid to ask for custom wording, fonts, or artwork if you don't like the standard styles offered. The stones are often cut from slabs of granite, so you can really design anything you want. I have seen stones of all shapes and sizes, and even benches.

Things to consider are what kind of stone do you want, including color, shape, and size? What pictures or etching will it have? What words do you want on it and in what font? How long will it take to be made and when will it be installed? If the adult child was a member of the military, what is provided by their branch of service, if any? Check with the Veteran's Administration for more information on services they provide.

Take the time to visit local businesses that provide headstones. Your funeral director can give you a list of local businesses. You may need to travel a bit to see what options are available. Do some research online or take some time to wander around local cemeteries to get a feel for what's available and what you like and don't like.

Some families find it is just too difficult and painful to shop for a headstone or marker right after their child dies. For some, it's years before they are ready and able to do so. Cost may also be a factor, as they can be expensive. I've seen beautiful markers simply made of a large rock with the child's name etched on to it with flowers or bushes surrounding it. I've seen markers that are simply an angel statue or a small memorial garden. Some people choose to create a memorial garden at their own home, as well. Be creative. Take your time. There is no wrong way to honor your child!

A Quick Note about Media Coverage

Although this was discussed in depth in Chapter two (please consider reading it if you have not yet), it bears mentioning again here that there is also the possibility that there will be media coverage to contend with, especially if the story surrounding the child's death was a matter of public interest or controversial in any way. You may get phone calls from local or national newspapers and TV stations. They may simply show up at any of the public events like the wake, memorial or funeral service, burial, or even at your home.

You should be prepared for this if you feel it is a possibility. Again, your funeral director can help you manage this and even point you in the direction of which media sources are "friendly" to talk to and which ones are not likely to be. You don't have to talk to them, but if you do, please, know anything you say can be used and not necessarily in the context in which you said or intended it. It's a deeply personal and emotional time. The awful school shooting tragedy in Newtown, CT in 2012 is an example of how the media coverage can be intense. You can also seek the help of the local police if you are being hounded by media.

It's all About Love!
Death is emotional. There are tears. There can be laughter. There is hurt. There is anger. There is sadness. There is *love*.

People worry about not knowing what to say or being upset themselves when attending services for a child. They feel as if crying in front of the family is somehow bad. When it's a child who has died, many people cannot get past their own grief to support the family of the child. Remember, everyone is in this together. It's often uncharted territory and the sea of grief can go from calm to a tsunami and back to calm again in record time. Everyone is in the same "boat" upon the same stormy sea.

The day after Meghan died was the second worst day of my life. It was Sunday. Most of my family went to church. They were invited to light the Advent candles. I stayed home. I just couldn't do it. I was pissed off at God. I didn't want to deal with people. I didn't want to shower. I did not find the notion of going to church or God comforting at all. They found comfort in it. I'm glad they went. Our faith community held them up and surrounded them in love as they all prayed for Meghan that last Sunday of Advent.

My husband and I had to go to the funeral home later that morning. A funeral home. We had to discuss what we wanted to do to honor Meggie's life and allow for friends and family to say goodbye. We had to plan her calling hours, funeral, and burial. It was surreal. How exactly does one do this? For their own child? Just one day after she died so tragically and unexpectedly?

As we parked the car, that chest pain and heavy legged feeling came rushing back, though not as strongly as the day before. I swear, we must have looked like zombies. I don't even know how we were functioning at that point, to be honest. Lost in a nearly blinding fog of sadness, we were deep in pain and depression. I had not eaten, slept, or showered since Friday evening.

Of course, the funeral directors do this all the time. It's their job. Still, the respect and reverence shown to us was touching. I'm sure it wasn't all an act. I really do think those who helped us through the process were emotionally affected by Meggie's death, too. I remember our funeral director later sharing that children's funerals were the most difficult for them, too.

In the previous day's conversation, they had asked us to bring some clothes for her and a favorite blanket. I chose Meghan's favorite pink pants with giant pink flowers, her pink shirt, and her white fleecy top with a kitty on it. I brought the pink slippers I had bought for Christmas and her favorite pink flower blankie. You might have guessed, she loved pink! For some irrational reason, I wanted her to be warm. I reluctantly picked up the bag they were in and got out of the car.

We walked into the funeral home... slowly and reluctantly. Unsure of what to expect, but knowing it was going to be awful. Further confirmation our little girl was dead. I was holding the bag of her things. We were greeted by the director and led to a warm and welcoming living room where there was a gas fireplace going and lots of tissue boxes about the room on various tables. We sat.

The director expressed his condolences and explained to us he would be going to pick Meghan up at the hospital after the autopsy later that day and bring her back to the funeral home. When she arrived, he'd call us to let us know and that we could come down to see her any time we wanted to. I found that very comforting. He "got" how parents need to know where their children are and that they are safe and cared for, even after they leave this world.

He slowly and gently walked us through the steps of planning a wake and funeral. I'm pretty sure it took forever because we kept breaking down and crying. I have no concept of time or how long we were there.

First, we tackled the "easy" stuff. We wrote her obituary together. This afforded us a chance to talk about her and what we wanted to say to honor her life. I remember some smiles and laughter here as we told him about her. He followed a worksheet asking us questions and letting us tell a bit about her and our family. He asked us about a charity, fund, or flowers. That was easy! We requested donations be made to the local animal shelter in lieu of flowers in her memory. Meggie loved kitties and it seemed tremendously appropriate.

Then, we decided on a day for the calling hours and for the funeral. It was somewhat dictated by the weather thanks to an incoming snow storm arriving the next day. It was also impacted by another wake and funeral and the fact our *church was having Christmas related services, as Christmas was only six days away. We discussed times and details. He suggested we bring some music to play that Meggie liked and some photos or things of hers to put around the rooms for the calling hours.*

He then showed us the room where she would be for the wake and explained the process to us. This allowed us to walk a bit and see the set-up of the rooms used for calling hours. The decor was warm and welcoming. The rooms were like large living rooms. He told us how guests would travel through the rooms and in what order. It was surreal, but on some level, I felt comforted. The curtain in the room was pink. I thought, "She'd like that!"

Then, we chose a prayer card, which was no easy feat. None of them resonated. There were really none that seemed appropriate. I got momentarily angry. How the hell was I supposed to choose a prayer card when I was pissed off at God? Why can't I choose this picture with this saying? Why couldn't I write my own? There was not enough flexibility in choice. I didn't want to choose one at all, yet I felt we needed to. I wanted to honor Meg and give those who came to see her one last time a keepsake of their own.

We ultimately chose one with her photo inside a heart. The background was a pale yellow. The heart was flowery, and frankly... old lady-ish. It had pink flowers cascading around the edges of it and her name on the bottom. Her picture didn't really look right inside the heart. It was laminated. It was ugly. But she was beautiful!

On the back it read:

"*In Loving Memory of*
Meghan Agnes Beck
October 23, 2001-
December 18, 2004

Little Angels
When God calls little children
to dwell with Him above
We mortals sometimes question
the wisdom of his love.
For no heartache compares with
the death of one small child.
Who does so much to make our world
Seem wonderful and mild.
Perhaps God tires of calling
the aged to his fold.
So He picks a rosebud
before it can grow old.
God knows how much we need them,
and so he takes but few.
To make the land of Heaven
more beautiful to view.
Believing this is difficult
still somehow we must try.
The saddest word mankind knows
will always be "goodbye."
So when a little child departs,
we who are left behind
Must realize God loves children -
Angels are hard to find."

I hated it. I hated the saying. What God takes MY child away? HE doesn't need her, I do! She's not really an angel. He has plenty of angels! She was dead and I was pissed. I was angry I had to do this. I was angry I was there. I was angry nothing did her memory justice. I damn near lost it. I didn't like icky pale yellow color of the card. I didn't like the way her photo looked. I just didn't like it at all.

The Director was patient; he gave us some time alone. He apologized for the lack of flexibility in choosing. I swear he just kept projecting love and compassion toward us and might have left the room to wipe his own tears at one point.

Then, we resumed. We settled on the guest book and thank you cards. Those I really liked. Then, we were done. He called the local florist, and she came to her store right away to help us choose flowers that same day, on a Sunday! One of the benefits of living in a small town with local businesses owned by folks who live in town is such amazing service.

It didn't take long to get to the florist shop. She greeted us with tears in her eyes and hugged us, offering her condolences. It's not as if there is much choice in funeral sprays. We asked for pink and white flowers. We chose a spray for her casket, a garland for the kneeler, and two side pedestal arrangements. We also chose an arrangement from her brothers. We were probably there less than fifteen minutes.

We also had to go to the cemetery and choose a spot for her to "rest." I think we actually did this the next day because I remember not actually being able to see the exact spot due to over a foot of newly fallen snow. It occurred to me when we were at the cemetery that we never picked a casket for her. I figured maybe there were no choices for small children, and that was why we were not given the option to select one. I wasn't about to go back to ask about it. At that moment, I really didn't care. I was barely able to remain upright and think.

We foolishly thought we'd be able to manage going to a store that day, after the funeral home. Our daughter had been dead barely 24 hours and we tried to go to the Paper Store to find angels. What the hell were we thinking? It was the most excruciatingly painful experience at a store I think I've ever had. The Christmas music, the happy people, it all made me want to scream. I could barely hold myself together. I must have looked like complete s*it. Oh, the horrible mixture of anger and profound sadness. How dare they smile? How dare they be happy? Didn't they know my life just fell apart? Didn't they know I was preparing to bury my child? Of course, they didn't. I was so jealous of them. They had no idea the horror I was living. They had no idea it could have been them. Bad. Bad. Baaaad idea to go shopping.

That said, I did find the most perfect ornament. A little blonde angel, dressed in pink, holding a white kitty. It was absolutely perfect. It was SO Meghan. I cried when I picked it up and smiled through my tears. It was the last one. That must be why I wanted to go. The kitty angel was for me! We found a few other angel and kitty things and left. In fact, I think my husband checked out and I ran from the store sobbing. It was not a second too soon. I got home and collapsed on the couch... utterly exhausted. I think I just stared at the Christmas tree the rest of the day. I vaguely remember others stopping by with food and hugs.

That night, it snowed. I took a walk down the street. It was dark, maybe 10 pm. I walked slowly, gazing toward the sky. Hot tears silently falling down my cheeks, I walked slowly, gazing toward the sky. It was so peaceful and serene... so quiet. I swear I felt her with me, keeping me warm, wrapping me in love and could almost hear her saying, "It's okay mommy, it's okay."

I thought to myself, as the soft, cold snowflakes hit my face and mingled with my tears, "Snowflakes are like kisses from Heaven!" They are pure, white, innocent, and full of softness and light. Each unique. Each beautiful. It brought me some much needed comfort. It still does, every time it snows.

The next day, it snowed... a lot. I forced myself to go outside to play with my boys. We made snow angels for Meggie, of course! It was so hard to try to be silly and happy when I was so sad inside, but my boys deserved to have fun. They deserved to enjoy the Christmas season as much as they could, even if it was the last thing I wanted to do. Just a little bit of time outside playing and you'd think I'd run an ultramarathon. I was exhausted on every level. Barely sleeping and barely eating, the pain of Meghan's loss was zapping every ounce of energy I had.

Preparing Children (and Yourself) for What to Expect at a Wake, Memorial Service, or Funeral

When a child dies, those attending the rituals of remembrance and closure are often even more uncomfortable with the experience than they would be if the deceased was an older person. In fact, many people simply may not be able to face seeing the bereaved parents so deep in anguish and sadness, or cope with seeing a small casket. Many people dread an open casket, especially when it's a child. In fact, many people simply can't bring themselves to attend because of their own issues around death or because it hits too close to home if they have a child of the same age. This can be upsetting to the parents whose child has died, whose anger can surface because they don't have a choice. They have to be there. It's their child that is dead!

There is often a lot of advice thrown about with regard to the siblings of the child that died and the children that might have known the child. This is especially true when the children are young or school-aged and have a concept of death. People tend to want to shelter young children from the rituals of death. I think this is part of the reason we are so uncomfortable with death as a society.

Kids are amazingly intuitive and empathetic. They are also resilient and self-limiting. They know what they can handle and will act accordingly. Trust them. Don't shelter them or shut them out; they are much more intuitive than you give them credit for.

It's important that you do not lie to them or use euphemisms. Instead, prepare and guide them through the process in terms they can understand. Offer them choices. Let them decide what they can and cannot handle. Don't force them to participate if they don't want to, instead, offer them the choice. Designate someone to care for them while at the events so you don't have to worry about them. However, make sure that person is not closely involved or deeply grieving, too. A friend or neighbor or even a trusted babysitter is a good choice.

Most people advised me not to bring my other children to Meggie's wake and calling hours. They thought it would be distracting or too difficult for me or for them. There was no way they were not going to be a part of this entire process. That's just not how I roll. Some people thought I was nuts. Telling me my boys were too young or that it would be too hard for them or me. Really, it was about how hard it would be for those people offering the advice. They were projecting *their* discomfort and opinions on to me. I got so angry. How dare they advise ME on what to do with MY children with regard to MY child that DIED?! The nerve! Grief is an ugly thing sometimes...

Some of those who had children who were close friends with mine tried to shelter their own children from the news of Meghan's death, some for a long time after she died. Some didn't tell them at all... for months! Others told their children, but did not bring them to any of the services.

Those children did not have an opportunity to truly understand the process or achieve the same level of closure they might have if they had attended the services. The choices made by these parents were largely because the parents were not comfortable with their own experience of death, especially a child's, not because the kids didn't want to come or couldn't handle it. Most were not even given the option.

While I understand their parents' choices at the time, I do wish in these situations, parents were better able to be honest and open with their kids, no matter how painful or difficult the situation is for those parents to explain or experience. Our inability to do so is why we, as a culture, struggle so much with death and the rituals around it. It doesn't have to be this mysterious and hard. It's a fear of the unknown and a fear of emotional pain that drives many of our decisions and perpetuates the discomfort we have around the rituals of death.

I wanted my boys there. They had been intimately involved up to that point. They were her brothers. They needed to be there. She was a twin! Her twin *knew* that Meghan had died, probably before any of us did. It's the "magic" of twinship.

My sons asked questions and I was honest and straightforward with them from the very beginning. I always had been. I always will be. No, it wasn't easy. We cried together. We laughed together. I involved them in the planning as much as they wanted to be. I respected when they did not want to talk or participate. I prepared them as best I could, in language they could understand, what to expect and why. They loved their sister just as we did. They needed to grieve. They needed to process. They needed to be with us and us with them through this most difficult experience. They needed to have closure. They needed to say goodbye. They needed the opportunity to have the experience and make of it what felt right for them at the time. This was something that was going to impact them for the rest of their lives

Explaining Death and the Rituals Around Death to a Child
Much of what you say to prepare a child will depend on your religious, spiritual, and cultural beliefs. Thus, it is unique to you. It has to be age appropriate and truthful, but the level of detail may be child led if you choose. One word of advice,

do not lie. Do not speak in vague terms. Don't say the child that died is "sleeping" or has "gone away." Say the word "death" or "died." Make sure they understand the permanence of death at an age appropriate level. The permanence of death is a difficult concept for toddlers and young children to comprehend, especially when not given truthful information and allowed the opportunity to learn not only about death, but how to cope with it.

If you are unsure how or what to say to your child about death, consult with your pediatrician or a social worker who works with children and families for advice. You could also contact a local hospital or clinic that works with children or provides counseling for children as well.

This is how I explained death and what to expect to my children, then age three and six:

In preparation for the wake, I explained to my boys that when people die, it's only their bodies that stop working. I likened our bodies to a house for our spirit. I explained our spirit, that which makes us who we are, our soul, never dies. It is energy, and we can never destroy energy. It's a law of physics. Energy can change form. I explained Meggie's energy, her spirit/soul, had finished its job early here on earth. She left her body here, so she could fly with the angels. We don't understand why she had to go now, but she did. She knew why.

I explained to them that even though we miss her because we are still here, but that she still hears us and loves us and watches over us. We could talk to her and pray to her and remember her and love her. Her energy, her "Meggie-ness" will always exist in energetic form. She would always be a part of us and a part of our family. She lives in our hearts and in our memories. Her energy is love, and love never dies. This explanation was based on my spiritual beliefs, and they understood it on their level.

I further explained that in our culture, we have these rituals called wakes, or calling hours, that allow those who loved Meggie and love us to come and say goodbye to her body. They also come to show us that they care about us, and they know how much our hearts hurt because we miss her.

I told them Meggie would have a very special white box that her body would be in. I told them she'd be wearing her favorite clothes and have her blankie. I asked them if they wanted to bring her anything to put in her special box. They wanted to bring her stuffed kitties because they knew she loved them.

I prepared them for what the room would look like with Meggie in the middle in her special box, the pink curtain behind her, and pretty flowers people had sent around her special box. I told them she'd look like she was sleeping but she was not. I emphasized it was just her body; they could touch her and talk to her, but she would feel stiff and not move. She wouldn't talk back to them. I reminded them her spirit was probably right around us, but we couldn't see it. We might be able to feel it though. Love. I reminded them she loved them... always.

When we got to the funeral home, we chose to take turns seeing Meghan in her "special box" for the first time. First, my husband and I. Then we brought in the boys with just us.

118

We gave them time to process and ask questions. Her twin went right over and said, "Hi, Meggie." We encouraged them to tell her anything they wanted to. They looked and touched a bit. My older son, then six, walked all around the box, looked behind the curtains, gazed at her from afar, but didn't want to touch her. We did not force him to. Both boys offered prayer cards to her and put them in her box. Lots of them. With the help of my sons, I placed some of her favorite stuffed animals, all cats, in her box. I included a Marie, from The Aristocats, that I had bought her for Christmas. She never saw it; she would have loved it.

Then both boys wandered off to play in the chairs, read their books, or play with their handheld games. As other family members took turns coming to see Meggie, the boys were free to come and go from that room as they pleased. One of the other adults kept an eye on them, as did the funeral home staff. They had time to adjust, to see all of us laugh, cry, and hug. Both my boys joined us to the level they each felt comfortable.

I emphasize again, there is no right or wrong. There is only what is right for you. When you are the bereaved parent, you can decide whatever you want with regard to your precious child who is deceased and any of your other children.

If the funeral directors are good at their jobs, and most are excellent, they will guide you to follow your hearts and do what resonates with you, while offering suggestions and recommendations based on their experience. They will also tell you that you can always change your mind.

As we were gently being encouraged to go home and change that afternoon, before the actual calling hours began, the funeral director asked us if we wanted the casket closed or open for the calling hours. We couldn't decide. I sighed and said, "I guess closed." The director sensed my hesitation and asked me why. I thought about it. My decision was not what I wanted. It was based on my not wanting to upset other people. He sensed that. He reminded us she was our child. She was beautiful and very viewable. If we wanted to look at her, then we should. If other people were uncomfortable, they could skip the viewing room. I felt like a weight had been lifted. I could have hugged him! Yes, I wanted to look at her! I wanted people to see her. She was beautiful!

As hard as it was for any of those other people, it was much, much harder for us. The harsh attitude of "screw them, she's mine" won out. I am so very glad it did. I don't think I could have gotten through it if that box had been closed. I needed to see Meggie's beautiful face. I drew strength from it. I didn't see just a body. I saw my daughter... only my daughter.

Tuesday, December 21st. The winter solstice. The day of Meghan's wake. Calling hours were from 5-8 pm only. We spent most of the day at the funeral home saying our private goodbyes with family and close friends. It was the first time we'd seen her since the hospital, the first time the boys had seen her since she died. She was in the most beautiful "special box." A white casket with gold and silver around it and golden angels on all four corners. There were beautiful flowers on pedestals on both sides and a spray on top. A cross with a ribbon that said, "sister" was leaning inside her

120

special box along with a crucifix. She looked like a little princess in there. Her favorite stuffed kitty lay at her side. Tucked in with her blankie.

When we arrived at the funeral home for her calling hours after going home to quickly change people were already gathering in the parking lot. We had a few quiet minutes with Meghan behind closed doors while a line formed in the hallway and in the first room. That first room had some of Meggie's art work, photos, favorite things of hers, and a slide show playing on a laptop which gave people something to look at and a glimpse of our Meggie for those who didn't know us well.

A queue was set up to funnel people through the pre-viewing room with velvet ropes like a line at an amusement park or theater. I thought it was odd, as I didn't expect that many people to be coming! First, attendees signed a guest book and received a prayer card. We had made a CD of Meggie's favorite songs which were playing on the sound system throughout the funeral home. It was quite an eclectic mix from her favorite Christmas songs to Disney tunes to "Mambo Number 5" by Lou Bega! It made me smile. I bet it made them smile, too.

As the guests approached the viewing room, we waited. My husband and I and our parents stood in a receiving line. Between the guests and us was Meggie in her special box. If they were not already crying, most people started to cry as they saw her there. Some audibly gasped, expecting a closed casket or being overcome with emotion. Others simply couldn't come in and retreated. My husband and I stood and waited as people knelt before her and had their moment to process and pay their respects to her. Then they came to us.

I am sure I've never been so thoroughly hugged in my life. Most went through the motions, clearly traumatized by their own grief, saying how sorry they were, through their own tears. Some couldn't speak at all. They were so overcome; they just hugged us. Some were crying so hard we were comforting them!

I'm sure I cried on and off but mostly I was disconnected from the experience somehow. The lack of sleep, the lack of food, the utter exhaustion of having to stand there and do this was overwhelming. I was there, yet I wasn't fully present. It was surreal.

It was non-stop for the entire three hours. The people were a blur. Some we didn't even know, they just felt compelled to come pay their respects. Others, I hadn't seen in forever. In fact, we had no idea how many of the guests had learned of Meggie's death. We were touched by each and every person who made the effort to come. Close to 300 people had signed the guest book; most waited in line for an hour or more.

We were especially fortunate for I am a doula, which means we had extra TLC and a bunch of surrogate mothers caring for us all. My doula sisters supported and mothered us the entire time. They made sure we had chairs and encouraged us to sit, even if only for a minute. They brought us water and fresh tissues. They sat there in the chairs and held the space. They sent love. They rubbed our backs. They helped others with water and tissues and hugs and support. They watched our boys. They stayed the entire night. Without being asked to do any of it. At some point, one of our neighbors offered to take the boys home for us as they were overwhelmed and tuned out. We let them.

One of the things I do remember about that night is the end of the calling hours. My uncle, the deacon, was there. Another uncle, one who usually didn't come to any family events and who I certainly didn't expect to see, came at the very end. Perhaps, most touching and surprising, our pediatrician came. She had in her hand two gift bags for the boys. In each of them was a Beanie Baby Angel Bear. She said they were the last two at the store. The boys still have them and cherish them. She hugged us through tears. My uncle gathered us in a circle and asked us to hold hands. I don't remember what he said, but I'm sure it was a prayer.

Everyone left. We, once again, were left alone with Meggie. We kissed her goodnight and went home. It was so hard to leave her. I wanted to stay and sleep next to her. Knowing the next day would be even harder than this one had been.

Memorial Services and Funerals
The decision on whether to have a memorial service or funeral is very individual. It may be based on your religious or spiritual beliefs and practices or on personal preference. Those who choose cremation often just opt for a memorial service and sometimes, a private burial. Others choose to have a wake, a memorial service or funeral, and then cremation and burial. Cremation also allows for the family to keep the remains in the home instead of burial, and this is often very important for parents of young children who feel

that having their ashes in the home is like having their child still in the home with them.

Those who do not choose cremation have options, too. They may do as we did and opt for the traditional wake/calling hours and then a funeral mass and burial that is open to all who wish to attend. Others might just choose a funeral or memorial service, but keep the burial private. Others keep it all private and small. It's a matter of personal preference.

One complicating factor of planning memorial services and funerals can be when parents disagree or are divorced, or there are different religious beliefs or preferences that cause a fundamental disagreement in when or how services are conducted.

When an adult child has died and their spouse and the parents disagree, it can cause additional stress, especially if that adult child had never made their wishes known. It's already a difficult task; finding compromise while in such pain and shock can be difficult. Hopefully, your funeral director and loved ones can help you reach a compromise that works for everyone.

It's important to remember the purpose of these services is to honor the life of the child that has died. As adults, everyone should be able to put aside their differences and focus on that, at least temporarily, for the sake of their child, no matter how old that child is when they die.

I remember the priest coming to the house, I think it was one or two days after Meggie died. He came to pay his respects to us, but also to assist us in planning her funeral mass.

Meghan was baptized Catholic and thus was going to have a Catholic funeral mass. The priest explained to us the order of mass for a funeral and asked us to choose readings and songs. He gave some suggestions to make it easier. The readings were a challenge. I really didn't like any of them. He tried to give us alternatives, but a funeral mass in the Catholic Church is pretty cookie cutter. There is not much wiggle room.

Ultimately, I just chose two readings because I had to, not because they resonated with me or because I liked them. I liked nothing about this experience, and I was getting pissed that I had to make these choices at all. Unsure how to comfort me, and probably expecting my wrath to burst forth at any moment, the priest looked a bit uncomfortable with the whole experience, too. I'm sure the number of funerals he conducted for children, especially at the holidays, paled in comparison to the ones he typically oversees. I'm not sure anything, even your faith in God, can prepare you for such an emotionally difficult experience.

The songs were easier to choose: "Amazing Grace" and "On Eagle's Wings." Standard songs, but at least they resonated more with me. I had no idea how beautifully they'd be played and sung. What a gift.

He also asked us, rather uncertainly, if we wanted the church decorated for Christmas, for they could wait to decorate until after her funeral if we wished. I was shocked he asked my preference. I had just expected it to be decorated for Christmas; it was only days away after all. It was kind of him to offer, but I didn't even think about it. I told him absolutely, decorate for Christmas. Meggie would have

125

loved it! It was mostly just poinsettias around the altar, some garlands, and the giving tree. She loved "pretties." It was an easy choice among impossible ones.

In preparing the boys for the funeral and burial, I explained to them what the day would be like. I told them when we'd go to the funeral home and that we'd get one more time to see Meggie inside her special box. I asked them that morning while we were there if they'd like to choose one of her kitties to take care of for her. They each chose one.

I opted to let her keep her favorite kitty and her blankies with her. I must tell you, it's the only thing I truly regret. I wish I had those things now. My mommy instinct was that she needed her lovies when in reality, I know she didn't. She wasn't in her body. *I needed them.* I do wish the funeral director had asked the same questions about her things as he did about open vs. closed casket for the wake. I might have changed my mind if he had.

I also prepared the boys for the ride from the funeral home to the church. I told them what to expect at the church and what to expect at her special place at the cemetery, where her special box would be put in the ground for safe keeping.

The day of the funeral dawned sunny and relatively warm. It was a Wednesday. December 22nd, 2004. Just three days before Christmas. Our family headed to the funeral home for our last visit with Meggie before her funeral. We all took turns saying our final goodbyes and our last chance to touch her, kiss her, and see her. As everyone said their goodbye, they took a pink rose from a vase for the cemetery and went to their cars. For the last time, we and our boys said our

126

goodbyes to Meggie's body, took our rose, and walked outside to the limo.

It was excruciatingly painful to know I'd never see Meggie's beautiful face again. I felt as if my heart was being ripped right out of my chest. As I sat in the limo, I wanted to run back in and get her blankie, to tell them no, don't close her box, let me keep her with me. But I was paralyzed with grief. The battle going on between my heart and my head was unbelievably painful to endure. It was visceral... overwhelming. I sat quietly and said and did nothing. Oh how I wish I had kept her blanket and kitty...

In the limo, her music CD was playing! It was a nice surprise. I explained to the boys how we'd all drive to the church in a line. Meggie got to go first in the fancy car, then us, and then everyone else. I told them there would be lots of people at the church, and we'd be the last ones to go in.
Then Meggie would be brought in in her special box on a wheely cart. They thought that was cool. We explained how the funeral mass would go as best as we knew. I had brought things to keep them occupied during the mass, and they both reverted to coloring and reading during most of the mass.

I did one thing that was a bit out of the ordinary; I asked a friend, who is also a photographer, to take a few photos of the services. I had actually taken some photos of Meggie in her special box and of her brothers and our family visiting her at the funeral home. I was worried her twin especially wouldn't remember it and might someday want to see some photos to help him understand. This appalled a lot of people who didn't realize I had requested it, but once again, I didn't care. She was my daughter, and I wanted photos. I am so glad I have them. I eventually scrapbooked them. It was incredibly therapeutic for me. Creating a memorial of her memorial helped me to process and heal. It is also a keepsake for all of our family. It's in a large pink album and sits in our living room for anyone to see at any time.

I remember seeing a woman, who was stopped by the funeral home to allow our procession through, make the sign of the cross as Meggie's car went by. I started to cry. I was touched by her gesture and the reality was slapping me in the face. I tried to hold it together because I had a long few hours ahead of me. The last place I wanted to be was in that limo, going to my daughter's funeral. I even contemplated jumping out and running away... as if that would have helped anything.

We arrived at the church and waited as late comers filed in. I wondered how I would manage to walk down the aisle of the church. I prayed I wouldn't pass out. I felt weak and shaky. When we were given the cue to enter the church, we were the last ones in. I was shocked it was so full... literally standing room only.

We walked, slowly and solemnly down the center aisle to the first pew on the right. It was the longest and most painful walk of my life. Meggie's photo sat on a table at the altar. All eyes were on us. All you could hear above the music were sobs and a few audible cries and gasps as people felt and saw our pain as a family.

Then, Meggie was brought in. The pallbearers were funeral home staff. I don't know if they even asked anyone from our *family or friends if they wanted to be a pallbearer. I'm sure no one offered or could have done it if asked.*

There were so many tears... We were invited to place the pall, a ceremonial cloth, over her casket. We tried to involve the kids in this ceremony, but they mostly watched. When it was done, her twin said very softly, "It's perfect." We took our place in the pew, and the mass began.

I don't remember much of it. There was the usual order of mass with readings done by one of the sisters of the church and another by a neighbor who volunteered. No one in our family wanted to attempt to read or maybe, no one was asked.

My uncle delivered a short homily about Meghan and death and something that was meant to be comforting about our faith. I honestly don't remember it. Although he did make us laugh briefly in sharing some memories of Meghan's strong and feisty personality. My eyes went to her face, smiling at us with those big, wise, blue eyes from her picture on the lectern.

Then, there was a surprise song. It was played on a CD player after the homily. He said, "... the song says everything perfectly, so let's just listen." It was called, "Visitor From Heaven" by Twila Paris. I think everyone cried as they heard it. Simply beautiful, and written specifically about the loss of a child, it spoke of what we felt in our hearts.

After the mass ended, Meggie was brought to the entrance of the church. We followed, as did our family, not unlike a wedding, pew by pew from front to back. There was a prayer said at the door of the church for her. Then she was brought back to her "fancy car" and us to our limo.

Throughout the funeral I was completely unaware of the friend who I had asked to take photos of the funeral. She captured some beautiful shots of the mass and the dedication at the cemetery. She made a slideshow set to music of them. I am grateful for them. They are a blessed supplement to what little memory I have of that day. I watch it every year on the anniversary of her funeral.

Burial

It's not as simple as it seems. Choosing a final resting place for a child can be complicated. It often means having to choose a plot for your family, or at least the parents and this child, especially if the child is young. If a family plot has already been purchased for the parents but there is no additional space to add a child to that plot, it can present an emotional and logistical challenge.

Then there are the rules of the cemeteries that should really be a factor in selecting a "special place" for your child to rest. Not all cemeteries allow decorations at gravesites. Some are very specific and restrictive about the type and size of headstone, type of flowers or shrubs that can be planted and when, what sort of items are allowed or not and when. For example, some cemeteries will only allow holiday decorations for a certain number of days before/after a holiday and then all items are removed. Some allow no permanent decorations.

For a child, particularly a young child, parents often decorate a child's gravesite seasonally. They may bring gifts: pumpkins in the fall, a tree a Christmas, a balloon for a birthday, bird feeders, personal items that belonged to the child, garden flags, and eternal lights. Not all cemeteries allow these gifts or decorations, and it can complicate grief if parents cannot bring their child gifts to their grave.

Some parents choose a cemetery in a town where they live, assuming that makes sense, only to later move far away and not be able to visit their child's grave. Others want to move their child with them when they relocate, which is possible, but very expensive. Some choose a place that is a midpoint between all those who want to be able to visit the grave, but then regret the inconvenience to them, as parents. Still others choose a place farther away because it's too painful for their child to be in the same town. Some choose cemeteries further away because they have more relaxed rules or a prettier or more peaceful setting, and that is important to them.

Choosing a headstone is also something bereaved parents are ill-prepared for. The choices available and decisions that must be made can be overwhelming. They are expensive and can take a long time to be made and then installed at the graveside. I was shocked at how long it took! There are usually very few options of where to shop for them and in some places, very few options for the style of marker.

Some parents really struggle with this and put it off for years; others are eager to get it done so the world knows their child is there, and they have their name. It will be forever the marker for your child's existence... their life and death. Take your time to find the right marker for your child and family. Shop around. Walk around local cemeteries for ideas. Design your own! Be prepared, though, that when you see it at the cemetery for the first time, it's like a punch in the gut. They typically don't notify you when a marker is placed, so it can be a trigger when you visit and find it's there. A bittersweet moment for many.

You can be creative and make a temporary marker until you find the right permanent marker. As mentioned earlier, finding a talented artist who can etch exactly what you want on a stone is worth searching for. I had received a sympathy card with a dove flying to the Heavens. I loved the image and asked that that be etched on the front of Meg's stone. It was a perfect replica!

As we sat in the limo waiting for everyone to exit the church for the short funeral procession to the nearby cemetery, I was numb. I think we all were. It was silent in the limo, even the kids, save for the sounds of Meggie's favorites CD playing. I gazed out the window at the people exiting the church. I didn't recognize some of them. There were others I never expected to see there, yet there they were. Some came to her wake and not the funeral, and others to the funeral but not the wake. Some came to both. I would later find out there were many community members who didn't really know us and friends/family we'd not seen in a very long time who attended the services.

After what seemed like a long time, we began to slowly move in procession. It was less than a mile to the cemetery. I remember seeing the officer that had stopped the traffic there. He appeared to wipe a tear from his eye as we passed.

He may have been the same officer who was first to arrive at our house the day Meghan died. I don't understand how these people do this all the time. It's got to be so hard, especially when it involves a child. I know Meggie's death hit others especially hard, even those who did not know us personally, because of the proximity to Christmas.

Once we arrived at the cemetery, we were told to wait in the limo for everyone to file in. Partially because it was cold and partially so they could get Meg's "special box" and flowers arranged. We got out and slowly walked to her special place. It looked oddly pretty, with the green fake grass carpet and Meggie's beautiful white casket adorned with pink and white flowers at the center. What they were hiding was the fact her casket was suspended above a hole, the one she'd be placed in after we all left. The snow had been shoveled aside, so we could all gather round. The dedication and commitment ceremony was brief. I really have very little memory of this. If it were not for the photos, I might not remember it at all. I know I was there, but so numb and so broken hearted that nothing registered.

Once the formalities were done, we each took our pink roses and placed them on her casket. I went first. I told her she always wanted to fly. Now she was free to "fly in the sky," just like she always wanted to do. Her father followed and then her brothers. Others followed suit, placing their roses on her casket. Some just simply touched the edge of the casket in a gesture of goodbye and slowly, the guests left. Some came to talk to us first, others just left.

Eventually, we were the only ones left. Her brothers were running through the snow. Her twin at one point started pulling flowers out of the arrangements to give her more on top of her special box. Then he said he wanted to go in there with her. A sweet gesture but... oh my God... the stab of pain and fear I felt when he said it!

The rest of the family and many friends were heading back to the house for the reception they had planned. I was in no hurry to go home. I still wasn't ready to leave her. The funeral director came over to us and commended everyone on the service and how meaningful and personalized it was. He asked us which way we wanted her oriented as the stone would eventually go near the cemetery road, did we want her head at the stone or her feet. We opted for a footstone. It just seemed nicer to have her head away from the road. It's so odd how we think with our human brains about such things. I thought it was nice of him to ask. Because we had purchased a family plot, we opted to put Meggie in the middle spot.

We made our way back to the limo to head home. He handed us a large bag. I wasn't sure what was in it, but he said it was the things from her calling hours like the stuff we had brought to display and the guest book. When we arrived home the Peter Pan song, "You can Fly" was playing. I smiled. How perfect! Her twin got out of the limo and immediately ran through the snow. He wanted to make a snow angel for Meggie!

I walked into MY house and it was full of people. I almost turned around and walked out. I wanted to be alone. I did not want to talk to or see anyone. I was exhausted. There was food everywhere. I saw no one. The last thing I wanted to do was eat or be social. I felt a wave of anger, then exhaustion, and then I was just completely overwhelmed. I was focused on feeding the boys because they were starving. It kept me distracted and focused on a task. I vaguely remember a few hugs.

That's all I remember. I think I might have sought escape in my bedroom, but I honestly just don't remember. Of all the things associated with those first few days after her death, that period of time is the one thing I really draw a blank on. I'm not sure why. I imagine it's because I shut down. I had hit the wall. I was exhausted in every way possible. I had just buried my daughter. I had still not eaten much or slept in five days. I didn't want to talk to or see anyone but her. I couldn't have that, so I basically ran and hid.

The next thing I remember is sitting in the living room later that afternoon, after most everyone had left. I had asked they donate the leftover food to a shelter, so someone did bring it somewhere. I remembered the bag the funeral director had given us. As I took the things out of it, I was surprised to discover a few unexpected gifts. The guestbook was one of them. I knew we had one, but reading the names and messages of love and support helped it sink in who was really there that night. We just didn't remember seeing many of them! There was also a keepsake book for us to fill in details of her funeral and burial and laminated bookmarks that had her obituary on one side and "Now I lay me down to Sleep" on the other. One for each of the four of us.

There were also several gifts from the funeral home that touched us deeply. Among them, a gorgeous heirloom Catholic Bible, a "Merry Christmas From Heaven" ornament, and a plaque that had Meghan's picture and a little poem about angels. The funeral directors were so compassionate and helpful. I know it's their job, but they went above and beyond and we owe them a debt of gratitude.

We later learned they gifted us her funeral. When we asked why at a later date, they simply said, "It was the right thing to do." There is some good in the world.

The rituals associated with death like calling hours, memorial services, funerals, and burials are emotionally charged, somewhat by design. As difficult as the process is to endure, it does give us a tremendous gift. It gives us some structure for our grief. It gives us a place to gather and share. It provides a place and time receive support. It connects us to each other when we need it most. It rallies our village.

The rituals and the people who dedicate their lives to serving those of us who have to do the impossible are guides for us during those incredibly difficult days. They are like beacons, showing us the way with love, patience, compassion and understanding. Gently, they help us to do the impossible. It's a thankless and difficult job. They deserve more recognition for what they do.

Perhaps if people knew more about the purpose of these rituals and what to expect during them we'd be in a much better place to cope ourselves and help others through such difficult days.

Perhaps if everyone knew what funeral directors really did when it comes to preparing families to say goodbye to their loved ones, there would be less fear and avoidance and a greater willingness to learn about and participate in these rituals. Most likely, we'd all be better equipped to help ourselves cope and more effectively help those who need us to help them.

These rituals are difficult to plan and participate in, but they are necessary to our healing. They facilitate not only a celebration of life for the deceased, but assemble a village to support the grieving family. It is an honor to be part of such a powerful ritual of love.

Love is what we celebrate when we honor a life. Love never dies.

Chapter Five

Understanding Grief: A Survival Guide

"The reality is that you will grieve forever. You will not 'get over' the loss of a loved one; you will learn to live with it. You will heal and you will rebuild yourself around the loss you have suffered. You will be whole again but you will never be the same. Nor should you be the same nor would you want to."

Elizabeth Kubler Ross

Things I Wish People Knew About Grief

There are many things about grief that I wish someone had told me or told those who tried to support me while grieving themselves. There are many, many things about the grieving process that you just don't realize until you are in it. So many things others don't realize, because they haven't been through it. Yet it would be so much better for everyone if we were better prepared for what to expect, how we might feel, and where to find support.

There is no handbook on recovering from the loss of a loved one. We are not taught about it in school. If you are lucky, you get a brochure from the hospital or funeral home on coping with grief with precious little information. You may turn to the internet to search for information, but it can be so overwhelming and time consuming. There are many books out there, like this one, which offer information and personal experiences.

Unfortunately, far too many people discover these resources too late, especially when looking for support and resources in the first few days and weeks after the death of a child or loved one.

Of course, the time when you ideally need all of that information is before you actually do need it. Plus, when you need it, you need it immediately, but you don't have the energy or ability to find it since you don't even know what you need when lost in shock, numbness and sadness.

Since none of us ever expect to lose a child or even a close loved one, especially suddenly, we find ourselves lost and without information and resources that would help us understand the process and make some of those difficult decisions.

What you really need is someone to hand you a Grief 101 book immediately after being told a loved one has died. One that explains what you can expect to feel, think and experience in the days, weeks, and months and even years following the death of someone you love. One that explains why you are feeling the way you are and provides resources to help you cope with such a profound loss and find your way to healing. One that teaches those who want to help you the best (and worst) ways to do so. I hope to provide that resource.

So here it is... Grief school.

Understanding the Grieving Process

So what is grief? Grief is often defined as the process one goes through when a loss is perceived and includes psychological, physical, social, and behavioral reactions. It is often very intense, varies tremendously from person to person and situation to situation, and can be quite confusing for those in and around it.

It's important to emphasize that grieving is a process and that it is normal! It is also a very individual experience and the intensity often varies depending on the significance of the loss.

Symptoms of grief can include:
- Physical pain
- Anxiety
- Anger
- Denial
- Crying
- Profound sadness/depression
- Irritability
- Hopelessness
- Fear
- Confusion
- Preoccupation with the person who died or circumstances of the loss
- Guilt
- Restlessness
- Shortness of breath
- Nightmares or difficulty sleeping
- Feeling empty
- Change in appetite

Some other responses or feelings one might have that are associated with grief include:

- Numbness
- Inability to focus or concentrate
- Obsessive-compulsive behaviors
- Feeling like you are on an emotional roller coaster
- A sense of loss of control
- A sense of loss about safety
- A crisis of faith
- Panic attacks
- Trust issues
- Forgetfulness
- Irresponsible behavior or reliance on medication, drugs, or alcohol to "cope" (risk for addiction)
- Withdrawal
- Overworking
- Relationship changes

Grieving is a process. When grieving the death of a loved one, it is a complex, lifelong, and highly individual process. It's a journey... a new road to walk. Emotions, like water, ebb and flow. At times they are soft, like gentle waves that soothe and appear to help the darkness recede and let in a little laughter and light with happy memories.

At other times, the ocean swells and the waves build with the power of a storm, crashing over you and pulling you under... over and over and over again. At times, you are certain you might drown, quite literally, in your sorrow. Then, the storm subsides, and the waves become soft and rolling once again.

Once in a while, there is rogue wave that comes out of nowhere and pushes you down again. Eventually, you will rest on the sand and feel the sun warm on your face. The sunny days will outnumber the stormy ones. Really, they will.

Over time, and the amount of time is different for everyone, the fog will gradually begin to lift. At first, just for short periods of time, but then, more brightness will be seen. The stormy season will subside and things will change and yes, eventually get easier. The sunshine and light will begin to emerge again.

No, it won't ever be the same. It won't ever be "normal" as you once knew normal to be, but you will find a new and different normalcy for you and your family. A state of being where you integrate your child's life *and* death into your life and move forward… together. Just in a different way than you once imagined.

Please know there is no right or wrong way. No time frame. It's a very individual experience, and it will evolve as you do.

Initial Grief: Surviving the First Week

The first few days are, of course, the worst. The varied emotions, rituals of grief, and decisions that must be made in first week following the death of a loved one were covered in the first few chapters of this book.

Knowing about and understanding the significance of the rituals of death and the importance of grief keeping to bereaved parents really speaks to the most difficult and profound parts of the grieving process in that first week. Just getting through it is exhausting.

Unfortunately, many people think that once that week is over, the worst is over. That it gets better... quickly. All too often, parents and those around them are shocked to find that it doesn't get better just because you've said goodbye. Grief is not that simple, nor should it be. Your child is still dead. That never changes.

Common Misconceptions about Grief:
- Time heals all wounds.
- You should stay busy.
- You shouldn't think about the child so much.
- You should give a grieving person their space.
- You should be "strong," particularly for someone else.
- You shouldn't feel bad or guilty.
- That the loss can somehow be replaced by having another child.
- You will eventually get over it and move on.

Much of what I've described in chapters two, three, and four describes what bereaved parents experience in the first week after their child dies. This is really only the beginning of the grieving process. It is only the very beginning of a long road of processing and integrating the death of their child into their life so they can find their way to healing.

The tasks of deciding how to honor your child and lay them to rest are overwhelming and exhausting on every level. When you are not tending to those tasks, you are often simply overwhelmed with the pain of your child's death or lost in numbness and sadness. Time, as you know it, ceases to exist.

Much of those first days and weeks is a blur, and few people remember much of it. It's very hard to lay down memory when you are in a state of emotional crisis, especially if you are also not eating or sleeping well. They are simply trying to survive it.

Most parents spend the majority of those early days deep in the first stage of grief, shock and numbness. They may not be sleeping or they may want to sleep all the time. Some will take sleeping pills prescribed by their doctor to help them sleep. They may have no appetite at all and not eat, or they may try to drown their sorrows in food, alcohol, or medications.

A heavy cloak of sadness and depression weighs them down, making it feel as if everything is a colossal effort and that they are moving in slow motion through a thick fog of physical and emotional pain. It is a dark and lonely place.

In these first weeks, it may feel as if the current of emotional sadness in and around you is pulling you under. You wonder if you can survive the pain. It's all you can do to keep your head above water. It's incredibly difficult to function on any other level than basic survival. Even though you may be physically doing nothing, the work of grief is absolutely exhausting.

Coping with Grief: Coping Styles

Not everyone reacts to the death of their child the same way. Not everyone will cope or grieve the same way and it is okay.

It can, and often does, change throughout the different stages of grief. There are two basic types of coping strategies that bereaved parents and their close family default to in these early days. There are those who are able and willing to honor their feelings and are willing and able to be with them, and there are those who just are not ready to go there yet. Both are normal reactions to a child's death in those early days.

It can complicate grief when parents and those close to them grieve in completely different and opposite ways, as it can leave them feeling isolated and alone. They are unable to comprehend their own experience, let alone be sensitive to the fact someone they love is not "doing" it the same way.

When those around them are unsure how to help or support the grieving parents, or are lost in their own pain, they tend to say or do nothing, further isolating parents in their sorrow.

Active grievers are just that. They are fully present in the pain. They process in their own way, but it often remains focused on the child who is now gone. They may relive memories quietly or want to talk about them with others. They may spend hours going through photographs and videos of their child. They may actively seek counseling and professional support or want to attend a support group right away. They may write to their child. They may read cards received over and over, wish to display them and the gifts they received as a tribute to their child. They may spend hours in their child's room or with their things, looking to connect, understand, and heal.

These are the parents who tend to actively search for information about the eternal question, "Why?" They try to understand the circumstances of their child's death, looking for answers, a reason, anything that can help them make sense of their loss.

As they ride the roller coaster of emotion, they may be more likely to share their experiences with others, often unprompted. They often seek to connect with other parents who have experienced the loss of their child. They may read books or articles trying to make sense of and validate what they feel. Tasks other than those related to their child and their grief are not important and often neglected. Household duties, work, and the mundane day to day things we all take for granted simply don't get done.

Others may react in just the opposite way. They are **non-active grievers,** or more passive. They find it's just too difficult or painful to dwell on their child or the fact that they are now gone. Often, these are the parents who dive back into work quickly and often spend more time than ever there, perhaps, as an escape from the pain of reality. They may gladly take care of the mundane tasks of day to day life, doing household chores and shopping. They may want to attend previously scheduled events and literally carry on as if nothing changed.

It could be that these things provide a welcome distraction from the pain they feel and are not yet ready to confront. Others often think they are "over" the death of their child quickly. The reality is they simply are not yet ready to go there.

I was at a seminar on death and dying and the instructor asked us what we thought the response, "Fine" really meant. The question asked to elicit that answer did not really matter. Think about the tone people often use when their only response is a one word, "Fine."

We answered, "They are not really fine." It turned out, the true meaning behind the response was often best represented by an acronym. I do not know who originally coined the acronym, but we all agreed it was appropriate in any circumstance.

F- F*cked up
I- Insecure
N- Neurotic
E -Emotional

Thus, if someone says they are "Fine," they are likely in need of some love and support. No matter what the question was. As a friend, family member or professional, we need to be sensitive to what is potentially hidden in a response of "Fine," no matter how it is said.

Active and non-active grievers often do quite the opposite of each other. The non-active griever may not want to talk about their child or the fact that they have died. They may avoid the child's room and their things. They may not be ready to read those cards or look at the photos and walk down Memory Lane. They often disappear when others come to visit and provide support. It doesn't mean they don't love and miss their child. It doesn't mean they are not deeply impacted by the child's death. They, too, are grieving. Just in a different way. For them, the thought of happier times is a place they just can't or won't allow themselves to go. The thought of moving forward through the pain over losing their child is unbearable. They stay in their comfort zone which is often a bubble of self-protection and avoidance. They may withdraw and appear depressed and sad all the time, or they may seem or say they are "fine" appearing to be their usual self. They may show no sign of acknowledging the child's life or death. They are not wrong or heartless or broken. It's simply a coping mechanism that allows them to function.

The Challenges of Different Coping Styles
When parents lose a child, they are often so lost in their own pain that they simply cannot support each other, especially if they react in opposite ways. In the first few days, they simply go through the motions. They are usually guided by the professionals around them like medical staff, clergy, funeral directors, and their close family and friends.

They often do simply what others tell them or suggest because it's just easier than thinking and feeling and, quite possibly, because they can't actually make decisions. They may remain connected to each other in their grief and literally cling to each other, or they may be together, but separate, lost in their own emotional storm, adrift from each other emotionally.

While this is not uncommon or abnormal in these early days and weeks, if it persists, it can strain the relationship between the parents. It's important to try to communicate with each other and acknowledge the differences in coping and that there is no right or wrong way. It's okay to grieve differently. It's important to seek professional counseling if your partner's coping mechanism is impacting your relationship with them or with your other children. You can always seek counseling individually as well as together.

Once the formalities of laying your child to rest have been completed, a new phase begins. The closure of burying your child or receiving their ashes brings a new level of painful reality. Everyone that supported you through the initial days and offered condolences returns to their own lives. The cards and flowers stop coming. The phone calls dwindle. The meal train may also dwindle. Your spouse or you may have to return to work. You may have to attend to the needs of your other children if you have them.

You have to begin to live a new life, one without the physical presence of your beloved child in it. While this may be on some level, more difficult for parents who have lost young children who still lived with them; it is no less painful for parents who lost adult children. It is just different in some ways.

The "Firsts"

The first week also brings the first of the "anniversary" firsts. The first meal without your child. The first morning that they don't wake up in your home. The first diaper you aren't changing. The first night you are not overseeing tubby time, reading them a story, tucking them in, and kissing them goodnight. Perhaps, the first day they are not heading to the bus stop or calling you to say, "Hi," and tell you about their day. It's the first Monday, Tuesday, Wednesday and so forth. Then it's the one week anniversary, the two week, the month. It goes on and on.

There are also the reflexive firsts. Sometimes these are even more painful, because they are out of the blue and done without thought, but rather out of habit. The first time you call their name or pick up the phone and dial their number as you always have and realize they will never respond again. The first time you set a place at the table for them, forgetting they are gone. The first time you go to the store and realize you put something in your cart for them, as if they were still here.

Then there are the public firsts. The first time you go out in public and have to manage your emotions in the face of strangers who are happy, who have children who are alive, who have no idea how much pain you are in. It can be unbearable. Especially when someone doesn't realize your child has died and asks how they are or even the innocent, "How many children do you have?" question.

Triggers for grief are everywhere, and you don't even know what they are yet! Parents are often unprepared for how difficult seemingly simple everyday tasks can be. Escaping the house does not always allow you to escape the pain. Sometimes, it actually intensifies the pain, especially in the early weeks.

Every day and everything is a new first that first week. As if you were not already exhausted from the work of grieving and trying to cope with the death of your child, these firsts just add more weight to that already heavy cloak you are wearing.

Perhaps the biggest and most difficult first is the first week anniversary of their death. The day of the week, the time of day you learned of their death, all the events of that day may come back in vivid detail. Some parents relive that day by the minute. Others simply block those details from their conscious awareness. The fact that it's been a whole week can be a painful reminder. A whole week that your child has been gone. Just like the first hour and the first day, that first week is a milestone of sorts. On the one hand, your child has been gone a whole week. On the other hand, you have made it through the first of the firsts and some of the toughest days you will ever experience emotionally. It still hurts like hell.

You may find this continues as the months go by. If your child died on a Tuesday, the 7th, every Tuesday and every 7th of the month, you may have a heightened awareness of the loss of your child. This is not true for everyone, but often people are blindsided by the fact that it can make for an emotionally difficult day... even decades later. For others it's the time of death or certain number sequences. Seeing their birthdate on a digital clock or looking at the clock and noticing it's the same as their time of death for example. Or seeing a picture of them cycle through their screen saver on their computer.

For me, that first week anniversary of Meghan's death was on Christmas Day. I don't need to tell you how difficult Christmas was that year or continues to be, even now, nearly ten years later as I write this. I, personally, found that for a long time, the day of the week and more specifically the actual calendar date, were triggers for me. If your child dies on or near a significant date for you like a holiday, birthday, or anniversary, it can complicate your grief and make those anniversary days a bit more challenging than if they were not associated with other important family events. Those days will forever hold a very different significance than they once used to.

Supporting Loved Ones in the First Week – How You can Help Bereaved Parents

Friends and family members of the bereaved parents often feel completely helpless and lost. They may feel as if they are walking on eggshells. Afraid to say or do the wrong thing. They are afraid they will make the parents cry or feel angry.

Supporters are often afraid of their own emotions; perhaps, fearful they themselves will cry and that would somehow be disrespectful to the parents. People are often unsure how to help someone in so much pain. Struggling with coping themselves, some friends and family members wonder if they have anything to give to the parents who are in even more pain. It's just so difficult to fathom.

Despite your own pain as a family member or friend, the parents desperately need support, help, love, and most of all, for you to remember their child. Please, don't be afraid to mention the child or their name. You won't upset the parents. They already hurt. As bereaved parents, we miss our children every day. We think of them every day. It is comforting to know others are thinking of them, too! Chapter six is dedicated to all the ways you can support the bereaved, including suggestions for what to say and do and what not to say or do.

It helps everyone whether you are grieving the loss of a loved one yourself, or supporting someone else who has lost someone close to them, to understand what the stages or emotional experiences of the grieving process are. We will all eventually lose someone close to us. We all need to know and understand the nuances of coping and recovering. It helps us help ourselves and help others in need.

Grief 101: The Stages of Grief

Grief is, by definition, the emotional reaction to a significant change in our lives. We tend to associate it with death, but we grieve other losses or changes in our lives in much the same way and with many of the same reactions. Our grief is often more intense, and appropriately so, when it's related to the loss of a loved one who was close to us.

Other losses in our lives where we might have had experience with the feelings and emotions associated with grief are:

- Death of a loved one or friend
- Divorce
- The loss of a pet
- Financial losses
- Moving
- Addictions
- Health challenges and illness
- Legal challenges
- Retirement
- Starting/ending school
- Job loss
- Children moving out or graduating
- Even the birth of a child is a loss in some ways. It represents a significant change in our previously single, non-parent lives

Much has been written by far more knowledgeable people than I about the stages one goes through in preparing for and after the death of a loved one. Perhaps the most popular are the works of Elizabeth Kubler-Ross and her book *On Death and Dying.*

Generally speaking, there are five major stages or phases of the grieving process. They are different for everyone; just as everyone's experience of loss is different. The stages of grief explained by Elizabeth Kubler-Ross are really about preparing to die, not coping after a loved one has died. However, they do apply equally well to coping with unexpected death, especially the death of a child, so I thought it would be appropriate to discuss here.

Many of these stages are really just labels for emotions we experience. It is important to remember there is no specific "stage." There is no correct order. There is no time frame. There is no right or wrong way.

You may experience some, but not all of them. You may experience them in a different order, or, more likely, find yourself bouncing around the different stages. There are also many other emotional stages or experiences you may have that are not listed here. You feel what you feel and it's all okay. Although emotions can be our friends, they can also be our enemies. There is a duality to them. As we used to say back in the '80's, they are "frenemies."

Denial and Disbelief
Denial is, in a way, what helps us survive the news our loved one has died. It is our protective bubble. It's our heart's way of saying, "No!" "I won't believe it" or, "I can't believe it."

We are not in a place where we are emotionally ready or able to accept the reality of the situation. It is really more a period of disbelief than true denial. We don't want to believe it's true. We just can't wrap our heart or head around the concept that someone we deeply love and care about has died.

The initial shock and numbness are, in a way, a gift. It allows us to just be wherever we are emotionally. It grants us time to absorb the news slowly. It stops us from our everyday routine life and makes us focus on the here and now. Few other things ever have that power over us.

It allows us to shut out thoughts and feelings we are not yet ready to handle, so we can wrap our brain around the reality of our circumstance. This is how the disbelief can be slowly transformed and the reality of our situation allowed to sink in and become accepted as truth.

Kids are naturally very good at this self-regulation of what they can and can't handle. Adults less so. Thus, the benefit of denial. Denial allows us to handle only what we, and only we, can handle at that very moment in time. It allows us the gift of time to process slowly… at our own pace. It is a stage of complete devastation where nothing makes sense and everything is surreal. It's a foggy place. It's a place of simply existing. Nothing makes sense in denial; it doesn't have to. It's not supposed to. How could it?

Some people linger in denial for a long time. There is no "right" length of time for these emotions, but typically, once one moves on from denial and disbelief, they don't go back. Once you have processed the reality of your situation, you are no longer in denial. If you or someone you know seems "stuck" in denial for too long, and it's a detriment to their health, professional help is advised.

As we emerge from the disbelief and denial, we begin to accept the reality of our child's death. It is then, we can begin to heal.

Anger

Anger is a powerful emotion and for many, it's a necessary part of healing. It's a defense mechanism of a different sort. It's a way that allows many people to feel in control of a situation. Anger is a way of being assertive and expressive. A way of saying, "NO!" A way to verbalize how frustrated and upset we are with our situation.

When a child dies, that anger may be even stronger than one might expect. The natural order of things has been disrupted. We lash out because we don't understand. Because we hurt. So. Damn. Much. Anger is born of pain. Pain we can't handle. Pain we don't want to know. Sometimes, the deeper the love, the more powerful the anger.

Anger is often associated with the question, "Why?" "Why my child?" "Why this way?" "Why didn't I..." "What if I..." If there is a question to be asked, most parents find it. Anger could be directed at your child, yourself, your spouse, the stranger that contributed to their death, whether it was intentional or unintentional, God, or anyone or anything at any time.

Sometimes, with anger, comes blame, especially if the child's death was accidental. Blame can be ugly and misplaced. It can complicate the process of healing. Where there is blame, there will need to be forgiveness to heal.

Anger can be helpful in that it inspires us to ask questions and seek answers. It can lead us to question our faith, doctors, first responders, other people who may or may not have been present for the circumstances leading to, around, and after your child's death. Some people are even compelled to pursue advocacy work or changes in legislation. This is a positive way to channel anger and grief.

Anger can manifest as irritability or sudden anger at something you normally wouldn't be upset about. You may become angry at someone for the littlest of things or at some seemingly insignificant event (Remember how pissed I was about the priest?) Of course, the anger is really based in something much deeper that you are unable to recognize at that time. For example, I thought I was pissed off at God, but actually, I was angry with myself for not getting up earlier, for not securing her dresser, and furious and overcome with grief that my daughter had died.

Anger is often an outlet for our pent up emotions of all sorts. It's a vehicle for change... an attempt to change a situation or a way of thinking. Anger can help us to move on, improve strained relationships, resolve our differences, and catalyze communication, so we can work toward healing.

However, anger can also be harmful to us or to others. Hurting yourself, someone else, or property or things solves nothing. There are healthy ways to deal with anger. Prolonged anger or holding on to anger can lead to problems with your physical, emotional, and mental health. It can strain relationships and create additional stress. If you feel unable to control your anger or find yourself or someone you love stuck in this phase, seek professional help to process and understand both the anger and where it is truly coming from, so you can work toward releasing it and healing.

Anger, an often necessary stage of grieving is a normal emotion that often comes and goes as it allows us to process our emotions "out loud." This may be especially true when our anger is accompanied by actual vocalization and yelling. It helps us identify what is really bothering us, so we can address it. It's a release. It's part of a process. It prepares us for the eventual acceptance of our child's death.

Despite all of that, sometimes we don't know how to deal with anger... either our own anger or that of another person that may be directed at us.

Here are a few tips for dealing with anger:
- Try to explain why you are angry instead of just yelling or venting at someone else. It will help you identify why you are feeling angry and help you communicate the source of your anger to yourself and to others. It also helps them to help you.
- Before lashing out in anger, take a deep breath. The old "trick" of counting to ten really does help!
- Find an outlet for your stress and anger that is healthy. Go for a walk or run outside, exercise, journal, punch a pillow, take a shower or bath, listen to relaxing music, try yoga or guided meditation.
- Try to avoid situations that will trigger your anger. If going to your sister's house for dinner stresses you out, politely decline.

- Talk to someone whom you trust to try to work through your feelings. This can be a friend or family member or perhaps, a professional counselor or therapist.
- Listen to music that you can identify with. There are many of songs out there about grief and anger. There are also many songs with messages of hope and healing. Find something that resonates with you and helps you feel calm.
- Consider treating yourself to a massage or a Reiki session.
- Nurture yourself. Be gentle with yourself. Be patient. Love yourself. Accept yourself and your feelings for what they are right now.
- Allow yourself be loved and to love. Love has a wonderful way of calming anger.

Coping With Guilt

Guilt is anger's evil twin. Many parents become angry with themselves or their spouse because they feel if only they said or did something differently, their child would not have died. They may take on responsibility not only for their child's death, but for not preventing it. Many parents feel guilty after the death of their child. They feel as if they have failed their child.

Guilt is probably the most useless emotion we have as humans, yet it's one we excel at. It's okay to feel guilt. You feel what you feel. While we can't help how we feel, it's important to realize feeling guilty won't change what happened, and we must forgive ourselves, and others, in order to move on and truly heal. Forgiveness can be challenging but it is a powerful catalyst for healing on all levels. You may require the help of a counselor if you feel very stuck in anger and guilt.

Bargaining

Bargaining is not a stage everyone experiences. It is most often experienced and typically begins *before* the death of a loved one. It is a way of processing and preparing for the eventual death of someone close to you and it may be the first stage many people go through. This is especially true for parents if their child suffered a prolonged illness with a poor prognosis or is in critical condition from an accident or sudden illness.

Bargaining is a stage where you try to make a deal with God or a higher power. Conversations with a higher power often happen where you ask that your child survive or be spared pain. You might say something like, "I'll never do ____ again if you will let my child come back to me," or "Please, take me instead, God, and let my child live!" Others might bargain with spirit and pray that the tumor be a more treatable or less aggressive type, or simply, bargain for more time with their child.

Many parents feel that the death of their child is punishment of some kind, and they promise they will change their ways and be a better parent or person and beg, "Please, please let my child be okay or bring them back to me. I promise I will change!"

The guilt that might have begun while you were angry begins to surface more in this stage. Or it may begin here, in the bargaining stage. This is where many parents suffer from the "what if's" and "if onlys." We, the bereaved, are still living in the past while we bargain. We want to go back in time and change things. We want to fix it and pray with all that we are that we can, somehow, make it all better. After all, we always told our children we would take care of them and make it better, right? Sometimes, all we find ourselves doing is begging to wake up from this awful nightmare because then, it wouldn't be real.

Then, despite all of our bargaining and praying, our child dies and it's all too real. It's so unfair. So very, very unfair.

Depression
Depression is exactly what you expect it is... profound sadness. When we reach the stage of depression, we are also moving into the present. We are now aware of, and deeply rooted in, the reality of the death of our child.

The depth of our pain is unfathomable to most anyone who has not had a similar loss. We feel empty, lost, and sad with little or no interest in doing anything that used to bring us joy. The simplest of tasks are overwhelming. We often want to withdraw and hide. We feel as if it will never end. That we will feel this way forever.

It's so very painful and utterly exhausting. We feel as if there is no future, no point in doing anything or in moving forward. It's as if we are in a thick and heavy fog. The world looks dark and gray. We feel trapped. We don't care. We care. We can't care. We don't want to be living this, yet we are. It saps our energy.

Depression is truly a gift. I know that sounds all kinds of wrong, but hear me out. It allows us to slowly begin to

162

integrate our child's death and figure out how to move forward without our child's physical presence in our lives. It helps us stay in the now while trying to integrate the past and begin to see there is a future. Depression is where we begin to process moving forward without our child. It is a difficult, but very, very necessary and important stage.

After the death of a loved one, especially a child, it's important to know that this depression is not a mental illness. It is a normal and necessary part of grieving. It often lasts longer than the previously published estimate of "normal" being a mere two weeks! Because it comes and goes and is a normal grief reaction, it is different from clinical depression, which is typically not related to the recent death of a child or close loved one.

One of the most frustrating things to parents who are in the depression stage is that many people around them think this is something to "get over." That there is some arbitrarily tolerable length of time for someone to be depressed after a loved one dies and then society expects us, as bereaved parents, to just move on and be our previous selves. This can lead bereaved parents back to anger quite easily!

Parents are angry at those who expect or tell them to "get over it" because those people clearly don't get it. Bereaved parents are angry because those other people don't have to live it. They are angry that their child is the one that died.

The reality is you never get over the death of your child. How could you? You will never forget them. They will always be your child. No, you won't be depressed forever, but it takes time to get through this stage... sometimes, lots of time. It takes time to process and integrate your child's death into your everyday life. And that's okay.

Depression may feel like it will last forever, but for most people it's a phase, just like the others. It may last a long time or come and go, but it's a very real and very necessary part of grief.

Many people are helped in this phase by support from others who have experience with the loss of a child. This may be in the form of reading books, articles, or message boards related to coping with the death of a child, or it may be in the form of attending a local support group. The Compassionate Friends is a fantastic organization with a wealth of resources and information for bereaved parents, grandparents, and siblings who have lost a child. I highly recommend them as a go to resource. You will find links to them and many other helpful organizations in the resource list at the end of the book.

Some people find that talk therapy in the form of a support group or professional counseling is very helpful to them in processing and healing from the trauma of the loss of a child. It is highly recommended for all bereaved parents. It's so hard to try to process all of this grief on your own. You should not have to. You don't have to! Sometimes just listening to others who have been through it or having the reassurance from a professional that what you are experiencing is normal is tremendously helpful.

Others may need antidepressant medication if their depression persists, is debilitating, or, if they had preexisting depression or other mental illness before the death of their child.

If you feel you are depressed, or you feel a loved one is, or are not sure if medication or counseling would help you, seek help from a physician or professional counselor. Don't try to diagnose or treat yourself. It's important to realize you feel what you feel and that help is available. Your child would want you to take care of yourself. Please do.

A Note on PTSD
Post-traumatic stress disorder is a very real thing. Most people only hear about it in relation to large scale tragic events like those who serve in a war environment or those who were witness to mass casualty events such as a school shooting. PTSD can happen to anyone and for any reason.

Any event that was especially traumatic to you can result in symptoms of PTSD. The death of your child can certainly qualify as such an event. Classic symptoms include a reliving of the trauma/experience, nightmares, and flashbacks of the event. It can also include a phobia or irrational fear that the event will occur again or of people and places related to the event.

It's not widely talked about as a stage or complication of grief, and it's not something the average person would necessarily recognize they have or something a loved one would recognize. Many of the signs and symptoms such as difficulty sleeping, memory problems, difficulty concentrating, irritability, and a withdrawal reaction are common and normal reactions in grief. The difference is that in PTSD, the symptoms last longer than 1-3 months and have to meet certain clinical criteria. In fact, many people don't share what they are feeling, so it can be hard to diagnose, even for a professional.

The circumstances of your child's death can lead to PTSD, or it can be a trigger from a previous traumatic event for yourself or someone else close to you or that child. It wasn't until I mentioned some of my feelings and experiences to my grief counselor a few months after Meghan died that she explained I had elements of PTSD. Because of her explanation I better understood the process, and that I was not alone or as afraid of what I was feeling. She was then able to help me cope and heal more effectively. It was very reassuring.

There are many strategies for dealing with post-traumatic stress. There is traditional counseling, talk therapy, support groups, and medications. There are also non-traditional, but very effective, treatments for example body work such as a massage or acupuncture. Eye movement desensitization and reprocessing (EMDR) is also an alternative and effective therapy.

Again, if you think you are having signs of PTSD, seek a referral for treatment. You owe it to yourself to love and nurture yourself, so you can heal.

Manifestations of Grief
There are many other important aspects of grief. Remember, not everyone experiences grief the same way. You may find the following examples of how grief may manifest helpful:
- It may make you afraid to get too close to people again for fear of losing them, too.

- You may push people away.
- You may feel changed... as if you are not the person you used to be... that you are a new and different person.
- You may be tempted to engage in risky or uncharacteristic behavior.
- It makes you feel stupid, confused, unable to make decisions or remember things.
- You may forget some things.
- You may remember things you forgot, and they will bring a smile to your face.
- You may behave in ways you've never behaved before.
- You may feel paranoid that everyone around you will die, or your other children will die
- You may feel anxious... crazy anxious.
- You may become hyper-vigilant to the point of not being able to sleep or focus on anything, especially if the death was accidental and unexpected.
- You may feel relieved or glad that your child or loved one has died, especially if they suffered or their dying was prolonged, as in the case of illness.
- You may have a heightened sense of your own mortality.
- You may find yourself wanting to significantly change your life, often for the better.
- You may fear answering the phone... especially if that's how you found out about the death.
- You may become anxious if you hear sirens or see an ambulance or drive by the hospital where your child died.

When grieving, it's also okay to:
- It's okay to laugh and have fun.
- It's okay to cry.
- It's okay to participate in life. Life continues to go on around you. Bills still have to be paid and food still needs to be bought and made.
- It's okay to grieve for people you didn't even know.
- It's okay to feel guilty, it's not uncommon. Work through it, but don't dwell on it.
- It's okay to ask, "Why," or "Why me?" Those questions are normal. Realize that actually getting an answer is rare.
- It's okay to ask for help. Be specific if you can in what you want or need.
- It's okay to accept help.
- It's okay to say, "Yes" or "No" to *anything*, or to change your mind.
- It's okay to be mad at the child or person who died for leaving you.
- It's okay to be angry that your child has died and someone else's has not.
- It's okay to talk or write about your child or how you feel. Anytime. Anywhere. To anyone.
- It's okay to talk to your child or loved one who has died.

Acceptance: Integrating Your Child's Death into Your Life
Acceptance is not the point at which everything is "okay" again. It is about accepting the reality of our situation. It's about accepting that our child is gone forever in the physical plane.

168

It's the stage of grief where we learn to live with the pain of the loss of our child. We begin to integrate their death into our lives. We begin to find a "new normal."

It's not that we can't experience any of the other emotions or stages of grief previously mentioned. You could be brought quickly and unexpectedly, but temporarily, back to any other stage of grief at any point in time. The difference in the return to these stages is that it's temporary.

This doesn't mean we forget about our child. Quite the contrary, many parents will tell you they think of their child daily... for years... forever. In fact, we received a sympathy card from a woman in her 80's that saw Meghan's obituary in the paper. She wrote us a beautiful note, sharing she lost her only child when they were about Meghan's age. She said Meghan would never be forgotten, because she still thinks of her child every single day. I was so touched by that sentiment when my grief was so raw. She gave me hope that I would be able to survive... heck, she did... and reassurance no one would forget my beautiful girl. Unbeknownst to her, that stranger, a fellow bereaved mother, she gave me the first glimmer of hope that I would be able to get through the loss of my child, too.

What many people don't realize is that grief is a good thing. It's a friend. It helps us to pace ourselves as we digest and process this tremendous loss in our lives. *It's normal and natural,* and it is born of the emotional reaction to a sudden and unexpected change in our lives. It feels awful when you are in the midst of it, but once you are on the other side, you can see the beauty and grace in it and in yourself. Don't be afraid of it. Embrace it and allow yourself to grieve however you feel you should for however long you need to.

In reality, the stages of grief are not a structured set of emotions one must go through in order. There is no time frame. There is no order. There is no limit to what you might feel, when you may feel it, or for how long. It's a lifelong process. There is a beginning but there really is no end… just a gradual accommodation to it being a part of your existence. The more time that passes, the more you begin to embrace and befriend grief.

Not everyone experiences the same responses to grief. The stages of grief are really just terms for the emotions many people have when trying to make sense of their feelings after a loved one dies. Some people move quickly through these emotional stages. Others, experience them in a different order or even after having reached a level of acceptance.

Acceptance is not a graduation, it is a transition. Sometimes, we spend mere minutes in an emotional state and at other times, days, weeks, or months there. I'm sure we move through them on and off for the rest of our lives. *There is no right or wrong way, only our way.*

When one is grieving the loss of a child, especially their own child, grief is further complicated because children are not supposed to die. The natural order of life, as we know it, is turned completely upside-down. We go through our lives expecting our children will outlive us, not the other way around. The love one has for their own child is different from that of a spouse or parent. The bonds are strong, deep and unconditional. It's no less important than the love we feel for our parents or significant other, but definitely different. Others around us who have not lost a child themselves will never be able to understand what the experience of this kind of grief is like. Even other bereaved parents will have different experiences and cope differently.

Unfortunately, our society doesn't often acknowledge how grief works, particularly when it comes to the loss of a child. It's often misunderstood or thought of as something that needs to be treated or "fixed" by giving it a label, a definitive time frame, or with medication. While at times, medication can be useful and helpful, and in fact, absolutely necessary, it must be for a correct diagnosis and followed up with medical care and treatment. For this reason, you should see your doctor regularly and seek the support of a counselor to help you process the death of your child and monitor your feelings, especially depression.

If you are appropriately depressed after the loss of your child, you are not necessarily clinically depressed, and you may not need antidepressants. On the other hand, you may. You need emotional support and guidance through the process.

There is a strong tendency in our society to want a quick fix to bury things, prescribe a magic pill, to just make it better, or go away. Grief doesn't work like that. The only way out, is through. It's a healthy, normal and necessary process. Some people, however, will need the support of medication to help normalize their brain chemistry and help them cope with the depression.

Losing a child changes you. As you work through the stages of grief and find your way to acceptance, you will find your perspective changes. You will begin to see your family, your friends, yourself and the world in a different light.

It's important and helpful to recognize:
- You can't change the past. You must live in the now.
- Grief can help you be creative. You may create a memory book or some other keepsake to honor your child.
- Life is short; say I love you every day.
- Sometimes the second year is harder than the first.
- Sometimes it's easier than you thought it would be.
- Losing people who once supported you in your grief can add another layer of pain, sadness and grief.
- There may be collateral losses… friends, family members. Close and significant relationships may end or change.
- Not everyone who said, "Let me know if I can do anything," means it.
- People say stupid things. It's usually not intentional. Even if it makes you angry, realize they were trying to help and just didn't know how.
- You may find your faith strengthened by grief.
- You may find you reject God, your faith, or religion as a result of your loss.
- You never "get over it." You will learn to integrate it into your life and move forward. It does get easier.
- You can't walk around the pain of losing your child. The only way out of the pain, is through it.
- There is no time limit on grieving. People may think you should "move on" but it's all in your own time. It often lasts a lifetime and changes as you do.

- Even an expected death of a child, or even an elderly person, can feel sudden and unexpected. It can, and still does, hurt just as much.
- Never ever think you are doing "it" wrong! The only right way is your way!
- It will get different and in that way…easier.
- Doctors are not always the best source for counseling. See a professional counselor if you feel like you need professional support or join a support group. Everyone can benefit from bereavement counseling.
- You may feel suicidal. Many parents do in the early days, but it's usually a reaction to the profound pain they are in. Please call the suicide prevention help line if you do have thoughts of ending your own life: 1-800-273-8255.
- Losing a child or someone close does not make the next loss any easier, no matter who it is or how old they are.
- You will be blindsided by unexpected triggers. These are often most intense in the first year, but can happen anytime.
- The first wake or funeral you attend after the one for your child will probably be incredibly difficult and bring back all sorts of feelings and memories. Especially if it is in the same place your child's services were held.
- You will grieve for what you will never have.
- It's best to not make any major decisions for at least a year after the death of a child.
- Having other children does not make the loss any easier.
- Having another baby does not replace the one you lost or your pain.

- There are no rules, no right and wrong, no time limits.
- Never let anyone tell you what you should or should not do or how you should or should not feel with regard to your child or your grief.
- Sometimes, complete strangers are the greatest source of support.
- Books, websites, support groups, and blogs can all be great sources of information and support.
- Never be afraid to say how you feel.
- Never be afraid to say your child's name or share stories about them.
- It's normal for your feeling to change… often.
- Grieving is a life-long process.
- You will grieve in your own way, at your own pace. You will heal… in your own time.
- Don't compare yourself to others. It's your journey to walk and only you know how to do it your way.
- Good things can come out of grief.
- Nothing can take away the love you have for your child. Love never dies.

It's important to realize that as difficult as coping with the death of your own child or one close to you can be, we, as humans, are resilient. With the right support, information, and resources and by tapping into our own inner strength and soul level knowing of our purpose in this lifetime, we can and will reach a level of acceptance and integration of our experience of our child's life and death into our lives. Remember, as the Compassionate Friends say, "You need not walk alone."

Grieving Future Losses

Whenever we lose a loved one, there are many collateral losses. When that loved one is a child, one of the most challenging emotions for parents goes beyond the present. It's more than just the loss of that child.

The grief is compounded by the fact that not only is their child gone forever, but so is all of the hopes and dreams those parents had for that child and their family. There is now forever a hole where their child was supposed to be in their lives and in their family. They must learn to go on without them, and yet they are always conscious of the fact there is child not there as they should be. As the parents always thought they would be.

Parents often grieve all the firsts they will never realize. Most obvious are the rites of passage; the first day of school, graduations, sporting events or dance recitals, first dates, the prom, marriage, even the loss of future grandchildren.

They mourn the experiences they and their family will never have together with their child. Birthdays, holidays, and vacations will never be what you once imagined they would be. Many parents who go on to have more children often grieve the fact those children will never know their older sibling.

These losses are often the ones that blindside us years after our child has died. Years after we've come to accept their death and integrate it and our experience into our everyday lives. These are the ones, especially if you have other children, that will hit you out of the blue. There is not much you can do other than to be aware that these milestones and

175

life events are likely to trigger your pain. You can use that information to plan for them as best you can and anticipate they may be difficult days. Be gentle with yourself.

Disenfranchised Grief

Disenfranchised grief is a fancy word that basically refers to grief over a loss that is typically not acknowledged by society or by your peers as "real", important, or worthy of the depth of grief you feel. It doesn't always have to be about the death of a loved one, although it often is. Any profound loss can elicit a grief reaction.

Sometimes, we experience disenfranchised grief because society says, "They deserved it," or, "They did it to themselves," as in the case of suicide, drug overdose, or drunk driving when the driver is the victim.

Disenfranchised grief is basically society dictating what you are allowed to grieve over and what you are not. They don't "get it" nor do they want to try to understand it. It's the "junk drawer" of grief. Unfortunately, like our junk drawers at home, it contains some very important items that are often just thrown in there because we don't know what else to do with them or how to label them.

Some examples of disenfranchised grief include:
- The death of a pet.
- The death of an online friend (one you did not know in person).
- The death of an "ex."
- Miscarriage or stillbirth.
- Infertility.
- The loss of a good friend or co-worker.

- A bad break up or divorce.
- The death or loss of a friend your family or friends did not approve of.
- The death or loss of a same sex partner, particularly if family and friends did not approve of the relationship.
- The "loss" of someone you love as they used to be because they have dementia or mental illness.

Remember this: *No one has the right to tell you what you can and can't grieve over or how to grieve. You are entitled to feel the way you feel and no one can take that away from you.*

Only you know how you feel. Only you had the relationship you did with the person or situation for which you are grieving. It's important that you acknowledge that you can go through all the stages of grief when coping with any significant loss, not just the death of someone you love. It's also important to realize only you can decide how you feel.

Don't let others tell you that you are not entitled to grieve or that you are wrong. No one can deny you your right to grieve. No one. No two people grieve over the same thing in the same way. The only way is your way.

Unresolved Grief
Sometimes it's difficult to resolve grief. This seems a bit two-sided to me. We've established that grieving the loss of a child is a lifelong process. Something we don't really ever get over. So isn't all grief unresolved?

Some experts say signs of unresolved grief are an inability to talk about the person who has died, only being able to talk about the negative or positive aspects of the child and their death, not both, or an unnatural fear and avoidance that is unhealthy.

While resolving the emotional impact of the death of your child is not likely something you'll do, since that would mean you could, in fact, get over it, we can and hopefully will, eventually integrate it. You will, eventually, get to a place where you can talk about your child's life and death and how it's impacted your life. This doesn't mean it can't be without tears or other emotions at times, just that you are not incapacitated by it like you might have been in those early days after their death. You are able to move forward.

For those who are unable to process their grief and move through the stages of grieving within a reasonable time frame, it is said their grief is unresolved. For these parents there can be additional complications and potential losses. There may be relationship changes with friends, family members, other children and their spouse and may lead to marital stress or divorce. There may be associated health or mental and emotional problems. There may be dysfunctional behaviors and addictions that begin benignly enough, but escalate. There is an increased frequency of auto accidents, suicide, and death from health problems in those who are deeply grieving or stuck emotionally.

Parents who are unable to function and work through the grieving process are also often unable to help their surviving children through it and this can lead to trouble in school, with their relationships, and addictions or behavioral issues.

Unresolved grief can also lead to dysfunctional relationships for the parents, job dissatisfaction or loss, financial stress, and other life choices that are not healthy. Until the grief is resolved, the emotions can limit the person's ability to fully live life and find a balance of health and happiness.

The good news is you don't have to do it alone, and you shouldn't try! While solitude, at times, is therapeutic, having someone to walk this path with you is vitally important.

Think about who you have in your life that might be able to do this with you. Hopefully, there are several people. They might be someone you know and love or, perhaps, a professional you haven't met yet! Resolve to seek out someone to guide you and help you. While it's true no one can do it for us, they can walk with us and support us in our journey.

At the very least, you have me by your side. As you read the following chapters, I will be your friend, your confidant, and your guide. Surrounding you in a bubble of white light and love, sending healing energy to you and to your family and guiding you through the process. You will walk through the darkness and into the light. You will get through this. Really. You will. If I can do it, you can, too.

Resolved Grief?
How do I know I've recovered from the death of my child?

It's pretty universally believed by bereaved parents that you never get over the death of your child. Some professionals may disagree by giving a label to us. They say we've recovered. What they really mean is that we've reached a level of acceptance of our child's death. We can now live our life having integrated our child's life and death into our everyday existence.

We haven't forgotten them. We still grieve, just not every day or with the same depth of emotion as we did initially.

We've made it through the most difficult part of the journey. We've grown and changed and continue to do so, but in a healthy way. We can experience joy again. Our once dark and gray world now has color once again. We now understand that it's okay to feel pangs of sadness and pain, but we know we'll be okay, that it's normal and we can talk about it.

We've found new rituals, new ways to incorporate our child's memory into the fabric of our lives. We can enjoy the memories of our child without those memories being tremendously painful.

The Importance of Connecting with Others who have "Been There"

I am but one bereaved parent. One thing that tends to happen when you are a bereaved parent is that you begin to find and friend other bereaved parents. We all share a bond we never wanted to have. Yet we are grateful for it. There is something so wonderful about a relationship in which you don't have to explain how you feel, because they get it, too. They've been there. No, their experience was probably not exactly the same. They may not be in the same stage of grief as you are, but the camaraderie is strength giving.

I know far more parents who share the experience of having lost a child than I ever imagined I would or ever wanted to. There are far too many of us. All members of a club we desperately want out of. There is no getting off this ride. It's a perpetual roller coaster. We are here for each other, in a way that only parents who have lost a child can ever possibly understand.

With deep sadness and loving open hearts, we welcome you to the club. Here, we understand. Here, you can say whatever you want. Tell us about your child, their life, their death, their legacy. Share your child's light with us. Share your pain with us. Share your child with us. We are here for you.

There are many organizations and support groups out there. The resource list at the end of this book lists many of them. Check them out!

On Being Strong: What is Strength?
One of the words you often hear tossed around when it comes to coping with the death of a loved one is "strength." We think we have to be strong for others. We are praised for our strength. If I had a dollar for every time someone praised me for how strong I was or am, I'd be able to retire.

Here's the thing. It's not about being strong. "Strong" is a term to describe physical strength. We don't define our ability to cope by our physical strength. How much weight I can lift has nothing to do with my ability to cope with the death of my child. What people are referring to is emotional "strength."

Unlike physical strength, this is not measurable. It's an opinion or a perception. People often perceive someone as being emotionally strong when they are not dissolving into tears constantly, or, if they are seemingly able to go back to work, talk about their child's death or take an activist or advocacy role after their child has died.

You've heard one should never assume, right? While it's true, some parents are able to do all of those things, it in no way means they are over their child's death or even doing well processing it. It may simply be a coping strategy, so they can get through the necessary tasks of daily living. They may have simply buried all those emotions and focused their attention on other activities to avoid having to face the pain. Or, maybe they break down into tears, get angry and collapse and pull the covers over their head when they get home, when no one can see the real them.

People label others as "strong" emotionally because when they think about how they would likely feel if their child had died, they can't fathom being able to function. It's definitely meant as a compliment and sometimes nice to hear, but it's not what it's really about and often not even true.

Unfortunately, when a bereaved parent, sibling, grandparent, or close friend or relative is perceived to be strong, there are few offers of help. Few acknowledge or recognize the pain they are still in and the difficulty they might be having coping with the day to day, especially around special or important days in their lives.

People often stop asking how parents are doing when they are perceived as "strong" because everyone thinks they must be doing well since they are so strong or because they are not wearing their grief on their sleeve 24/7 anymore. Often, it's just not true. Those parents may receive less support than the ones who are perceived as a mess emotionally. Yet they need it just as much, if not more.

My personal belief is that it's not about strength at all. It's about love.

Let me say that again. It's not about being strong. It's about the depth of love we have for our children. We don't stop loving them just because they have died. Their love for us was real and persists through their memory and the connection we'll always have with them in our hearts. *Everything* I have done since Meghan died has been born of love. The love I have for her. The love she showered on me. My love and caring for others, including those I don't know, to the point that I don't want any other parent to ever feel my pain. Every word I've written, every word I've spoken, everything I've done with regard to Meghan, her death and Meghan's Hope is about love. It's how I continue to mother her.

It's not about strength. It's about love.

Love is powerful. Love is good. Love will always prevail. Love never, ever dies. We are not strong. We are love.

Chapter Six

Supporting the Bereaved: How You Can Help

In this chapter, primarily written for those who are the friends, family, co-workers, and the professionals who care for and provide support to the bereaved parents, we will discuss valuable insights and tools to facilitate coping and healing for everyone affected by the death of a child.

In this chapter you will learn how to support the bereaved parent and learn both what is helpful to say and do, as well as what is not. You will also learn how to care for yourself and navigate your own grief, while supporting a bereaved parent through theirs.

Bereaved parents will also find this chapter helpful; as many of the suggestions for support may help you identify what you may need and want to ask for. You, as the parents, must also support each other and any other children you may have. The question and answer section addresses common questions asked by bereaved parents. The discussion on the 3 C's, in particular, is tremendously important for both the bereaved parents and all who support them. They are life skills we all should have and honor.

What is bereavement? Bereavement is defined as the total reaction to a loss. It goes beyond the stages of grief to include the process of healing and recovering from the loss. It's not a stage, but a journey that lasts a lifetime. Like any path, it winds and turns through hills and valleys.

Bereavement encompasses cultural practices, religious and spiritual beliefs, memory making and keeping, and the creation of meaningful tokens of remembrance. Everyone who is bereaved needs support. Many also need education and guidance.

In order to support someone who is coping with the death of a loved one, especially with a child, you need a few special tools in your coping toolbox. Among the most important are patience, compassion, flexibility, the ability to listen, an awareness of potential triggers and reactions to them, and the ability to put aside your own "stuff" to help them with theirs. Any and all support you give should be heart-centered and non-judgmental.

Remember, the bereaved parent is the expert. They will teach you what they need.

If you are a friend, family member, or member of the medical profession supporting someone through the loss of their child... thank you. Thank you for being there for them while you are likely coping with your own grief as well. Thank you for taking the time to care enough about them and yourself to seek out a resource to help you through. No one should have to walk this road alone or blindly. We're all in it together.

A Unique Grief
The most important thing for you to know and understand if you want to support a bereaved parent are the truths and realities of their experience.

It goes without saying that losing a child is a deeply profound loss. Many say it's the worst kind of loss one can experience. They may not tell you or even be able to recognize or articulate it themselves. The first several chapters of this book clearly outline what a bereaved parent experiences from the moment they learn their child has died throughout the grieving process. If you've not read them yet, I recommend you do. You will likely find it insightful and helpful for your own future reference.

Truths and Realities About Bereaved Parents
They will never, ever "get over it."

Nope. Never. They will heal. It will get easier. It will take a long time... a lifetime. But they will never be the same. Their family will never be the same. The death of a child is not something you truly ever recover from. It changes you and your world forever.

Know that you can never, ever, possibly know what they are feeling, so don't ever say, "I know what you must feel like." That is, unless you, too, have lost a child and can truly relate. Even then, every experience is different. Every coping style is different. It doesn't mean you cannot provide wonderful support; it's just that you have to realize the death of a child is not like any other death. Not to that child's parents.

Losing a child is not the same as losing a grandparent, pet, spouse, or even a sibling. You cannot compare it. It's not that those losses are not painful or worthy of grief. It's that the pain of losing a child is a unique grief. Parents are not supposed to outlive their children. It doesn't matter how old that child was. A miscarriage at six weeks of pregnancy or the death of an adult child is still the loss of a child, *their* child. Age has no bearing on the depth of pain a parent feels when their child dies.

Another very important truth is *they will never forget their child.* The thing that all bereaved parents fear is that their child will be forgotten. When those close to us don't say our deceased child's name, don't talk about them, and act as if they never existed, we feel as if they've been forgotten. That can be deeply painful and upsetting and makes us angry and sad. Many people are not sure what to say, so they don't say anything, and that can make it seem like they don't care, which is often far from the truth.

We want to hear their name. Yes, their name. Don't be afraid to say it. Share *your* memories of *their* child. What you loved about them. What you remember. Talk about their child. To them. With others. Acknowledge the child's existence. Their life. Their death. Their importance in our lives. We think of our children every day. You aren't reminding us. We never forget. You aren't making us upset, you aren't making us cry. You are showing you remember them, too.

One of the many reasons I wanted to write this book is to provide a resource for those of you who are providing support to bereaved parents. Understanding what they go through is necessary for those who are trying to support them. A parent's grief is unique and profound. Knowing what to say and do as well as what not to say or do can make a big difference in the healing process and in your relationship with them in the long term.

I am forever grateful to the many friends, family members, and members of my community, some of which I didn't even know, for the tremendous support they offered and gave in the days and weeks following Meghan's death. I do not know how I'd have gotten through it without them.

As bereaved parents, we are so lost in our grief, we are often unaware of the help that we need. We also often lack the foresight or capacity to ask for help, even if we do recognize we need it. There is simply not enough energy or drive to do so. Depression is heavy and difficult to recognize, let alone reach out through. Anger may be directed at the very people who are trying to help us, because we feel safe with them, inadvertently pushing them away.

We are in it Together; yet Separate

Furthermore, those who are closest to us, as bereaved parents, are also bereaved. Those who we often rely on the most to support us when we need it are in a similar emotional place to us.

They, too, are trying to cope with the loss of our child. They are also trying to go about their daily lives, for they must go back to school, work, parenting, and their usual day to day tasks. They are often unsure of how to help us. They don't know what to say or do, so often, they do nothing and wait for the bereaved parents to ask.

It's difficult to summon the energy to help others when you, yourself, are also in pain. It's unfair to feel as if you have to, or to expect that you should, ignore your own needs because the parents need your support.

It's a delicate dance on a slippery floor. No one knows the moves. Yet the music keeps playing.

Bereaved Parents Probably Can't See Your Pain
It wasn't until years after my own daughter's death that I really became aware of how completely oblivious I was to everyone else's pain over her death that first year and even beyond.

I was so lost in my own experience, my own pain, as her mother, that it just never occurred to me that others close to her and I might also be feeling a similar depth of pain. It also never occurred to me they had no idea what I was really feeling. Why I was making the choices I was, especially uncharacteristic behaviors for me.

It never occurred to me they might need help. It never occurred to me that they didn't feel comfortable talking to me about how they felt and what they needed. It never crossed my mind to ask them.

In fact, it wasn't until doing some research for this book that I asked my close family and friends what their experience of her death was. How did they find out? How did they react? How did they feel? What did they do? What do they remember about us and our reactions?

This was incredibly eye-opening to me. I actually learned some things I never knew! The PTSD my sister has when she gets a phone call from my cell phone… especially in the morning… especially at Christmas. To this day, the stress my parents feel about not being able to get here fast enough from Florida to see her at the hospital. The guilt they harbor for not coming up for the twins' third birthday party a few months earlier. The friends that were hurting so badly themselves that they couldn't bring themselves to call, send a card, or come to her services. They felt guilty they were not there. I feel guilty that I don't remember if they were there or not!

As I interviewed friends and family, I felt suddenly guilty that all these years had gone by, and I had never bothered to ask any of them about their feelings. It also boggled my mind that they never voluntarily shared how they felt with me or brought it up. I tend to say what I feel, so maybe they didn't feel they needed to ask me anything. They didn't realize I couldn't articulate it.

Maybe they felt their experience and their pain was somehow less significant or less important than mine, which is so not true. Maybe they felt I'd be angry with them. Maybe they were afraid of what I'd say or think or how they'd react to acknowledging their own grief.

This leads me to one of the most important tenets of supporting a bereaved parent or anyone who is suffering the loss of a child close to them: Love. Yes, love. Not just the unconditional or obligatory "because you are family" love. Rather it's a true, honest, heart-centered love for someone who is hurting, love. Don't assume anything.

As I was thinking about a way to capture what bereaved parents need in a way that would help those who support them remember the most important aspects, I kept coming back to the concept of love.

This acronym for love came to mind as I was writing.

L - Listen
O- Offer to help
V- Validate their feelings
E- Express your feelings

Listening is so very important. You may need to ask a question to start the conversation, but then, sit quietly and listen. Listen not only to their words, but to their body language. The story of their child's life and sometimes their death needs to be told... sometimes over and over and over again. It may make you uncomfortable, but open, active listening is crucial to facilitating the healing process for both of you.

Offering to help can seem like an easy thing to do, but when you ask if you can do anything for the bereaved family, you often hear, "No, thank you" or "I don't know." There are other ways to help. Sometimes informing the family of your intention to help works better. You could say, "I've arranged for a meal train for you, so you don't have to cook for the next two weeks for dinner. Let me know what foods you like or don't like and any allergies: I'll take care of the rest." You could do similar things for house cleaning, shopping, or support check-ins.

I was so appreciative and touched by the generosity of both those who knew us and those who did not who offered to and brought us meals for weeks. We didn't ask for it; it just happened. If they had asked, I'd probably have said we didn't need it. The truth was, we did. I was so grateful. I was especially touched by those who took the reins in organizing it and providing me with a list of names and phone numbers of people who were willing to be there for me anytime day or night if I wanted to talk or needed anything. Just knowing I had that support out there was tremendously helpful, even if I never took advantage of it.

This brings me to another truth about grief. There may be a slew of generosity and offers of help, but the bereaved rarely agree to accept help when it is offered. Even more rarely do they ask for help.

It's not because they don't want or need it, but because they don't want to inconvenience anyone… because decisions are just too hard… because the thought of having to be "on" or even dressed for others is overwhelming. Or, perhaps, they might not want to admit that they need the help. This is especially true for men, because they perceive they must be "strong." They feel obligated to be the breadwinner or "hold everyone together" and as a result, they don't ask for help, even if they recognize they need it.

If that help is simply given, if someone reaches out to them one on one, they are more likely to agree. For example, I had a wonderful spreadsheet of doula sisters who were friends and colleagues who support women through childbirth and "mother the mother," who were willing to help me. There was literally a weekly schedule for six months after Meghan died of women who volunteered to, at a minimum, call me with no expectation that I would have to answer the phone.

Some would just drop by and bring or leave food, offer a hug, ask me if I wanted to talk, offered to care for my children or have a playdate with theirs or just sat quietly and shared a cup of tea with me. I don't think I ever called any of them, but if they called me, and I felt up to it, I'd say yes to their offer or sometimes it was just nice to hear someone simply ask, "How are you doing? Do you need anything?" or, "I'm thinking of you." I've said it before and I'll say it again. Doulas rock! You don't have to be a trained doula to provide this kind of support. Anyone can!

Validating feelings is tremendously important to processing and healing. Validating involves active listening. Instead of offering your unsolicited opinions or suggestions, or telling the bereaved what they should and should not feel, or should and should not do, you simply listen to how they feel.

There is no right or wrong, only what they feel at that very moment in time. They are entitled to feel however they feel. Acknowledge that whatever they feel is part of the process, and they should honor their feelings. Certainly, if they are expressing active suicidal or homicidal thoughts, you need to get them help immediately, but a roller coaster of emotions is perfectly normal.

Many people find it helpful to think out loud and talk about their feelings. You may hear them say the same thing over and over as they try to process and make sense of it. Reflect their statements back to them and open a conversation about it. Be with them. Support them. Laugh with them. Cry with them. Ask them to tell you more or elaborate on a topic or story. Hug them. Love them. Be there for them. Let them know they are safe to share with you... anytime... anywhere... about anything.

Express feelings freely. Many bereaved parents express they feel like they are riding on a runaway train, and they can't get off. Much like a roller coaster, there are times they feel as if they are moving slowly against gravity, and then suddenly they feel as if they are free falling, unable to control how they feel and where they are going. Then they hit the bottom and begin to climb out again, only to find out it's not over and there is yet another hill, another slow agonizing climb, another free fall and suddenly, a corkscrew, and everything is upside-down and twisted. They feel disoriented and lost. Then, the ride may slow down or stop abruptly, only to suddenly take off again, and they continue on the same wild emotional ride.

They desperately wish they could get off this ride and escape this unending roller coaster. They'd trade places with anyone, but, of course, no one wants to get on *this* ride. No one.

Encourage the bereaved parents to express how they feel. Offer to go on that ride with them. Hold them when they cry and feel free to cry with them. Tears cleanse the soul! Laugh with them when they laugh. Pray with them if they find comfort in prayer. Hold the space when they get angry. Surround them with love when they withdraw. Reminisce with them about their child. Listen when they tell whatever story they want and need to. Even if you don't understand their train of thought, encourage them to share and express it. Share your feelings, too. Simply share how you feel. Don't compare. Don't judge. Just share from the heart.

If it's difficult for you to hear or think about their experience, imagine for a minute what it's like to be them. They need *you.* Be with them with, and in spite of, your own grief. This is what it means to be a friend.

The 3 C's

I find associations to be useful learning tools. In writing, an acronym of sorts came to mind. It is alliterative, too; the 3 C's. They are the hallmark of another set of tenets of supporting the bereaved. In fact, they are the survival guide to any relationship: communication, connection, and community. All three are necessary to processing, integrating, and healing.

Communicate

Communication is vital to healing. It's so easy to get lost in our own world as we try to make sense of it all. Before we know it, we drift away from others. Isolation can happen quickly, easily, and without recognition that it's happening. As we've previously discussed, bereaved parents are unlikely to reach out to others, so we, those who love and support them, must reach out to them.

It's important to check in with those you love and care about regularly. Daily for those who share your home or close family. Check in every few days for extended family and friends. It can be an email, phone call, a text, or ideally, a real person to person conversation. Stop by with flowers or a prepared meal for the bereaved parents or send a card to let them know you are thinking about them or their child. This is especially appreciated on anniversary days (first week, month, six months, every year) and other difficult days of significance like birthdays, Mother's and Father's Day and holidays.

Ask how the bereaved parents are doing, frequently. Ask if you can do anything for them, or if they need anything. Don't be surprised if they say, "Yeah, bring back my child, that's all I want."

It's not about them answering you or taking you up on your offer, although it's wonderful when they do. It's about the bereaved parents knowing you care enough to check in on them. About them knowing that you are there for them if they need you. Even if they don't say it at the time, it means a lot to them, and they need it.

Sometimes the stress of the loss of a child can cause couples to drift apart from each other, especially if they have vastly different coping strategies or are in very different stages of grieving. In some instances, there may have already been stress in the relationship. In other instances, it may just happen gradually over time. Good communication can help to prevent this drifting apart and prevent assumptions that are often wrong about what the other person is thinking feeling or doing with their time.

Take the time to share your feelings, your wants, and your needs. If something is not right about your relationships, say something. Lovingly and gently express how you feel and why. It might just lead to a wonderful open conversation that brings you closer and brings you peace. This applies to your relationship with your spouse or significant other as well as your relationships with friends and family members.

When you as a bereaved parent or close family member go back to work, be sure you are ready. Set boundaries for yourself. If it's too much, tell your supervisor or boss. Tell them why. Inquire about working from home or cutting back hours to gradually return to work if possible, and if you have a job that allows for that.

Some people don't want their colleagues to know they've lost a child. Some need colleagues to know, so they don't have to explain their behavior or mood. Some people can't function at work, where others might thrive because it's a distraction from the pain of their loss.

Unfortunately, bereavement leave is but a few days for most companies unless you take sick time and even then, it's limited. Some people end up losing jobs or resigning because they can't cope with work. That can lead to additional financial stress.

Often, one of the parents wishes to seek counseling but the other one does not. You don't have to go together. One can go to a counselor or a support group without their significant other. You could even bring another family member or friend to a support group.

The most important thing is that you seek the help and support you need. You can encourage your significant other, friends, and family through your open and honest communication, but in the end, you can only be responsible for yourself and your needs.

Connect
All too often when a child dies, we, the bereaved, are so wrapped up in how we feel that we forget to connect. We lose touch with the world around us and the people and

things in it. Grounding and centering is important to our ability to cope. There are many ways to connect.

Connect to Nature
There is something incredibly soothing about being out in nature. Some find peace in the warm embrace of the sun or in the light of the moon and beneath the stars. Some find solace by the ocean, a lake, or a stream. Nothing speaks to the emotions like the movement of water. You might find walking in the rain or snow quite literally cleansing for the head, heart, and soul. Walking outside quite literally grounds you to the earth. Being outside, especially at night, also affords you the opportunity to gaze to the heavens and ponder the next place. It may help you connect to your faith and the deceased child. In the silent darkness of night, one might find some peace.

Connect to your religious or spiritual beliefs
Many people find comfort in their faith. Going to church or synagogue, praying, or reading scripture may help to lend comfort and insight. For those more spiritually inclined, meditation or connecting with a spiritual practice that resonates with you may bring about healing and peace. Many people will search for and receive signs from their loved ones after they pass on. We will explore this more in later chapters.

Connect with the child and their memory
One can connect with the deceased child through their things, photos, memories, and their energy. Talking about the deceased child keeps their memory alive. Having mementos around your home can help you connect, although some people find it too painful right away. You could also write to

the child or about them in a journal. Scrapbooking photos or creating a photo album, creating a quilt from their clothes and bedclothes, and even just spending time with something that was theirs or in their room, home, or a favorite place can help you connect.

Some may seek the assistance of someone who is psychically gifted or a medium to try to get a message from their loved ones. If this resonates with you, it is a perfectly normal desire of many who have lost someone they love.

Connect with your spouse or significant other and surviving children
Make time each day, even if only for fifteen minutes, to check in with your spouse or significant other. Talk about each other, not the child who has died. Not that you shouldn't talk about the child. Just for a dedicated amount of time, devote time to you and your relationship.

Yes, it's hard to relate sometimes, but it's really about checking in with each other and communicating. Ask each other how you are doing... really doing. Be honest. Be open. Share what you are feeling and needing. As petty as it sounds, talk about work, talk about the bills that need to be paid, talk about who is making/bringing dinner, talk about the tasks that need to be accomplished. It's important to talk about your child, but not exclusively. It may seem difficult, but it's important.

Take time to connect physically: share a warm and loving touch. Hold hands. Offer a hug, hold each other while you cry. Simply sit together, or snuggle in silence. Although physical intimacy may be the farthest thing from your mind, or feel disrespectful to your child's memory, know that it's normal both to want to have sex (it is life affirming!) or to have no desire to be physically intimate in any way. If you feel the urge, there is nothing wrong with pursuing it. Endorphins are a good thing. Often, parents are in two different camps on this one, and that can create tension and a distancing physically and emotionally. Again, communication is so very important.

Be sure to connect daily with your other children. Try to stick to routines as best you can. Encourage them to express their feelings. Be honest with them. Choose your words carefully. Kids are very literal. Respect that they may be very clingy and need to be held, hugged, or just near you more than usual. In contrast, they may distance themselves from you and withdraw. They may continue as if nothing is different. They will take their cues, in part, from you.

Younger children will often act out their feelings in play, so be attentive to signs they are processing or perhaps having a difficult time coping.

Older children may seek to spend more time with friends and out of the house. If they are school aged, let their teachers know about the loss of their sibling, and ask them to keep you informed of any behavioral changes or dropping grades. If they seem to be struggling, or you are concerned about their behavior at school or at home, discuss your concerns with their pediatrician. The deceased child's siblings may need professional guidance, talk therapy or a support group specifically for bereaved siblings. The Compassionate Friends has some great resources for siblings on their website.

Connect with extended family

It's so easy for everyone to get lost in their own grief that they forget to check in with and connect to those closest to them. Often, families gather in the same physical space like the bereaved parent's home, but they don't have a lot of interaction. Conversation may be superficial or limited, or it may be deep and personal. Not everyone is in the same stage of grieving and that can make it difficult to connect.

What is most important is *being* there for each other: offer hugs and food, share stories, tears, and memories. Check in and ask how others are feeling, and how they are coping with the loss of your child.

If extended family is too far to physically be present, they can still connect with a card, a phone call, an email, or via instant messaging or Skype. These types of communications are important and appreciated, not just in those first few weeks, but periodically over time. Sending a card or a token of remembrance is so healing, especially for important days like birthdays, Mother's/Father's day, holidays and, of course, the anniversary of the child's death. Not just the first year, but every year. Remember, parents never, ever forget their child.

Connect with friends

Close friends *are* family for many people. Chances are your closest friends will flock to support you, especially in those early days after your child dies. They are often the ones that rally others to help. Although they are close to you and, therefore, likely were close to your child, their relationship is on a different level than that of close family. They certainly have their own grief, but it is usually not as intense, and they often are able to function at a more normal level than your family. This allows them to be a tremendous source of support and assistance.

Friends often offer the general, "If I can do anything, please let me know." This is often difficult for the bereaved parent because they either don't know what they want, don't want to impose or deal with it, or simply, don't care at that particular moment in time.

It's often more helpful to be specific with offers of help. Perhaps, saying, "I'd like to bring you supper tomorrow night, is that okay? I'll drop it off, complete with paper plates and all, so you don't have any clean up." It's a lot easier to say yes or no to a specific offer than it is to come up with a plan yourself when you are lost in the fog of missing your child.

It's usually your closest friends who will sit with you, shop for you, cook for you, take care of your other children for you, or arrange play dates for them, and listen to you talk about your child. They will sit by your side as you go through pictures, share memories, sort through their clothes, and tell their birth, life and death story.

They are probably the ones who tell your other friends and colleagues about your loss, the ones that arrange a meal train or a memorial fund for your child. They often assist with the phone calls that need to be made and may even be instrumental in helping you to plan memorial services for your child.

Your friends are more likely than not the ones who know you more intimately and better than even your closest family members. They are often the ones who are able to hold your hand and protect your heart and your child's memory as you walk this rocky road. They rally around you and your family. They are often your rock and your anchor. I don't know what I would have done without the amazing support of my own close friends. They were there not only in those first few days, but even today.

An important thing to realize is that the death of your child will show you who your friends really are. Just as the birth of your child changes you and your relationships with your friends, particularly those who didn't have children yet, so does the death of your child.

Many people, especially those who don't have children, don't get why it's taking you so long to get over it. They can't relate and often, they drift away. They are just moving on in their lives while you are standing still for a time. It may be temporarily, or it may be forever.

Others, particularly those who have their own children, may find it hits too close to home for them, and distance themselves as a coping strategy.

It's not that they don't want to be there for you, because they often do. It's just that they are not equipped or able to handle their own emotions and grief, and they purposefully distance themselves from you until they feel they can. This may mean they miss your child's calling hours, funeral or memorial service.

While this is understandable, if they don't communicate that and no one is supporting them through their pain and encouraging them to connect with you, those relationships can drift apart. When anger surfaces, it may be directed at those friends. This is most likely due to a lack of communication and understanding, especially if you don't live in close proximity to each other. It's all too easy to let good friendships end because it's too difficult to reach out in your pain. Should this happen, it's never too late to reach out and re-connect!

I don't know how I would have managed if it were not for my friends. I remember calling my best friend a few hours after we got home from the hospital. I both needed to hear her voice and knew I needed to tell her first. I knew she and her husband would call our other friends and be able to share the sad news in an appropriate and supportive way.

When I called, my other best friend, her husband, answered the phone. I asked for her, but she was not home. He could tell I was upset and asked what was wrong. I don't quite remember what I said beyond somehow conveying Meggie had died. Nor do I remember what he said in reply, but I remember feeling the love and support through his own shock and sadness. While I was talking to him, his wife called in, she sensed something was wrong. He wisely waited for her to return home before telling her, knowing she'd be upset and had to drive home. At my request, they began the phone tree and shared the news with other friends.

When Meghan's calling hours and funeral were planned, it was my friends who got the word out. I am eternally grateful for their friendship, love, and assistance not only in those early days and weeks, but for years to come.

The day after Meghan died; friends and family came to our home. Including the friends I had called the day before. I don't know if they called first or just came. It wasn't like we were going anywhere other than to the funeral home. They brought food. They brought love. They cried with us. They laughed with us. They listened as I told the story of her death. They held the space. They comforted my family. They brought Meggie gifts. A kitty. Flowers. Love. They brought love. They bolstered my ability to cope. Two of my friends offered to wrap the Christmas gifts for the boys because I just couldn't bring myself to do it.

My best friend asked for some pictures and if she could make a scrapbook for Meggie. She spent a good part of the day creating that scrapbook. She did it as much for me as she did for herself, it was healing. It's still something I look through often. It holds a special place in our family room, along with some other items gifted to us after her death.

Community
The support of your community can be absolutely amazing. When a child dies and so close to the holidays, communities rally. Even those that don't know you personally feel for you and want to do *something* to help. Losing Meg was horrifically painful, but the love, compassion and generosity shown by our community and even those who just read Meg's obituary and felt compelled to reach out to us, was absolutely overwhelming… in a good way. I was blown away by the support of our community, so many of whom I didn't even know.

Our neighbors astounded me. I'm pretty sure most of them were in our home at some point between the time we called 911 and the time we got home. We had just had our annual neighborhood holiday party the night before. They literally flocked to us to help, some still in their pajamas!

One of our neighbors assumed a position of chief neighborly helper. She was the one who took the boys to her house until we got home. She shared the news with our church, our other neighbors, her family and friends. There was a meal train arranged. There was a prayer vigil arranged for the neighbors at her house with our priest, that we were invited to, but I did not attend. She collected money people donated to help offset costs for us. She arranged for memorial masses long beyond Meg's funeral mass. Their generosity was humbling.

The day after Meg died, neighbors stopped by with cards, gifts, and food and just to give us their condolences and a hug in person. I was and am so grateful to live in this community and especially my neighborhood. Granted, many neighbors are "helpers" by trade: EMT's, nurses, teachers, a respiratory therapist, first responders, and even a physician. Even so, they abandoned their plans that day to support us.

Being that the day after Meghan died was Sunday, one of the neighbors mentioned it at their church service (not our church). A letter of support and condolence was handwritten and signed by the parishioners and hand delivered to us later that day by the pastor. Some of those who signed it knew us or our children; others had no idea who we were. I was so touched. At our own church, parishioners also rallied and put together a list of people to bring meals for us. They lasted for weeks! The outpouring of support and love by our community was absolutely amazing and so helpful. My gratitude is difficult to convey.

Community can go beyond geography. Your community includes your co-workers, those you might know through clubs or activities, friends of friends, or those who have crossed your path in some capacity in the past. With the social media platforms today, even total strangers can become part of your community.

I remember being surprised to see former co-workers come through the receiving line at Meg's wake. I had no idea they knew. Maybe I emailed one of them, but never expected them to come! Old friends I had not seen or talked to in years and former neighbors from my childhood also came and lent support. I had been a childbirth educator and birth doula for several years before Meg died. I was touched and surprised to hear from and see many of my former students and clients at her wake or funeral. Many other distant friends or acquaintances sent cards. I don't know how they all found out, but the support was so helpful in healing.

One of the greatest gifts I received was from my doula community. Doulas are women who are trained in supporting others through childbirth. They are, by nature, very loving, giving and compassionate women. They excel in mothering the mother. They are on call nearly constantly if they serve as a doula full time. It is a calling. The death of a child is not unlike the birth of a child in many ways. They need for unconditional non-judgmental love and support is the same. The experience is different for everyone. The need

208

to tell your child's death story, just like mothers tell their birth story, is often very similar. Doulas excel at active listening... at holding the space with love... at setting aside their feelings and opinions and making it all about the mom. They nurture and care for the mama and everyone around her.

I have never felt as loved in all of my life as I did when my doula sisters showered me with love and support. It began within hours after they found out Meghan had died... the emails of support... the cards. In fact one of the first people I reached out to the night Meghan died was a doula friend. Many came to her wake and/or funeral. A few, and one in particular, stayed for the entire wake. She sat quietly at times, beaming love and support to us. She rubbed my shoulders; she brought us water and tissues. She made sure we had chairs behind us in case we wanted or needed to sit. She tended to our family and friends, even though she didn't know them before that day. She did not know me very well at that point, but it didn't matter. She was my self-appointed death doula. My gratitude for her foresight, love and support is beyond measure.

The thing that blew me away was that same doula sister that cared for us so lovingly at Meghan's wake also compiled a list of fellow doulas who offered to help. She created a spreadsheet and assigned them all a week. It was a rotating schedule and went for six months! They committed to call me at least once a week, perhaps more often, to check in, to offer support, to bring a meal or do some errands, or simply to come give me a hug and wrap me in doula love. She sent me a copy which included their names and contact information.

They made it clear that I did not need to feel obligated to answer the phone or email, but to know they were on call 24/7 for me if I needed anything. They were my death and bereavement doulas. Everyone deserves a doula to support them through loss. Everyone deserves to be mothered, nurtured, and loved by someone who was there in that moment only for you. In birth and in death.

Nurturing Yourself

Self-nurturing is also very important to healing. This is true not only for bereaved parents, but for anyone who is bereaved, including those who are supporting bereaved parents. You must take care of yourself so that you can take care of others.

Self-nurturing is about caring for your health on all levels; physical, emotional, mental, and spiritual. There are so many ways you can care for yourself, nurture your mind, body and soul and help yourself integrate the experience of grief as you heal your heart.

Suggestions for self-nurturing
- Connect with the earth and ground yourself - go outside in nature.
- Balance being still and quiet with the benefit of being with others.
- Meditate.
- Exercise - walking, gentle yoga, dance or a more vigorous workout are great outlets for emotion and for tension.
- Anticipate and set limits for yourself with regard to participation in events.

- Don't be afraid to feel and be with your grief, seek help and support and accept it!
- Be grateful - start a gratitude journal. It can provide perspective and help you see the good in your life despite your pain.
- Be careful with isolation - let others share and love you, include them.
- It's ok to feel happiness, joy and other positive emotions.
- Seek comfort in your faith if it helps you.
- Laugh, even if it's through the tears.
- Express yourself and your feelings - write, dance, yell, cry, throw things in a non-hurtful or destructive way, or talk to others.
- Get a massage, energy work or Reiki, a chiropractic adjustment, acupuncture or any other spa treatment that resonates with you.
- Accept and forgive both yourself and others.
- Find a ritual of remembrance that resonates with you.
- Just be - whatever you feel, it is okay.
- Get regular health checkups.
- Seek support. Consider counseling, talking with a close friend, or attending a support group like the Compassionate Friends or a loss support group at your local hospital or funeral home.

Ways to Support Someone Who is Grieving (and what not to say or do)

There are many, many ways you can support someone who has lost a loved one. There are general things you can do like sending a card or preparing a meal. There are also more specific and meaningful things you can do to honor the deceased and support those who love and miss them.

Bereaved parents are a unique group. Losing a child, of any age, is so profound and so wrong on so many levels that it can be hard to find the right thing to say or do. The unfortunate thing about this is that people act in ways that inadvertently don't help or say/do nothing out of fear of simply not knowing what to say or do.

There are most definitely things that do not help bereaved parents. One of the most powerful ways to understand what helps and does not help a bereaved parent is to understand what it's like to be in their shoes. What it's like to be in the club no one wants to belong to.

So, what's it like to belong to the club no one wants to belong to? I wrote a blog post in an effort to explain what it's like. I also offered suggestions for what helps a bereaved parent and what does not. Many people said they found helpful and wish they had known what it is like when they were in similar shoes, trying to support a bereaved parent. It was part of the inspiration for this book. Sometimes the best way to know what it's like is to hear it from someone who has been there… to walk in their shoes.

Does Anyone Want to Try on My Shoes?
What happens in the "My child has died" club is something everyone should be aware of. This is not a book club. It's not a club anyone wants to be a part of. This is actually the "I can't believe I'm living this nightmare" club.

The club shouldn't be a secret. It shouldn't be hush-hush. It should be talked about, shared, supported, and known across the land. We are hurting. We need love, understanding, non-judgmental and unconditional support. We need to be listened to, not told what to do or how to feel. We need time. We need tissues. We don't need to eat, sleep, "get over it" or "move on." We don't need to hear how much better off our child is, how it was somehow for the best, or at least they didn't suffer or are no longer suffering.

WE are suffering. WE are hurt. WE need to walk our own road, at our own pace, in our own way. WE will never, ever be the same. We are not bad, stupid or neglectful parents. Although depending on the circumstances of our child's death, some say we are. I don't have to tell you how painful THAT is. We are parents who loved our children, and now they are gone. Time may heal, but it doesn't cure.

Joining a club is typically a positive experience, one made voluntarily and with great enthusiasm for the subject. Not so with our club. We are a unique group. We are the club no one ever wants to belong to. We are the person you never want to be. We are the person some of you can't handle being around, we "bring you down" because you can't deal with our pain. We have no choice. We are parents who've had to bury our own children. We didn't expect to join this club and we are beyond pissed that we had no choice but to become a member.

To the members of the club who have reached out to me in comments on my blog post about Meghan's Angel day, on her Facebook page, and through her website, I most sincerely, lovingly and with an open, but heavy heart welcome you to the club. I've heard from so many of you who are also members, far more than I ever expected. Some of you have very recently lost your children. You've lost your unborn babies, infants, toddlers, teenagers or adult children.

They've been lost to cancer, accidents, overdoses, suicide, murder, and medical illness. None of us ever expected it would happen to us. Yet here we are.

All of you who have reached out to me have commented that in reading my words, you realized you were not alone. You realized you had similar feelings and experiences. You felt the pain, the guilt, and the anger. Some of you said you have never shared with anyone, even your own spouse, how you felt or feel, until you responded to my post. It helped to validate how you felt and that you were not alone; that you were not "broken."

This post is for both those who have lost children and those who support them in their loss. We cannot bring our children back to us in body. What we can do is honor our feelings, remember our child and the joy they brought to our lives preserving their memory and love them always.

Many of those who lost children or grandchildren, especially recently, have asked how I coped. Does it ever get better or easier? Is it a life sentence of guilt, pain and depression? Will my marriage survive? How am I going to do this? I hope to help answer some of those questions for you here.

Although specifically about the loss of a child, much of what I say here is appropriate for the loss of any loved one.

Of course, I can speak only for what I found helpful and that which worked for me. Know you will find your own ways of coping, processing, and integrating your child's death into the rest of your life.

It is my distinct hope that in sharing what I've done to keep Meg's spirit alive in our family, will help you. That the growth and change her death catalyzed in me, and how I've gone through the stages of grief it will give you hope that you, too, will get through it. It is my hope that it will help you either in your own journey living your life with a spirit child, or in your role supporting a loved one who is. Please, feel free to take from this only that which resonates with you and leave the rest.

You already know about my experience of Meghan's Angel Day and how I honor her memory and remember her death every year. You already know how Meghan's Hope began, what it is, and why I devote so much time and energy to educating others about the dangers of furniture tip-over and child safety. It is how I continue to mother her. It is how I honor her life and her death. It is perhaps, her purpose in my life and in yours. In her death, in sharing her story, she has saved thousands of lives, at least I hope so. That brings me some peace. It, however, does not lessen the pain of her loss.

Questions and Answers About a Parent's Grief
The following is a question and answer section I posted within the above blog post. These are the most common questions that bereaved parents or their close family members and friends asked me about or wanted me to share with others about what helps them and what does not. Chances are you have the same questions or want others to know these things, too.

So, What is the Experience of Losing a Child Like?
It's a living hell. You've not known pain until you've held your dead child. Until you've seen their tiny lifeless body in

a casket. Until you've planned and attended their funeral, buried them, and came home without them. You can never, ever know what it's like unless you've experienced it. It's almost indescribable.

Don't Say You Know or Understand What They are Going Through

As someone supporting a bereaved parent, don't ever pretend to know what it's like. Don't ever say you understand how that parent feels unless you've lost a child yourself. Even then, your experiences and feelings could be very different. That which comforted you may not provide any comfort to them, and, in fact, may anger another person. Losing a pet, spouse, or sibling is tragic, but very, very different than losing a child. Please, think before you speak. That is my first piece of advice.

Don't Touch Their Child's Stuff Without Asking First

The day Meghan died, neighbors held vigil at our house. One of them was a police officer. He wisely told the women who, in wanting to do something to help, wanted to clean for us. He told them not to touch anything, the house needed to be exactly as I left it. They had no idea what or where Meghan's memory would be for me, and I needed to have that part of normalcy untouched. I am so grateful for his words.

I went to that last cup Meghan drank out of in the sink and held it, smelled it; put my lips where hers had been. If they had washed it, that opportunity to reconnect with one of the last things she touched would have been forever lost.

In a similar story, my mom, in trying to be helpful, vacuumed Meghan's room a few days after she died. I was sad and angry. She vacuumed up bits of Meghan that day: her hair, her skin, her smell. The energy of where she last lay, played, died was disturbed by the vacuum. I couldn't have known I'd feel that way. Neither could my mother. Let it be a lesson, parents, especially mothers, need to touch, feel, smell their children. I sniffed her shoes, her clothes, the floor. Any way I could connect with her, I tried. I still do.

Many people are unsure what to do with their child's room and "stuff." The answer is nothing, until you are ready. Some people have kept their child's room exactly the way it was left the day they died for decades. Others tweak it over time.

After about a year, we took Meg's day bed down. We moved her dresser, the one that killed her, to a different place in the room, and I moved my scrapbook and beading supplies into her room. It's now "our" space. Some of her toys, pictures she drew, a box she painted, her hair pretties and other little things that were hers are still there.

Other things I've packed away and ritualistically go through periodically. That was what resonated with me. The windows still bear her finger prints. The lamp that was on her dresser still has the creased lampshade from when it fell the day she died. It's a blend of her life, her death, and my love for her. A place for me to be with her, to channel creativity, to meditate, to just *be* with her, for it was the last place she was alive in our home. For me, it's sacred.

Don't Hound Them About Eating

I lost nearly twenty pounds in the first two or three weeks after Meghan died. I had no appetite. Everyone told me I had to eat. I got angry at them. I ate enough to survive.

Every person who told me to eat only pissed me off more. I picked at eggnog, sweets, and pasta. My go to comfort foods.

I did greatly appreciate the non-stop food train that came to our house for weeks after she died. That is so helpful. Neither I, nor anyone else in my family, had to worry about cooking or cleaning for weeks. Food arrived, fully prepared, often hot, the containers it arrived in were either disposable or left on the porch the next day to be quietly picked up. What a Godsend!

Do that. Arrange to bring or prepare meals for the bereaved family for weeks, if not months. There are great services out there like Lostsa Helping Hands and Meal Train to help organize it.

At first, I picked at food. I just wasn't hungry. Eventually, I began to eat more. I slowly regained the weight, but it took years. I was not overweight to begin with but I was not underweight, either. I just ate a lot less. I was also exercising and moving a lot less than I had prior to her death. I simply had no appetite. Depression and the work of grieving will do that to you. It's not unusual.

Some people will have the opposite reaction. They'll eat non-stop and gain weight. Some will turn to alcohol or sleeping pills, and sometimes abuse them. We all cope differently. For a time, it's to be expected. Be sure you get regular health care checkups in that first year and beyond and take care of any medical conditions you have.

Sleep May be Elusive or All You Want to Do

I couldn't sleep at all the first week, and I slept fitfully in 20-30 minute bouts for months. I later learned this was an element of PTSD. Every little noise I had to investigate, because I never heard the dresser fall. With a 3 and 6-year old, that was constantly. I compulsively checked on my kids every half hour at night to be sure they were still breathing.

I'd lie in bed at night, desperate for sleep but unable to sleep. Every time I closed my eyes I relived everything about Meg's death. When driving, I'd pull the car over frequently to be sure the kids were breathing if they were quiet. I was afraid to cross railroad tracks. I was petrified to let them out of my sight. Meg's twin slept in our bed more often than not. Sometimes my older son "camped out" on our bedroom floor. I lived in constant fear of something happening to one of my other kids. Constant fear...

Several people suggested sleeping pills but I was petrified to take them. I already had tremendous guilt about not waking up and saving Meghan, the thought of chemically knocking myself out and potentially not hearing something that could save one of my other children was unbearable. Besides, I don't tolerate medicine in general and I avoid it unless necessary. It may be very helpful and appropriate for others; it just didn't resonate with me.

Other parents may find that all they want to do is sleep. They can't pull themselves out of bed to save their soul. They nap constantly. They give in to the emotional and physical exhaustion, perhaps, to escape, perhaps, because it's what their body needs to cope and heal.

Inane and Mundane Stuff Will Piss You Off

You feel as if you are operating in slow motion, everything is foggy. It's hard to feel anything other than sadness. If you smile or laugh, you almost feel guilty. If someone else is smiling or laughing, you hate them. How dare they be happy when you are in so much pain?

You find the mundane things you used to enjoy either don't hold the same appeal or are downright annoying now. Seeing other children who look similar, act similar, or seeing children's things your child would have liked can rip your heart right open.

I can't tell you how many times I'd have something in my hand to buy for Meghan before I realized she was dead, weeks and months after she died. I still sometimes call the cat "Meggie" if I'm thinking of her! I couldn't even walk past the little girls' clothing section of stores for years without dissolving into tears and feeling like I got kicked in the gut. It still bothers me, especially at Christmastime.

I partially cope with this by purchasing trinkets for Meg's special place at the cemetery, her memorial garden at our home, or buying something she'd have loved and donating it to a charity or a family in need.

Trigger Days and Being Blindsided

There are certain "trigger days" when you can expect a resurgence of emotion. They are the difficult days. The firsts of the first year are usually the most difficult and expected. For a while, for me, it was every Saturday. Meghan died on a Saturday. I was hyper-aware of days, times, and how it correlated to the day and time of her death and my experiences that day. Much like a mother remembers her birth story and the birth day of her children, she remembers their death day. At least I did.

Then it was the 18th of every month. She died on the 18th. Even now, on the 18th day of every month, I think of her angel day. Now it's nothing more than "another 18th" without her. But at first, it was a marker of some kind emotionally. I was more aware and it hurt more on the 18th's.

The big triggers, of course, are the major family holidays, Mother and Father's day, the child's birthday, and their death day. I was surprised how much my own birthday was a trigger for me. Then there are things like the first day of school or what should have been their first day of school… every year. Going through the milestones of your other children, without the one you lost, wondering what it would be like if they were there for this event, or their own graduations, proms and other rites of passage. You can prepare for them in some ways, but in others you can't. I found I dreaded them. The anticipatory grief was almost worse than the actual grief and pain of the day.

You will be blindsided at times. You'll think you're fine, having a good day, going about your business, even years later, and then, out of the blue, something will pull at your heartstrings: a song, a person, something you heard, a child that looks like yours did. It could be anything, anytime and anywhere.

It's to be expected, and even now, years later, it still happens once in a while. Not nearly as much as it used to, but I expect it will happen forever.

For me, a year or so ago, it was a Seventh Generation ad. There was a little blonde girl wearing a pink shirt looking through a washing machine door. My heart nearly stopped. She was a ringer for Meghan! It blew my mind. Her twin brother asked how it was possible she was living somewhere else doing magazine ads! Those are the triggers you just can't anticipate.

Counseling is Helpful; Depression is Normal for a Time, Please LISTEN

The loss of a child is up there on the life stress scale. You have every right to be depressed and for the better part of the first year. It's an expected grief reaction. It's not something you get over.

There is help out there. The Compassionate Friends is a bereavement support group especially for parents who have lost a child of any age. They have a wonderful website and local chapters that offer support meetings. There is a national conference every year and a walk to remember, where walkers carry the name of your child. They sponsor a candle lighting memorial around the world in memory of the children gone too soon so that "their light will always shine" on the second Sunday of December every year. I can't recommend them enough for parents, siblings, grandparents, and friends.

Grief counseling is tremendously beneficial. It can help you express and validate your feelings while helping you navigate and process grief. It's a process. Many people find it helpful. I did.

Sometimes, antidepressant medication is helpful, too. I strongly recommend it be used together with talk therapy. Far too many primary care physicians are willing to write prescriptions without understanding why that person is requesting or needing them and without appropriate follow up.

Depression following the death of your child is a normal grief reaction and is not the same as clinical depression, although it can evolve into it or another mental illness. Masking it with medication without appropriate medical oversight could potentially be detrimental to the process of healing so please, seek professional support and help if you feel depressed or have a history of depression or mental illness for yourself or in your family history.

As a friend, you can offer to listen. Don't try to fix it or them. You can't. Give them permission to call you anytime, anywhere, for any reason. You may hear the same thing over and over. Listen. Only offer your opinion or advice if they ask for it, especially initially. Hug. Say, "I'm sorry." Be there. Offer to help by doing housework, shopping, cooking or errands. Don't be afraid to say their child's name, ask what they are thinking or how they are feeling. It's okay to cry, yourself. Don't judge. Just be there.

How do You Answer the Question, "How Many Children do You Have?"

It may well depend on the day, how you are feeling, and who is asking. In the first few weeks after she died, I'd just cry if anyone asked. Avoiding human interaction was my chosen coping strategy at the time with anyone who didn't already know. Thankfully, I'm pretty well connected with some pretty amazing people, so I had a lot of support and understanding around me.

Many people don't acknowledge to strangers that they've lost a child. It may be too painful to say out loud or, many of us simply don't want to have to deal with the person who is asking's discomfort or reaction to our answer. Yet then we feel as if we are denying our own child's life.

It can be emotionally exhausting to deal with the fallout of such an unexpectedly loaded question for both parties. I think that's unfortunate. Our children's life and death both deserve to be acknowledged.

In my professional bio, I say that I am the mother of three; two boys who walk this earth with me, and a daughter who flies with the angels. The majority of the time when I am asked, I say I have three children and leave it at that.

What if they ask a more specific question, like how old are they or are they boys or girls? Then, I typically say I have two sons and a daughter. I often elaborate on my own and say my youngest son and my daughter are twins, but she died when she was three and give the current ages of the boys, because, well, at that point, full disclosure is easier.

You'd be surprised how expressions change and that abruptly ends the discussion. Some say nothing. That hurts the most. Some say they are sorry. I appreciate that. Some ask how she died. I tell them. Sometimes I tell them even if they don't ask. They are often moved to tears. Some open up and share that they, too, lost a child and an amazing opportunity to share and heal unfolds for both of us. Sometimes, it provides an opportunity for discussion about safety because of how Meghan died. Sometimes, I end up comforting them.

What do You Say When People Say "At least you have your other children." Or, "You can always have more children."
Yeah, never, ever say that to a bereaved parent. Like never. I mean really, which child of yours do you feel you could live without right now? None of them, right? You don't want any of your children to die. You cannot replace the pain of the loss of a child with another one. Don't belittle their child's death by somehow making their other children matter more or by the notion that the loss can somehow be replaced by another child. We want *all* our children to be with us.

As a bereaved parent what I would say is exactly what I referenced above. "Really? Which of your children do you feel you could live without?"

Some Relationships Will Change
Death has a way of showing you who your true friends are in life. There are those that are the "fair weather friends" who are there for you when it's sunny, but become scarce when the stormy emotional weather moves in.

Then there are those who will sit with you through the storms, through the flood of tears, the violent tornadic winds of emotion and offer you a life preserver of unconditional and non-judgmental love and support. Those are your true friends. You might be surprised to discover they are not who you thought they were.

Family and friends will all cope differently. Some cope by not coping at all. They avoid contact with you. They don't want to talk about your dead child. They dive into their work or hobbies. They become "busy" and unavailable. You may find that fundamental differences can no longer be dealt with or tolerated.

Some people you were once close to may drift away, and those relationships may end. Others may become closer and stronger. New relationships will blossom, perhaps, with those who've had a similar loss or experience.

I lost some really good friends after Meghan died. Some were because of the complications of grief. Others largely drifted away because neither they, nor I, understood our emotions or the personality changes born of grief.

Some drifted away because they just couldn't deal with the "new" me. Some family members became closer, others more distant. I found some new, really amazing friends. I am grateful for all of them and what they brought to my life in the time they were an active part of it.

Will my Marriage Survive?
People often ask me about their marriage. Will our marriage survive? I don't know the statistics specific to bereaved parents. I do know nationally, in the U.S., the divorce rate is over 50%. Whether or not your marriage survives may well depend on how your child died, if blame is placed on the

other parent, or if there was already animosity or difficulty in your relationship.

If your marriage was anything but perfect, with fantastic communication, before your child died, it's going to take a lot of work and understanding to weather the storm of losing a child. It will take open and honest communication, understanding, and, perhaps, some individual and couples counseling as well as tincture of time.

Be gentle with each other. Be honest with each other. Talk. Losing a child and working through your grief may actually make your marriage stronger. It may not. The general advice is not to make any drastic changes for at least a year after the loss of a child because it takes time to process the grief.

My marriage did not survive. It's a long and personal story and not one I have the intent of ever sharing in a public forum. Suffice it to say that our marriage was not ideal before Meghan died. Her death certainly did not help that at all. There were fundamental reasons why our marriage failed. It was NOT because Meghan died. Her death did catalyze a tremendous change in me, my beliefs and my view on life. The decision to end my marriage was not made lightly, but it was, in the end, the best thing for all of us.

And for those who have asked, I recently re-married. I, of course, never expected to date, let alone marry again. In a twist of fate and the way the Universe works is amazing way, my new husband was actually at Meghan's wake. He was a friend of my sister's, although I did not know him until years later. He had also seen Meghan alive, a little over a year before she died, at my sister's wedding. He is now the proud step-dad of a spirit child. He spoke of her in his wedding vows to me. Not a dry eye in the house...

Ways to Preserve the Memory of your Child and Creating New Traditions

Memory keeping is a wonderful way to remember and honor your child. It's tremendously personal and meaningful. I encourage you to consider ways you can honor the memory of your child and incorporate their life into yours.

- Ornaments. Every year, Santa leaves a Tinker Bell ornament in her stocking. Her twin usually hangs it on the tree. This year, it jumped off the tree and shattered. Instead of getting upset, we laughed and said, "Oh, hi Meggie! Guess you didn't like that one."

- A memorial garden. I created one area in our yard that is a Meggie garden. Pink roses, a butterfly bush, bird bath, kitty garden statues, and Tinker Bell decor abound.

- Personalize their cemetery plot. If your cemetery allows, make it about the child. We chose her stone carefully. We choose flowers in colors she'd like. There are always kitty and Tinker Bell trinkets. We bring new decor now and then. Bird feeders and colorful twirly things decorate it in the summer time. A pink tree at Christmas. A bunny and a basket of eggs celebrate Easter. A kitty pumpkin and black cats mark Halloween.

- Celebrate their birth day. Meg was a twin, so we still celebrate her brother's birthday every year. It is exquisitely painful to me on this day, probably, the second hardest day of the year for me, because I see one where two should always have been. I bring her flowers and a balloon. Every year since Meg died, we have a family cupcake picnic at the cemetery on their birthday. We sing happy "bird" day with a suet cake with candles. We eat our cupcakes. We blow some pixie dust to the heavens and then we run around silly, just like she used to, and sing "Tinker Bell all the way." Anyone else at the cemetery that day thinks we're nuts. We don't care. It's about Meg, remembering and celebrating HER essence, her joy, her spunky-ness. What better way than to emulate her?

- Gifts of honor. I received many notices of masses in Meg's honor, memorial candles with her prayer card on them, a tree planted in the Children's Forest in Israel, donations made in her memory to charitable organizations and especially to the Sterling Animal Shelter, where they received so many donations, they renovated their kitty adoption area and named it after Meghan.

- A memorial quilt. I wanted to have a quilt made of some of Meghan's clothes. Someone quickly volunteered. Although I hated to part with that box of clothes, the gift I received in return is beautiful and now I can wrap myself in her in a way. I can tell you what every scrap was from and what I or she loved about each item.

- Incorporate their life into yours. Perhaps this is best noted as how I involved Meghan in my wedding day. We had a chair for her. I had a tiny picture of her on my bouquet. We had her special candle centerpiece that we lit as we said the "We Light These Five Candles" poem. We created and played a memorial slide show honoring all our deceased relatives and friends.

Perhaps, the greatest gift you can give someone who has lost their child is remembering their child out loud. Say their name. Talk about what you loved about them. What you remember about them. Send a card or post on their Facebook wall where everyone can see every year on their birthday, their angel day, Mother and Father's day. Let them know you are thinking of them. That you know it's a difficult day for you, even if it's years and years later. I promise you, their parents are already thinking of them. To know their child was not forgotten is the best gift.

Specific to Meghan, the greatest gift I can receive now is the sharing of her story, the sharing of Meghan's Hope. Telling others about the danger of furniture tip-over and how easy it is to prevent by securing furniture and TV's to the wall. That honors her life.

If you are a parent who has lost a child, the greatest gift you can give yourself is patience. Allow yourself to feel what you feel. Know it's a process. Connect with those who you feel called to. Be gentle with yourself. Know your child's spirit and light will always live in your heart. Let it shine!

Use Your Ears and Your Heart
If I've said it once, I've said it a zillion times, the most important thing you can do as someone supporting a bereaved parent is listen. Listen with your heart. Keep your head out of it and your opinions to yourself unless asked directly for them. Do not judge. Do not criticize. Be there. Be empathetic. Be compassionate. It is okay to cry... in

body, in mind, and in spirit for them and with them. Bring love. Bring acceptance for the bereaved and whatever they are feeling, want or need in the moment. Be with them.

Things NOT to Say to a Bereaved Parent
Often, people are afraid to say anything to the newly bereaved because they don't know what to say, are afraid of saying the wrong thing and upsetting the person, or because they are afraid of their own emotions getting in the way.

Well-meaning and commonly offered platitudes may fall flat or even exacerbate their pain for parents who have lost a child. We often say what we think we are supposed to say or what we've heard others say before, without really thinking about how it might be received or interpreted by the bereaved.

One should not say something just for the sake of saying it. One should also think about the context of the death, the age of the child, and your own relationship with the child and their family. Now that you know the truths of a newly bereaved parent, you can use that knowledge to help in your support of them.

Whatever you say or do should come from your heart, from a place of truth, honesty and feeling. It's okay to cry when you do. It's okay not to cry. It's okay if the parents cry. Don't fear the sadness or the pain.

I promise you, they cannot feel any worse than they already do. I can also promise you, they are already thinking about their child, so avoiding talking about it and pretending it didn't happen is about the worst thing you can do. *Parents want the life and death of their children acknowledged.* Their child lived. They will always be part of the fabric of their lives. This is true no matter how old the child was when they died and even if that child was never born or was stillborn.

That said, there are things that can irritate bereaved parents and are not helpful to them or to their healing, even if well-intentioned. Here are a few. These are things people often say and bereaved parents almost universally report that they wish people didn't say them because they didn't help or even angered them.

These Words Don't Help: What Not to Say

- You can always have more children.
- At least you have your other children.
- You could always adopt.
- You're still young; you have your whole life ahead of you.
- Now you'll have your own angel in Heaven.
- This was God's will.
- They are with God.
- God needed another angel.
- Don't be angry with God.
- They are in a better place.
- It's for the best.
- I know how you must feel (unless you have lost a child yourself).
- I understand (unless you have lost a child yourself).
- It's probably best that you forget about them if it hurts so much.
- You'll be fine.
- They are better off now.
- You'll get over it.

232

- It will get better.
- It's been ("x" amount of time), don't you think you should move on?
- Why do you talk about them if it makes you so sad?
- Why haven't you given/put away their things yet?
- You need to put this behind you and get on with your life.
- You shouldn't blame yourself.
- There was nothing you could do.
- You shouldn't feel that way.
- Their suffering is over; you should be glad and move on.
- They are safe now.
- You'll see them again (when you die).
- They are with _____ (another deceased loved one).
- Why do you do this to yourself? (especially around ritualistic remembrance or trigger days)

Things You SHOULD Say to a Bereaved Parent
- I'm so sorry.
- I'm so sad for you and for the loss of _____ (say their name!)
- Share a memory what you loved about their child
- Say their child's name or ask if you don't know
- What happened?
- How old was your child?
- I can't imagine how incredibly painful (or devastating, or hard or heartbreaking or impossible) this is for you.
- I know this must be very hard for you.
- What can I do for you?
- I'm here for you, anytime, anywhere.

- Tell me how you are feeling.
- I have time, is there anything you want to share/talk about? Tell me as much as you want.
- Tell me about _____ (their name).
- How are you doing managing all of this?
- I've been thinking about you. Is there anything I can do?
- I love you.
- I am sending love and wishes for healing your way.
- Call me anytime. I'm here for you.
- I can't imagine how you feel, when I lost (a close loved one), I remember I felt...
- I'm heading to the store; can I pick anything up for you?

Things You Can Do to Help
- Offer to help address thank you cards.
- Offer to do the shopping, laundry, or household tasks or drive them so they have company.
- Offer to make phone calls that need to be made.
- Recognize everything has changed. Don't pretend that it has not or tell them it will ever get back to normal.
- Invite them to dinner or offer to bring them a meal.
- Offer support.
- Send a card, let them know you are thinking of them and recognize how difficult this is for them. Especially at holiday times, birthdays, anniversaries and Mother's or Father's day.
- Reminisce with them about their child. Share what you remember or loved most about them. Listen while they reminisce. Bereaved parents want to hear

their child's name and know they have not been forgotten.

- Acknowledge that they are hurting. Support them through their grief but know you cannot make them go through it any faster. Only they can walk that road. It's a much easier road when others are there with us, supporting us.
- Offer to care for their other children so they can have some quiet time.
- Provide resources for support.
- Offer to attend a support group with them.
- Send a gift on a special day or just because you are thinking of them.
- Offer to help plant flowers at the cemetery or memorial garden.

Gifts of Remembrance

When a loved one dies, especially a child, people often want to honor that person somehow. The ways this can be done are as numerous and unique as your child was. Sometimes the most meaningful are the simplest or the unexpected.

Perhaps, as the bereaved parent, you have an idea of tokens of remembrance you might like to have. It's okay to ask someone to help you make it a reality. I discussed many of these in Chapter three, if you are looking for some ideas; refer back to that chapter or to the resource list at the end of the book.

Unexpected Financial Burdens

When a child dies, especially unexpectedly, the families are faced with tremendous expenses. If their child had been ill, especially for a long time, there may be medical bills to pay.

Getting a bill for an ambulance ride, an ER copayment, or medical procedures for the day your child died can be excruciatingly emotionally painful, let alone the stress of having to find the funds to pay for it.

Then there are the costs associated with the calling hours, funeral, burial, cremation, and memorial services including things like the viewing room rental fee, the casket, limos, the cemetery plot, and all sorts of other small fees that add up. Sometimes they are detailed out; sometimes it's just a set fee.

Flowers are an additional cost, as are obituaries, and some papers charge by the word! Incidentals like the guest book, prayer cards, and thank you notes all add cost. The police who escort the processional and stop the traffic have fees. These are often all taken care of and sent in one itemized bill from the funeral home. Then there is the cost of a headstone, which is often separate.

Average funeral expenses can total $7-10,000 quite easily. The costs are not related to the age of the person who has died, but to the goods and services associated with these items.

Because most parents don't have life insurance for their children or $10,000 lying around, this can be a tremendous burden. Some simply cannot afford to give their child the funeral they feel their child deserves or that they want to, and choose cremation over burial because it's less expensive. Some parents have to cash in retirement funds or take out a loan to bury their child!

Many times, a memorial fund is set up at a local bank by a friend or family member that donations can be made to help cover the family's expenses. You may be able to assist with this either in setting up the fund or spreading the word to your social network or media to get the word out.

Sometimes, complete strangers who hear of the death of the child through the media or word of mouth will donate. This is a wonderful gift to the family and a practical one, too. A new way to offset funeral expenses is crowdfunding through organizations like Go Fund Me, where accounts can be set up for donations, often attracting donations from complete strangers.

Sometimes, parents will suggest a donation in lieu of flowers in their child's obituary. It might be to a charity organization near and dear to the parents or related to the child's death. It might be a scholarship or memorial fund that was set up in honor of their child. Sometimes it's to a local organization.

We chose to suggest a donation to the Sterling Animal Shelter, a local no-kill shelter in our town, in lieu of flowers. Meggie loved kitties. It seemed to make perfect sense that she could help kitties out as part of her legacy. When the shelter read her obituary and learned about our request, they reached out to thank us. We stopped by a few days later to introduce them to Meghan. We brought pictures of her and her many kitties. We told them how they shared her "special box" (casket) with her. Little did we know how many people would make those donations! I received an email from the shelter a few weeks after Meghan died. They had received literally thousands of dollars in donations! They were absolutely blown away, as were we. Some came with cards signed by family or friends. Others were anonymous.

They received so many donations in her memory that they went forward with a long awaited renovation to their kitty adoption room. They named her "The Kitty Angel" and a watercolor was commissioned and donated by a local artist of Meghan holding a kitty. The original hangs in the shelter today along with some of Meg's personal pink kitty artwork and a newspaper article about her. We were invited to the dedication and grand opening about six months after her death. Several kitties were adopted that day and week.

That day, our beloved Rusty adopted us! My oldest son opened his cage and he walked out onto his shoulders, draped himself across his neck and began to purr and nuzzle. He looked at us wide eyed and asked if we could keep him. Of course, we said "Yes." The shelter gifted our beloved cat to us, but we have always viewed our love muffin purr monster of a kitty a gift from Meghan to her oldest brother. Rusty has been tremendously instrumental in healing my eldest son's grief.

Beyond monetary gifts, there are many ways to honor and remember a child. Many of these were discussed in chapter three where I discussed the many memorial keepsakes that are available. Religious stores, gift boutiques, and many online stores sell beautiful and unique memorial gifts. Several specific to child loss are listed in the resource list at the end of this book. Or, perhaps, you could make something very personal and more meaningful to the bereaved parents yourself.

I've said it many times, and I'll say it again, the best gift you can give a bereaved parent is your unconditional and non-judgmental love and support. Acknowledge their child by name, be with them wherever they are in their grief, and be sure to take care of yourself in your own grief.

Offer to walk the path with them. Remember. Listen. Love.

Chapter Seven

Expecting the Unexpected: Triggers, Holidays, and Anniversaries

In this chapter we will explore what triggers are, how they can make you feel, and tools and tips for coping with them, especially on the most emotionally challenging of days; the child's birth day, the anniversary of their death, and family holidays. It is my hope this chapter not only gives the bereaved parent and those who support them a better understanding of what can set off grief, but also some creative and beautiful ways to honor the deceased child's life through new traditions.

Triggers are the things people tend to forget to tell you about when you are newly bereaved. They are the things that can suddenly turn on your grief or send you into a different stage of grief like the flip of a switch.

Although some triggers can be anticipated, like holidays, they often are unexpected and out of the blue, and in situations where you didn't think or expect you'd find yourself suddenly thinking of your child or feeling the pain of their loss sharply again.

You can quite literally go from being happy and functioning to suddenly angry or dissolving into tears because you saw a child that looked like or said something like yours or you noticed the time on the clock is the same as the date or time your child died or was born. Or, perhaps, you reached out to buy something for your child reflexively, only to realize they were not here anymore to receive it. The unexpected nature can make these triggering events harder to cope with for you and challenging for those around you to understand.

Triggers are most common in the first year, but can happen anytime... forever. Over time, you may learn to anticipate what things may trigger your grief and be able to prepare for it. It's important to recognize that anticipating a trigger does not necessarily make it any easier to cope with. You can also be blindsided by triggers years later. It's part of the journey.

Common Triggers
- *Expected or Anticipated Triggers*
  - Holidays
  - Birthdays
  - The anniversary of the child's death
  - Visiting the cemetery
- *Often Unexpected Triggers*
  - Dates and times - seeing numbers on a clock or the calendar that remind you of your child's birth or death day or time or other important numbers.
  - Places of significance - passing the hospital where your child was born or died.
  - Dates of significance – birthdays such as your own, anniversaries, the first day of school, etc.
  - Going to the funeral home, church/synagogue or place of worship where your child's services were held.
  - Hospitals, ambulances, police and fire vehicles, sirens.

- Anything associated with the day your child died. What you were doing, eating, wearing, where you were or whom you were with, etc.
- Your child's favorite things or belongings.
- Family events.
- Milestones - ones for other family members, especially siblings, or ones your child should be having or participating in, but are not, such as the first day of school, first dates, prom, graduation, marriage, anniversaries, milestones for other family members, particularly of the children of your deceased adult child.
- Receiving mail for your child, especially bills related to their illness, death or burial/cremation.
- Seeing Facebook or social media posts about/from your adult/older child or those that are automatic such as birthday reminders, their photo cycling to the top of your friends list, or if a friend or family member posts a photo of them and tags them or you, etc.
- TV shows/news stories about your child's circumstances of death or ones that are similar.
- Something on TV or in print that reminds you of your child or is about your child.
- Hearing a favorite song of your child's or one you associate with your child.
- Ringing phones, particularly from the person/number who called you to notify you the day your child died if you were notified by

phone. Seeing your child's name or phone number in your contact list.

- o Coming across pictures/videos of your child.
- o Going through or finding items your child made.
- o Noises that remind you of the day your child died such as medical beeps and alarms (even if on TV or read about), sirens, sounds of a crash (if it was a motor vehicle accident), any sound associated with your child's death or death day.

Sometimes, the best way to understand triggers is to read what a bereaved parent's experience is like. I wrote a blog entry about triggers and the pain of grief using an analogy to shoes that are ugly and too tight. The feedback I received was positive, both from fellow bereaved parents and those who were not bereaved parents, but found it most helpful to understanding how grief comes and goes and what that feels like to a parent who has lost a child. Perhaps, it will help you, too.

A Walk in my Shoes

It's that day again. The first day of school! I don't know about your house, but it was a first day of school miracle here. With two boys, one in 6th grade and one in 10th, the fact they woke up ON THEIR OWN, were not only downstairs and ready before they had to be (with everything they needed, even), but ate breakfast and got out the door on time, without nagging, left me both flabbergasted and tickled pink at the same time. It made the hassle of shopping, organizing and trying to get them to participate in preparation quite rewarding at 6:30 this am. If only it could last all the school year...

Speaking of pink, this day is never an easy one. As I watched my youngest head off to the bus stop, so independent and SO excited to be in middle school, I couldn't help but wonder, as I always do on the first day of school, what it would've been like if his twin sister was racing him to the bus stop.

That's the way it was supposed to be, you know. With her pretty new back to school dress and platinum blonde hair in a ponytail with a pink bow, giggling as they shared yet another exciting adventure together.

I was supposed to be back to school shopping for girly things: the clothes, the shoes, the backpack, the school accessories, the dance or gymnastic outfits. We were supposed to get our toes painted together and get our hair cut. I was supposed to hug my three babies and send them off for another year to learn and grown. She was supposed to come home with her brother, telling me all about her middle school adventures and what sports or clubs she wanted to try out for or join. I was supposed to get a hug and kiss from my twins, my son and my daughter.

Instead, my boys got on the bus, and I drove to the cemetery. To visit my daughter's grave. There is pink there, among the trinkets and tributes left for her. There is no backpack. No new shoes. No pretty new clothes. No pink hair pretties. Dreams of watching her dance and jump and play died nearly 9 years ago when she did. I sat there. I stared at her headstone. I felt guilty I've neglected the flowers the past few weeks, and they died in the heat. I saw the resilient roses on the rose bush and smiled. There will be pink! She always was persistent...

I felt a heaviness in my heart. I asked, to no one in particular, "Why?" Why was I robbed of the joy of raising a daughter? Why were my boys robbed of their sister? Why was it MY little girl and not yours?

Why do I have to wear these shoes? They are ugly and tight and they hurt like hell. I will never, ever be able to get them off. When everyone is posting back to school photos and complaining about something or other, I am sitting at my daughter's grave site. Alone. Alone with my sadness... my guilt. Alone with the pain of what could have been, but will never be. I won't ever get another hug from her. I'll never run my hands through her silky hair. We won't ever giggle over the power of pixie dust. I just have to keep putting one foot in front of the other, walking further away from the last time I held her... heard her voice... smelled her scent. The last time I snuggled her.

I sigh. Tears spring to my eyes. For some reason, I'm always surprised by how easy it is, if I let myself just stop for a moment, to feel the pain. As years go by, you get good at keeping it under the surface, so you can function and live life. Yet it's always there. Just like those shoes. They seem to pinch a lot harder on these trigger days. Perhaps, it's because on these days, the pain of her loss swells, making the walk that much more painful.

I'd give anything to give away my shoes. The truth is, none of you want them. I don't blame you. The trade is not a fair one. It's not even one I'd wish upon my greatest enemy (if I had one). It's my path to walk. I accept it. I have no choice. That doesn't mean I don't feel the pinch of my too tight, ugly, and permanent shoes. It doesn't mean I don't want to give them away.

It just means I want you to remember, that I am not alone. There are thousands of other parents who wear this style of shoe and who feel this pain. They may not say anything about it, but they may be cranky and irritable. They may not call you back. They may cut you off in traffic. They may yell or overreact. It's because they are hurting. Please, remember them. Me. Us. We have many days like this every year.

So please, don't make fun of our shoes. Walk with us in them. Just for a moment. You are lucky. You can always take them off...

These triggering events seem to happen more frequently in the first year and even more frequently in the days and weeks after your child's death, but can happen at anytime and anywhere. They are different for everyone. Some things may always trigger your grief; others may only for a while. Then it bothers you less and less.

Sometimes triggers set us off more if they are close to a significant date or event or, perhaps, if you are already tired or irritable. They may be less apt to set us off if we are in an otherwise happy and healthy space.

Sometimes, we realize we've been set off by an unexpected trigger or even an anticipated one. We feel it emotionally, but we don't express it or recognize it at that moment for some reason. This can cause our grief to manifest in other ways. Irritability, sudden extreme fatigue, loss of appetite, nausea, headache, or a desire to withdraw are all common manifestations of the pain of grief. Some people are not fully aware of what might trigger them, or has triggered them, and therefore are not fully aware of why they feel or act the way they do. They may only recognize it in hindsight, or if someone helps them understand what triggers are for them.

Others might be aware of what triggers their grief and go out of their way to avoid it. Being aware of it doesn't necessarily take away the pain or sadness it can cause.

Once you realize what triggers you, it becomes less of a surprise and more of an anticipatory thing, and often, a tactic of avoidance is the #1 coping strategy. For me, it means I avoid stores after Halloween because I cannot stand the holiday decorations, music, and parents buying gifts for their children. I can't stand to see pretty little girl dresses and shoes. It kills me. It's irrational, but I hate it. So I've learned to just avoid the stress of it if I can. It's made me a more efficient shopper!

Unlike other triggers which may blindside you, holidays, birthdays, and anniversaries are days that you can at least plan for a bit in advance.

Anticipatory grief is a whole other kind of grief, and it is common before important days and events. I have found that at least for me, anticipatory grief is sometimes worse than the actual day it leads up to. I've learned I am more irritable, tired, and tend to not want to do anything. The more I try to keep busy, the more exhausted and cranky I get. Once the day or event arrives, I find I am in a better place to cope. Sometimes the waiting is the worst part.

Knowing Meg's Angel Day is a huge trigger for me, I have a ritual I've developed around it. I always take that day off of work. If it's a weekend, I try to isolate myself as much as I can. I *need* to be alone. I need to be alone with Meggie. I tend to become increasingly withdrawn and irritable as the day draws near. I become forgetful and apathetic. I don't eat well. Everything related to Christmas and little girls triggers me. Pretty much everything triggers me. *Everything.* I sleep poorly the night before.

I often allow myself to relive our last happy moments together. I wake up early on her anniversary. Sometimes I go to her room, sometimes I sit quietly and watch the sun rise. I insist on being alone for the day. I don't answer the phone. I often spend much of the day writing to her. Once everyone is gone for the day, I begin my ritual.

I wrote about it on my blog on the 8th anniversary of her death. If you read the first chapter of this book, you have read it, too. It was the first time I felt comfortable and ready to share with the few people who I thought would read it what it was really like to be a bereaved mother. Why I do the things I do with Meghan's Hope. Why I speak, why I teach. Why I write. Really, I just wanted people to secure their furniture and understand that they could avoid my pain, and save their child's life, by doing so. I wanted to save others' lives because I couldn't save my daughter's.

Little did I know, it would be a post that would go viral, and that would travel around the world. That Meggie's story would touch so many and inspire them to action… it was a dream come true… a painfully bittersweet dream come true.

Holidays

Holidays can be one of the most difficult times for those who have lost a loved one. This is especially true in the first year following their death. When that loved one is a child, it goes beyond the physical loss to the loss of your hopes and dreams. The loss of the way you envisioned the holidays would be for your family with your child present, through the years as they grew. Their absence is painfully obvious, year after year.

Holidays are traditionally a time for celebrating with friends and gathering with family. It is a busy time, often involving parties, shopping for gifts, and travel to see family and friends.

For those who have lost a child, it is often a long and painful road. One many bereaved parents dread. Someone important in our lives will always be missing from these celebrations. Relationships will change. Family dynamics will change. Traditions will change. Priorities will change.

Not only is our child sorely missed, but the future losses we grieve are very raw for some at holiday times because there is so much focus on family. It's so obvious someone is missing and terribly missed.

The realization that it's not just this year, but every year, from now on, that we won't share these special times with our child. We won't see them grow. They won't have their own family to share it with someday.

It can drain the energy and joy of the season right out of you. Whether it's the summer holidays or the winter holidays from Thanksgiving until New Year's Day, instead of looking forward to the holidays and the events that usually surround them, they are often something that becomes dreaded.

Parents sometimes want to skip them altogether and often can't wait for them to be over. It's always hardest the first year. They don't have to be this way forever, but those firsts are so, so difficult. Eventually, the bereaved parents find new ways to cope with and manage the holidays. New traditions may emerge. Holidays and special events will get easier over time, but they are different than they once were... forever.

While they may always be difficult on some level, the way you ultimately cope with the holidays is up to you. The glasses or lenses, through which you choose to look at these days, as is true of every day, truly do make a difference in what you see.

There are ways to remember, honor, and even involve the memory of your child or other deceased loved ones in your holiday celebrations. There are new traditions that can be created that focus on the love, light, and joy your child brought to your lives. There is a way to find joy and peace.

Much of our own suffering is perceived or is what we allow it to be. We always have free will with regard to how we choose to feel and act. That said, it's hard not to feel physically and emotionally drained or even plum exhausted during the busy holiday season, at least once in a while.

That first year, and for many years after Meghan died, I wanted to cancel Christmas. Before she died, I used to go all out to deck the halls. We had advent calendars, decorations all over the house inside and out. I loved to bake. The kids did holiday crafts. We hosted parties. We attended parties. Choosing and decorating the tree was always something I loved. I loved Christmas music and couldn't wait to play it while decorating on Thanksgiving.

Because Meghan died just a week before Christmas, the holidays are, perhaps, even more painful for us than others. Maybe not. I only know our experience. We buried her 3 days before Christmas. The last thing I felt like doing was celebrating anything. Yet I had two young boys who deserved the joy of Christmas, especially after their painful loss.

I did not want to get out of bed Christmas morning, even though I didn't sleep all night. I didn't want to face the day. I remember feeling like a caged animal, wanting to scream, desperately wanting to run away from the day... from the pain. Some of Meggie's gifts remained in the attic. Never to be given to her.

There was, however, an ornament in her stocking. That angel we had purchased the day after she died. The boys found it and hung it on the tree. They thought it was so cool Santa left Meggie something special! I fought tears all day, trying to fake it and make it for my boys. I am not sure they noticed. We were all trying to find the joy and latch on to their excitement over opening gifts and singing carols. Sadness literally hung in the air. The heartache was palpable. I ate next to nothing. I was tempted to have an entire bottle of wine but could barely choke down a few sips. The next day I wanted to put Christmas away forever.

Every year since, I've dreaded the holidays. It has gotten easier each year. The pain is still there, but I've learned to manage it with new traditions. I don't decorate like I used to or as early as I used to. It's really the bare minimum. The mantle and the tree are pretty much it.

We bring a tree to Meggie's Special Place at the cemetery and decorate it, complete with solar powered twinkle lights! Many of the ornaments are the ones people hung on the tree our neighbor placed there just a few days after she died. We've added more over the years that we think she'd like. Others have done the same. We try to do it as a family but it doesn't always go as I'd hope. That exhaustion and anticipatory grief can make me pretty irritable.

Every year, on Meg's anniversary, I have developed a few rituals. One is that evening; I sit in front of the tree, in the dark, and stare. Alone. Kenny G's Christmas Album playing softly in the background. Not unlike I did the night she died. I cry silent tears. I often swear I can feel her with me, snuggling up like we used to. It's not the painful stare I had that first year or two, but instead, a more peaceful and loving one. It's a way to honor and remember her.

Yes, I do allow myself to remember the pain I felt that night, but I also thank her for all she's taught me and given to me since. I take the time to be still in the moment. I have always loved the tree, its peaceful white lights. I gaze at her ornaments and smile. She'd love them! A tree full of kitties and Tinker Bell! I remember her decorating the tree the year she died. How she put all the ornaments in the same spot on the bottom right hand corner of the tree. They were mostly cat ornaments. Guess what? I still put those same ornaments in that same spot every year! A tribute to her.

Her stocking still hangs on the mantle where it always did. Every year, there is a new ornament in it on Christmas morning. Usually Tinker Bell themed or a kitty. Her twin loves to be the one to put it on the tree. The boys check her stocking when they take theirs down to see which ornament has been chosen this year. She gave us that new tradition.

We don't do a big dinner anymore, but instead, fondue and appetizers. It's non-traditional, but new traditional. We light Meggie's candle centerpiece, as we do at all family celebrations. We reminisce and ponder what she'd be like now. We visit her special place. I've purchased new holiday music and listen to that instead of the traditional music I used to listen to. My tolerance is not great, but much better than the first few years when I literally had a visceral nearly PTSD inducing reaction to any holiday music at all. Frosty still gets me every time.

I still put Christmas away on December 26th. That is the day I look forward to. It is the day that marks the end of the "dark months." The day it all goes back to the attic... until next year.

Coping with Social Events and Obligations around the Holidays

Social events can be a challenge. There is pressure, either from friends and family, or, simply self-imposed, that you have to participate in certain events. Attending parties, going to church or synagogue, hosting events you've always hosted, baking or cooking as you've always done, or travelling elsewhere for traditional events can be overwhelming.

Here's the thing. You can say no! It's okay to say, "No." It's okay to say you are not sure. It's okay to say, "Yes." and then change your mind. It is okay to go to an event and then leave if it's too much for you.

It can be difficult to know how you are going to feel at any given moment in time, so keep an open mind. After some time, you will learn which events are more challenging or difficult emotionally. You will come to know what anticipatory grief is, what triggers it for you, and be able to plan for it. But in the beginning, you just won't know until that very moment. That's okay.

Here are a few suggestions to make coping with the holidays easier:

1. Know that they will be hard. It will help if you prepare yourself and those around you. Talk with your immediate and then extended family about how you want to celebrate. Be as honest and specific as you can be.

2. It's okay to say, "No." It's hard to know how you will feel any given day. So it's okay to say "Maybe." or even "No." to the party invitations. It's also okay

to get to the party or event and realize you can't or don't want to stay and to leave. You do not need to feel obligated to bring a gift or food. If you do, ask someone else to bake and shop for you unless those things bring you comfort and peace.

3. Sometimes people want to involve you in planning, preparation, or invite you to events to help distract you from missing your child. What others don't understand is that nothing will make you forget. Not only that, but it's healthy and normal for you to be feeling more grief at the holiday times. Others who have not been there don't realize it's not something you can escape, even if you desperately want to. It's with you. That said, if you do find the distraction helpful, then by all means, get involved!

4. Shopping can be very difficult. Triggers abound. Energy is often low, and the ability to cope with stress is minimal. Having to deal with traffic, parking challenges, crowds, happy people, mall Santas, and even the music and decorations can prove to be overwhelming. Instead, try to shop throughout the year, online, or ask others to shop for you.

5. It's okay if you don't want to decorate or follow the usual traditions. Perhaps, you only do the bare minimum. Maybe, you don't decorate at all. Maybe you get a new decoration instead. Maybe putting electric candles in the windows to honor your child, instead of a Christmas tree, is more meaningful and less stressful for you this year... maybe every year.

6. Don't feel as if you need to send cards or bake, even if you have always done these things. If you traditionally host, it's okay to say you are not up to it.

7. Consider attending a remembrance or memorial event or creating one for your family and friends. The second Sunday in December is the annual Compassionate Friends Worldwide Candle Lighting. Many chapters hold events so that bereaved parents can gather together. Our local chapter has a dinner and remembrance evening that is beautiful. At 7 pm, local time, candles are lit in memory of our children, "So that their light may always shine." You can light a candle at your own home; you needn't attend a formal event. The vision is a 24 hour wave of light around the world in memory of all our children who are gone too soon. It's a beautiful sentiment. Perhaps, you could create a special candle just for your child. We made up tea lights for Meghan and gave them to our family and friends for the first candle lighting. Of course you can do this any time.

8. If there is an Angel of Hope statue from the story, "The Christmas Box," nearby, consider visiting it. There are several, all around the United States, in Canada, and even one in Japan. There is a remembrance ceremony on December 6th every year at these memorials, but you can visit them anytime.

9. Consider creating a new tradition to honor your child that you can grow and honor them with every year... an ornament or a special candle centerpiece. Bring a gift to their grave, perhaps, flowers, a wind chime, an angel statue, or some token of love and honor.

10. Try to find one thing to be grateful for each day. It helps us refocus and take a breath. It helps us realize there is good in the world. In our lives. In us.

11. Set a place for them at your holiday table or create a small remembrance table for them in a common area

of your home with their photo, perhaps the "Five Candles" poem, and a candle.

If you are supporting someone who has lost a loved one during the holidays, here are some things you can do to help them:

1. Have no expectations of how they will act or react.
2. Respect their need for privacy or solitude.
3. Be a calm, loving and understanding presence in their life. Say, "I love you."
4. Be available to them, anytime day or night. Both before and after the holidays.
5. Ask them how they are doing. Listen. Listen. Listen. Acknowledge this is difficult for them, out loud. Invite and allow them to share their thoughts, feelings and stories. Over and over and over again if necessary.
6. Say their child's name. Share a memory. Give them a gift that honors their child.
7. Ask them, "What would help?" or, "What can I do for you?" Be sure you are prepared to follow through on whatever they request.
8. Offer to help them with everyday chores like cleaning, food shopping and child care. Offer to help with holiday chores and preparations. Offer to shop, wrap, cook, address cards, deliver gifts, decorate, and whatever else they may need or want to do, but are having difficulty managing or finding the time do or to finish.
9. Only give advice if asked.
10. Encourage them to connect with nature. Walk with them literally and figuratively.

One of the most unexpected and yet loving and giving things you can do, anytime of year or for any difficult occasion, is to bring the bereaved parent an unexpected gift or even just send a card or a simple flower arrangement. Let them know you are thinking of them. These unexpected tokens of love and friendship mean the world to a bereaved parent or any bereaved person. To know that someone else remembers their child and the importance they held in their life, someone who can acknowledge how difficult emotionally this time of year can be, is an uplifting and beautiful gift.

It's difficult to put into words how touched bereaved parents are when others reach out to them in such a way. An ornament in memory of their child, a gift basket perhaps with a candle and cozy socks or slippers, a prayer shawl or wrap, a new mug and warm beverages of choice, a card with an inspirational or meaningful saying, a memorial donation, or something specific and meaningful to them with regard to their child are all lovely ideas. Of course, you know that person best. I promise you, they will be so grateful for your kindness.

Some of the gifts I received over the years include:
- Ornaments with my daughter's name.
- Her photo and a poem in a Tinker Bell frame.
- A memory quilt of her clothes. The quilter did not accept payment despite my desire to reimburse her. (Always get the parent's permission before doing anything with their child's possessions)
- Donations to and fundraisers for the local Animal Shelter as we requested in her obituary.
- A mother and child necklace.
- Mother's bracelets with her name.

- A five-candle centerpiece and a framed "We Light These Five Candles" poem.
- Flowers and cards at random times from a good friend.
- Tokens of love left at the cemetery for her, some by strangers. Flowers. Kitties. Ornaments for her tree.
- A pink rose bush for her memory garden at our home.
- Many angel themed items such as collector plates and figurines, Willow Tree Angels, angel sun catchers and ornaments, pins and jewelry.
- A stepping stone with an angel and inspirational saying.
- A tree in her name and memory in the Children's Forest in Israel.
- Many, many mass offerings and prayer vigils.
- Food... I don't think we had to cook a meal for months!
- Beautiful hand knit shawls. One a prayer shawl, the other a comfort one. I still use them!
- Gift certificates for massage, bodywork and Reiki. Many offers of distance Reiki for our entire family.
- Dish gardens, plants and flowers, both indoor and out.
- A stained glass plate with a replica of her hand and footprints.
- A pin made out of one of her drawings.
- A flag, flown over the US Capitol in her honor with a certificate.
- An Irish Blessing, framed, with petals from flowers taken from her funeral sprays by a crafty cousin of mine.
- Memory candles, made with her prayer cards for all of our family.

Coping Mechanisms

How we cope with the inevitable stress of the big trigger days is, in part, reactionary and in part a conscious choice. Initially, we simply feel. It's all we can do.

As we move through the stages of grief and come to accept and integrate our child's death into our everyday existence, we can begin to be more conscious about the choices we make. For some, it's a longer and more difficult process than others.

How we frame the concept of death makes a big difference in how we cope and how we ultimately involve our child or any deceased loved one into our lives, rituals and family events going forward. For many of us, this in part comes from our upbringing, cultural practices, and personal experience. Beyond that, personality and desire to change play a big role in coping and healing.

As we've discussed previously, there are basically two styles of coping people fall into when processing or coping with the death of a loved one. Those who are stuck in their pain and either stuff it all, never publicly acknowledge it, or are unable to get away from the darkness and depression, and those who are able to process their grief, and learn to integrate their child's life and death into the fabric of their lives.

Many of those who get stuck in the pain of grief find it too painful to have any reminders of their children around. No photos, no mementos, no old holiday things that were made by or given for their child. There is a difference between normal grieving, depression and sadness, clinical depression and victim consciousness.

We discussed depression as a normal part of grieving in Chapter five. Those who are clinically depressed, either before or after their child dies, should ideally be receiving counseling or, perhaps, need medication or alternative therapies to assist them in managing their symptoms. If you are not sure if you are depressed or think that you or you think a loved one may be, please, please, please be pro-active about seeking professional help.

It can be hard to tell the difference between the normal grieving process depression and something more profound and severe. Depression may come on gradually over time and if you are the person who is depressed, you may not recognize it in yourself.

As their spouse or significant other, you, too, may still be grieving and unable to recognize it in yourself or in others. It's often someone beyond your immediate family, like a close relative or friend, who realizes you may be suffering from depression.

If you are, or think you are, please seek help or encourage your loved one to seek help. As a loved one, offer to make the appointment, drive them there, and wait for them. Research local bereavement support groups, present the information to them and offer to drive and/or accompany them to the support group.

Those who choose to be victims may have a difficult time moving on. They may feel as if this happened *to* them and expect someone else to fix it or make it better. They may or may not be stuck in depression or anger. In fact, it may look as if they are fine, but they are not. Often, they have never truly processed and accepted their child's death. Sometimes, they blame others or simply say, "It's over," and dive back into life. They may say all the right or expected things, but you see no emotion behind it. They may have a difficult time separating and moving forward, carrying the memory of their child with them. Or sometimes, they detach from the child and their memory.

Perhaps it's because they are afraid they will lose their connection to their child if they do either. They may cling to their child's death instead of to their life and their legacy. Or, they let their child go entirely, neither attaching to their life or their death. Either way, they often bypass the difficult and painful work of grief, maybe for a short time, maybe for a lifetime. They fail to recognize or acknowledge the gifts their child has unknowingly given to them both in their life and death.

It's unfortunate, because these parents and loved ones who become clinically depressed, or, who consciously and intentionally avoid the work of grieving might never be able to truly heal and find peace in their heart and lives. Especially if they don't get the help they need. The difference is depression is not a choice. It's a chemical imbalance in the brain. It's no one's fault. It can be helped with counseling and possibly, medication.

Victim consciousness, blaming someone or something else, and feeling as if this was done to you, is a choice. Free will allows us to choose to avoid the work of grief or to do it. It's really that simple. Although in reality, we know the work of grief is the hardest work any of us will ever do. We don't all do it the same way or in the same time frames, but if we don't do it, we can't truly heal.

The other style of coping includes those who are able to process their grief, come to accept their child's death, do the work of grieving and forgiveness, and truly integrate their child's life and death into their own lives. They are able to function in a new place of "normal" and often keep their child's memory active and involved in their family's lives and especially special days and events. It's not that it's any easier for these parents. They will still have trigger days. They will still get angry, sad and cry at times. It's just that they are able to take their grief, couple it with love, and use it for the greater good and to heal.

A "New" Normal?

Many people, most of them people who have never lost a close loved one and especially not a child, think that a day will come where everything returns to normal. Or, they'll say you can start anew.

They may be very well intentioned comments but any other bereaved parent will tell you different. They'll tell you it's not new. They don't want it to be new. It's certainly not normal as they knew normal to be. It's just different. It will change over time. You will never forget. Your child's memory, their life and their death, is always with you. It has changed you. How could it not? Yet, you are still living *your* life. Life goes on.

The obvious difference is that there has been a crisis and significant change in your life. It's even possible that your child's death will lead to more changes down the road. It is still *your* life to live. Your path might be very different than you thought it would be or even than it was yesterday, but it's still your path. You have the wonderful human gift of free will, the ability to make choices. While this is difficult to realize and to do early on, you will ultimately and always be in a place of choice. You will choose your path. When presented with forks in the road, you get to choose which way you will go. We will address the "new" you in Chapter eleven.

I know right now, especially if your pain is new and raw, that seems like it is all but impossible. Trust me, anything is possible. Join me in the next chapters to see what I mean.

Chapter Eight

Out of the Darkness: Finding Your Way to Healing

Your world seems dark, gray, and devoid of color after a child dies. Grieving is a lifelong process and is quite possibly the most difficult emotional work you will ever do.

You now know it is also a journey along a new path. A path out of that darkness and into the light. A path to seeing the world in color again. If you are willing to walk that path, you can get there. You can walk out of the darkness, holding the love for your child in your heart forever, and move forward in your life. You've already begun to find your way out of the darkness, for you are reading this book and walking with me.

When you are at the beginning of this path, when the death of your child is so raw and new, it can be difficult to find your way out and to see the light. The only way out of the darkness, is to go through it. But how? How does one even begin to heal? It feels impossible. In the beginning, you feel as if you will never feel joy and happiness again. Many feel guilty if they do have moments of happiness.

What many people, especially those who have not lost a child, don't realize is that there is never really full closure when you lose a child. No one wants closure, because that would imply we get over it. There can, however, be a transformation and integration. There needs to be.

Losing your child changes you. Forever. It has to. It's not unlike other major life changes such as birth, marriage, or divorce. Just as the birth of your child changed you, your perspective, and your priorities, so does the death of a child.

The challenge is in figuring out how to get through the pain, navigate the emotional hills and valleys, and find your way to the light and out of the darkness, in the best, most resonant way for you.

Everyone grieves differently. The way you grieve and the things that bring you insight, comfort, and ultimately healing will probably change over time and ebb and flow, just like grief itself does.

We've discussed the myth that bereaved parents "get over" the loss of a child. We don't want to forget our child. How could we? Even if we try, we know they existed. We know they have left this earthly plane. Death may have ended their physical life here on earth, but it does not have to end our connection and relationship with our child. It certainly doesn't make us forget them!

Pretending we are "over it" is a coping mechanism and often rooted in denial and fear. Our child was such an important part of our family and of our lives… quite literally woven into the fabric of who we are. That doesn't change just because they've died. That bond of unconditional love transcends death. I absolutely know it does. I will share much more about this in coming chapters.

The question most often asked by bereaved parents, after, "Why?" is "How? How do I do this?" It hurts SO much right now that you can't imagine life beyond today. As a newly bereaved parent, you can't fathom a day when you won't feel this much pain. Having someone who has walked this path before you can be a tremendous source of support and hope that you, too, will find your way to healing. Please, don't feel as if you have to walk this path alone. Remember, you have me right now.

One of the greatest misunderstandings among those who have not lost a child is the fact that bereaved parents often want and *need* to stay connected to their child. It wasn't that long ago when all grievers were told to move on and forget their loved ones that had died. Even children! They were advised to put away the photos, to not talk about them, to get rid of their personal items. The belief was really rooted in out of sight, out of mind.

Nothing could be further from the truth! How sad and unfortunate for those who followed that advice for they have probably never had the opportunity or guidance on how to heal. Nor did those around them learn that grief is normal, important, and necessary.

I've met several elderly parents who lost children when they were young, some lost several babies. None of them have ever forgotten their children. Most, confided I was the only person they had talked to their child about in years, if not decades. One, in particular, dissolved in tears after she shared that she, too, had lost a daughter, and I asked what her name was. She had not talked to anyone about her daughter in almost 40 years, since she buried her at the age of 21! I was the first person who had asked her to tell me about her daughter, her life, her death, and asked her name since she had been buried! She thanked me for asking and told me she still thinks of her every day and misses her just as much as the day she died. She wished her family understood and would talk about her, too.

It's probably why, especially if you lost a young child, your family might have disagreed with many of the things you've said and done. Simply because they don't understand what it's like. Perhaps, they offered advice that did not resonate with you regarding your choices regarding your child's rituals of death and remembrance and how you are grieving and remembering them. They may think you are taking too long to move on. They lack the knowledge, insight, and tools to help you. Unless they, too, are reading this guide.

Remember this. *You don't need anyone else's permission or approval to grieve.* You get to do it your way, in your own time. Because it's your child and your road to walk. Others may walk with you, but they are on their own journey and just sharing the path.

We know now that forgetting our loved ones or sweeping everything under the rug and ignoring it is not healthy or even possible! Our children are very much on our minds, in our hearts, and a part of our lives. As I write this, Meg has been gone almost 10 years. I still think of her every day. Every. Single. Day. Her photos, drawings, and other reminders of her life and death are all over the house. She is a part of every celebration, every holiday, every day.

Having no reminders of her around my home would not erase the fact she existed. It wouldn't fix my broken heart. It wouldn't erase the connection we had as mother and child. It wouldn't take away the pain. I would never, ever be where I am today if I were not able to keep Meggie around me in the way that I have.

Putting off coping with the death of your child does not make the pain go away. It may temporarily stuff it somewhere else, kind of like throwing clothes that don't fit right in a drawer or closet somewhere so it's out of sight, out of mind. However, it doesn't magically make it disappear. Eventually, you have to clean that closet and make a decision about what to do with those clothes that don't fit right. Eventually, you have to process your child's death, so you can truly heal.

Parents who have lost children often actively seek a connection with their child, to their energy, their smell, their essence, and their spirit. This is healthy and normal. It's a way to continue a relationship with their child. I often refer to the ways I connect with Meghan as how I continue to mother her. By nurturing her memory and connecting to that Universal love.

You can both love and miss your child at the same time. You can be sad about their loss, but function again. The day will come when you will be able to talk about your child and even the circumstances of their death without falling apart. Sometimes tears will fall. Sometimes, they will not. It's okay. The day will come when you, too, will be able to help someone else walk this path none of us ever wanted or expected to walk.

So how do you connect with your child? How do you maintain a relationship with them when their physical presence is gone?

Often, it begins with how you normally process stressful situations. Sometimes it will depend on your religious or spiritual beliefs. Ultimately, it will depend on what resonates with you. You may even find yourself drawn to or exploring avenues for healing and connection that you'd never even have considered previously such as seeing a medium.

You will develop this relationship with your deceased child or any deceased loved one slowly, over time. As you move through the stages of grieving and integrating the loss of your child into your life, your thoughts and your life will become more organized and purposeful again.

Parents often feel stuck in their pain, particularly in the first several months following their loss. Especially if those around them are not able to provide the emotional support they need. The process of developing a relationship with your deceased child or your child's memory is as unique as you are. Just as all relationships are learning experiences; they change and grow over time. Just as you learned to parent your child in their life, right from the moment you found out about the pregnancy, you will learn to parent them after they die. Love never dies. Never.

There are many ways you can stay connected to your child. Know that it's perfectly okay and normal to experience a range of emotions while going through these exercises. It's part of the process. Don't be afraid to experience it. If you want, you can invite someone to join or help you through some of them. Choosing to do these things in solitude is also perfectly normal and okay. As Martin Luther King said, "You don't have to see the whole staircase, just take the first step."

Ways to stay connected to your child

1. *Write to them.* This was advice I'd been given shortly after my daughter died and I read about from multiple sources. You can write a short and simple note, or you can write a letter. Maybe several letters. I remember sitting down at my computer late one night because I still wasn't sleeping well about two weeks after Meghan died. I wanted to write to her, desperately. It was as much an outlet for my grief as it was a longing to have a conversation with her about how I felt, why she left, and everything that was swimming around in my heart and in my head. I sat and stared at the blank page and had no idea where to start. So I started with saying how much I missed her. How I was sorry. I asked her what happened, how did she feel? I thanked her for all she gave me. I told her the story of how I felt, the amazing things that happened in the first week or two after her death, the kindness of those around us. Once I began to write, it came easily. I wrote. I cried. I even smiled through the tears. I wrote some more. That letter is now over 400 pages long. It is as much a personal journal as it was a place to put my grief, my questions, my experiences and my love. It's fascinating to go back and read it today. I'm so glad I did it, for I would not remember many of the things that happened if I had not written them down.

2. *Start a journal.* A place to privately record your thoughts, your feelings, anything you want. No one else has to see it, just you. My letter to Meggie turned into a journal over time. A combination of a way to stay in touch with her and a place to put everything I was feeling and try to make sense of it. I kept it up for years, until I moved to blogging and eventually, writing this book. I still write in it occasionally and on her Angelversary.

3. *Be creative in memorializing them.* Look through photos. Connect with important milestones and memories in your lives. Make a scrapbook or collage. Frame your favorite photos and place them around your home. If your child was school aged, display some of their art work or awards. When you are ready, consider making a quilt or pillow from their clothes or bedding. I was actively scrapbooking at the time Meghan died. I actually made a scrapbook dedicated to her death. I included her obituary, newspaper articles, photos of her and from her wake and funeral, memories, the little cards that came with flowers and food baskets, and her prayer card. I also made small scrapbooks for each of her brothers and her father using photos of her with each of them. A friend made a small scrapbook for me of all photos of Meggie. It sits on my coffee table today. The quilt I had made is a precious gift; it's like wrapping myself with Meggie's love. I also made eye pillows from some of her clothes for close family and friends as a way to stay connected.

4. *Make a perspective list.* This can be anything from a list of ten things you miss the most about your child and even ten things you don't miss. Or ten things you

are sad you won't get to do with the deceased child and ten ways you can actually include their memory in doing those things or instead. Perhaps, five things you used to think or believe about death and five things you now believe as a result of your child's death. Another idea is a list of things you thought were really important in your life before your child died (in order of priority) and things you think are really important now in your life (in order of priority). You could also make a list of things you want to do to honor your child in the next two years. It can be anything you want it to be although it often helps for it to be a comparison in order to allow you to gain perspective about then and now and even give you a sense of direction.

5. *Brainstorm ways to include your child and their memory in your life.* How will you honor their birthday, the anniversary of their death, holidays, Mother's and Father's Day, your birthday (an often surprise trigger day), every day? Involve your family and friends if you want to. Create new rituals, ways of honoring and celebrating them. Perhaps it's doing something they loved to do, baking their favorite kind of cake and eating it at the cemetery or setting a place for them at the table. Maybe you wear their favorite color or watch their favorite movie. It could be anything that is meaningful to you.

Finding and Getting Help

There are many sources of help out there. Please, please, please find at least one or two and utilize them. I've said it before, and mention it here again, I strongly recommend the Compassionate Friends. They are a group with a tremendously informative and supportive website and many local chapters that hold meetings and events. They have an annual conference and a walk to remember. Their worldwide candle lighting memorial is always the second Sunday in December and is a beautiful way to honor all our children gone too soon. Anyone can participate from the comfort of their own home to a public remembrance event. They have a virtual guest book that day where you can write your child a message. They provide support for not only bereaved parents, but also for siblings, grandparents, and friends and extended family. They also provide wonderful articles, resources, and a social media presence as well.

There are a myriad of books available on coping with grief. There is a boatload of information on the internet, but please do be careful. Not all of it is written about the loss of a child, which is a very unique loss, and not all of it is going to resonate with you. That's okay. Take what helps and makes sense to you and just let the other stuff fall away. Be mindful that some of it is also opinion or personal experience rather than professional or evidence based research. All of it can be helpful; you just need to remember it won't all feel right to you.

There is no shame in seeking professional support and guidance after the death of a child. There is no "right time frame" for doing so. Help can be healthy. Anytime! It's not just available right after your child dies. Some find they need professional support months or even years after their child has died. Sometimes, the need is on and off.

Help is something in general we are very good at giving and very bad at asking for and accepting. We all seem to have this unrealistic notion that we should be able to function normally despite such a massive loss in our lives, despite being in crisis mode. For bereaved parents, we might be willing and able to accept help in the first days and weeks after our child dies, but then we, and society at large, think we should be able to pick up the pieces and move on.

The reality is that's a whole lot easier said than done. As we've already talked about, grieving is a process. One that is lifelong, but most intense in the first year. It's not fair that we impose expectations on bereaved parents or on ourselves that we can both actively grieve the loss of our child and function as we were before their death, especially in those early days, weeks and months. Yet that's what society expects of us in so many ways.

Bereavement Leave

In the United States, bereavement leave for most people's jobs is a maximum of three days and it's not always paid. There is no way this is enough for the vast majority of parents, especially those who have lost young children!

Many companies allow families to use saved vacation, sick, or earned time if they need extra time off. Still, not everyone has that option and it's still not enough for most people. Some larger companies may allow for time off without pay, but it's usually quite limited, and not everyone has the financial ability to take time off unpaid. Some companies will grant FMLA time, but legally, only have to hold your position or three months and it is often unpaid. With the unexpected financial strain of the costs of funerals, memorial services, and burial or cremation, this is often just not feasible for most families to be able to do from a financial standpoint.

It puts bereaved parents between a rock and hard place where they feel the need to provide financially for their family yet need to provide for their own healing, too, for their own good and the good of their family. It makes the work of grieving that much harder, not to mention the challenges of being able to fully attend to one's job responsibilities while grieving. It's just not fair. We need a better system. We need better support. We need a better understanding in our culture and society about the work of grieving.

For families where only one parent works or there is not a financial concern, there is still the challenge of trying to run a household and care for any other children while trying to process and heal yourself. I've mentioned how the work of grief is exhausting. There is often nothing left energetically to go shopping with, cook with, clean with, or attend to other daily chores and errands. Many a day, simply taking a shower was a colossal effort and a tremendous accomplishment for me in those early weeks.

Helping others and ourselves
In order to be able to survive this challenging time and give ourselves the time and space we need to self-nurture and heal, we need the help of others. In previous chapters, we've discussed what kind of help is most needed and appreciated by the newly bereaved. That help is beneficial throughout that first year and beyond, especially at difficult times, for example, the holidays, and when those triggers blindside bereaved parents even years later.

One of the problems with our societal construct of grief is that friends and family are really wonderful at supporting us in that first week or two. But then, just as after you have a child, the well-wishers and helpers vanish, going back to their own lives. They think that you are doing the same and managing just fine. Particularly since they often assume if you needed help, you'd surely ask for it.

I've also talked about how the newly bereaved often don't realize the help they need nor do they have the energy to ask. They may feel badly asking for help or, perhaps, it's just not culturally correct or accepted. They may feel as if they are imposing, or that they should be able to handle everything by now on their own. They may simply be appropriately depressed and just don't care about anything in the moment.

Of course, that would imply they have done the tremendous work of grieving quickly, something that we know for most people takes the better part of the first year and of course, lasts a lifetime. Some bereaved parents or even close family members of the deceased child don't want to admit they need help because they've been led to believe it's somehow a sign of weakness.

Nothing could be farther from the truth. The ability to ask for and accept help is a sign of inner strength. A recognition that, right now, your needs are paramount. You need to take care of you, so you can take care of the rest of your family. There is no shame in receiving help in that, no matter how seemingly little and insignificant or, how big and significant that help may be. Remember, if you don't ask or say, "Yes," to offers of help, others cannot provide that help. If you don't tell them what you need or ask for help, they don't always know you need it. Friends and family wouldn't ask if they could do anything to help you if they didn't really want to provide support!

As someone providing support to a bereaved family, specific ways you can help the bereaved can be found in Chapter six.

Support Groups
One of the greatest gifts you can give yourself is the opportunity to connect with other parents who understand because they, too, have walked the same road. With them, you don't have to explain anything to. They "get" it.

They don't mind if you share a story, cry, laugh, or show them photos. They will ask your child's name and say it often. They love it when you say their child's name and you know how important it is, so you make sure to! They don't think it's odd that it's been 30 years, and you still cry when you light a candle for your child, or make them a birthday cake. They sing "Happy Birthday" with you! They hug you and cry with you. They celebrate with you and they support you when you are having a rough day because you will do the same for them.

The bond you will have with complete strangers because you are now members of that club no one ever wants to belong to can be a powerful and healing one... for all of the members. Some of the fellow bereaved parents I've met have become wonderful friends. We support each other in our grief but we also do the normal things friends do.

There are many wonderful support groups and resources out there where you can find information, support, and connect with other bereaved parents. Your local hospital, funeral homes, or local chapter of the Compassionate Friends are good places to inquire about support groups. You may even want to start your own. Some people find them tremendously helpful and attend for years, eventually becoming facilitators themselves. Others attend just once, for a few times, or only at certain times of year, such as the anniversary month or try out or attend several different groups until they find the right fit for them.

Others find that online communities or the social media sites for these support groups are more to their liking. They can ask questions or simply lurk, reading what others post and finding comfort and support in that.

There is an extensive, but not exhaustive, list of national support groups and websites in the resource section. I plan to keep an updated and ever growing one on the Out of the Darkness website. If you have one to recommend, let me know. Many of these organizations also have state and local chapters and groups as well.

Professional Counseling
I think everyone who loses a child can benefit from some professional counseling or a support group, or both, at least for one time. I think this is important to process not only their grief, but the emotional challenges of collateral losses or changes in relationships or perspective that often occur in the months and years after a child dies. Especially if you and your spouse or loved one are coping differently or struggling in your relationship, it helps for you to have someone to help you through this experience. Someone unbiased, non-judgmental, and able to hold a loving and respectful space

and guide you, helping you understand why you feel the way you do and suggest healthy ways to process and recover from it.

Personally, I found it tremendously useful. I went to a therapist for several visits, then took a break for a few months, then ended up going back for a while. It was immensely helpful to me on many levels. Many other bereaved parents have said the same.

Counselors can also refer you to support groups and help you find ways to nurture your healing. They can refer you to someone who can prescribe medication if they feel you would benefit from it. Talk therapy is tremendously powerful and a wonderful vehicle for processing and healing.

The physical, psychological, and emotional experiences of grief can be overwhelming and confusing. Sometimes they can be a bit scary to you or those who care about you, because of the lack of understanding of what you are feeling and why. Having a professional guide can be a tremendous source of support and also one of validation that what you are feeling is normal and they can provide suggestions for ways to positively cope with it.

Often, health insurance will cover professional counseling, at least for a certain number of visits. Check into your benefit and consider it as an option to facilitate your healing.

Your Health and Healing: Self-Nurturing
An often overlooked part of help and healing is self-help. The bereaved parent has to find a way to nurture and care for their own physical, mental, emotional and spiritual health.

One way to do this is to try to take some sort of "me" time every day. Go for a walk, do yoga, meditate, sit quietly and listen to relaxing music, snuggle or play with a pet, or do a more intense workout or run.

Body or energy work can be tremendously healing. Consider a massage, reflexology, acupuncture, or Reiki. Even a manicure or pedicure can help you to process, relax, and nurture yourself. These can be both relaxing and healing, facilitating a release of pent up physical and emotional stress and the toxins of stress that accumulate in your body as part of the normal grief reaction.

Some people find comfort in seeking readings with tarot, angel, or oracle card readers, psychics, or a medium. They can often be found at local new age book stores, psychic fairs, in spiritually minded magazines, and on the internet. If these things resonate with you, there is no harm in doing so. Losing a loved one often opens the mind to spiritual avenues you might not have otherwise considered.

Even if you feel as if you don't have a normal appetite, try to eat at least one healthy item that brings you comfort each day. It could be a smoothie, a piece of fruit, a glass of juice, a protein shake, or something more substantial. Perhaps try some organic chamomile tea for it has relaxing properties to it.

If you are not eating a full and normal diet, consider supplemental vitamins. Do be careful with any herbal supplements as they can interact with other medications you may be taking and are not regulated. They can and do have side effects that you need to be aware of. Always check with your doctor before taking any herbal supplements.

It can be difficult, but be sure you attend to your own health needs. Take your prescribed medications as directed. Keep and make appropriate doctor's appointments and tests for yourself. It may be the last thing you want to do, but you do need to take care of yourself, so you can heal inside and out.

In order to heal, we have to take care of ourselves on all levels: physically, emotionally, mentally, and spiritually. We cannot care for others without first caring for ourselves. It is not selfish, it is necessary to our healing. Our child would want for us to find happiness and be healthy. We need to find balance in our lives, support and healthy coping strategies.

Remember the love? It all comes from the heart. Our heart may be broken, but it can heal.

Chapter Nine

The Gifts of Grief

The gifts of grief? What are you? Crazy?

I know. It seems ludicrous. How can there possibly be anything good about losing your child? Any loved one? How can there possibly be a gift of any kind that comes with such a lasting and life changing pain? This dark, heavy cloud can't possibly have a silver lining! I know it seems unbelievable. I know, right now, you probably can't fathom there could be anything positive that could come out of this experience. I couldn't either in those early days, weeks and months.

I can tell you, without a doubt that wrapped up in the pain there are gifts: amazing, powerful, life-affirming, strength giving gifts. You may not see them now. They won't be gift wrapped with a bow and a gift tag. They are not always obvious. They are usually subtle but powerful shifts in your core beliefs... your values. How you think, act, and live your life.

As the pain of the loss of your child becomes softer, as you heal and come to accept your life as it is now, without your child's physical presence, you will change. You will retain all of the memories and all of the love held in your heart, as you integrate who you were then with who you are now, and you will likely have an entirely different perspective on life.

They say the greatest catalyst for our personal growth and change is a life changing crisis. Losing a child certainly qualifies. We all have the capacity to grow and change, even in the face of horrible tragedy, pain, and sadness. Even when right now, it feels like we've lost everything and have no strength or energy to even begin to see a light at the end of this dark and lonely tunnel. For some, they may even find transcendence.

Bear with me and let me show you the light.

I often say that I am eternally grateful to Meghan. Not only for the gifts she gave me in her short life, and they were many, but most importantly for the gifts she gave me in her death. I am a different, better, and more authentic person because of her. I would not be who I am today, doing what I am doing, surrounded by the people I am blessed to have in my life, if she had not lived *and* died.

Don't misunderstand me. I miss her so much it hurts. I'd take her back in a heartbeat and give just about anything in order to go back to that day and change the outcome. I wish with all that I am that she was still here with me and that the nightmare of her tragic and preventable death didn't happen.

But it did. I had two choices. I could wallow in my guilt, my pain, and my loss, changing nothing about my beliefs, my life, and who I am, or, I could embrace what the pain of losing my beautiful daughter taught me, and use it for the

286

greater good of myself and others. For within grief is the gift to expand our capacity for love.

It is often said that out of crisis, comes strength. I think, instead, that out of pain, comes a new depth and understanding of love, a true understanding of the fragility and true meaning of life and love. The loss of a child changes your perspective and priorities in life. If you can allow yourself to truly experience the depth of the loss and take the introspective journey such a profound and life-altering loss can be, you will likely emerge a very different person. It's virtually impossible not to change in some way after such an experience.

It is not a journey that is easy by any means. It is a lifelong journey along a very winding road. There are seemingly insurmountable mountains and deep, deep valleys. It's like being on a roller coaster that never stops. As I've said previously, the only way out of grief, is through. It's a daunting journey, especially when you are just starting to walk the path.

There is also tremendous beauty, bright light, and a flowing river on this path. If we willingly walk that path, we will uncover our truth, our inner strength, our true self. Sure, we will stumble now and again. We will struggle with those mountains and steep climbs, and we will fall into the valleys. At times, we won't want to get up and go and go any further. Yet, we will also draw strength from the beauty and love around us. We will discover our soul's purpose and find our way to healing and peace.

The death of a child changes you. It has to. It has got to be the greatest and most painful loss there is. When a child dies, there are unexpected and collateral losses. It's so much more than the loss of a child.

Relationships change. Your relationships with your spouse, your other children, your own parents, friends, extended family, and even co-workers all may change. Some relationships will grow apart, some will become stronger. You often find new friends, often fellow bereaved parents.

You might find that things you once loved to do no longer hold the same appeal. You may find you are more strongly drawn to your faith or spirituality or, perhaps, find yourself questioning or rejecting previously held beliefs because they just no longer make sense or resonate with you.

You may find there are financial losses. Loss of income, expenses related to their medical care or services like a funeral or memorial service, or sometimes related to reflexive spending on others, especially surviving children, in an attempt to make them, or you, feel better.

It's not these things that are the gifts. It's what you learn from them. It's about how you use the lessons and energy shifts that happen within you because of the loss of your child, to move forward in your life and fulfill your life's purpose.

When a child dies, you might find yourself with a very clear picture of how truly short life is. You suddenly have been forced into the reality that you just don't know if today is your last day on earth or the last day of someone you care

288

about. You are all too aware how lives can be taken suddenly or unexpectedly.

As a result of this awakening to the reality of how short life can be, you might decide you want to live your life the way you really want to... starting right now. Things that you were putting off for "someday" may move to the top of the list. Waiting for the right time may mean you never realize your dreams. You may choose to start living every day as if it's your last.

Often, our values shift. Our priorities shift. Our tolerance for bullshit and the stupid and petty little things changes in that we become less tolerant of it. When we are ready, we might begin to make changes and choices in our lives that we might not have otherwise made had our child not died.

Before I go any further, please, know that it is widely recommended by professional counselors and therapists that you avoid making any major decisions, changes, or purchases during the first year after your child's death. The first year is a very difficult year in every way. Parents often must go through the grieving process for the entire first year, before they are in a place to be able to make rational decisions and not ones made in anger, frustration, confusion, or depression.

It's also recommended that both parents, either alone or together, as well as siblings; seek support and professional counseling if needed to help them process not only the child's death but any collateral losses and major shifts in how they feel.

Opportunity for Growth and Change

I don't have to tell you that losing a child, no matter how old that child was, has to change you in some way. We, the bereaved parents, grandparents, and siblings, are so deep in our own grief, that we are unable to see the changes as they happen. It's often only after we begin to emerge from acute grief and start to integrate our child's death into our life and figure out how to move forward in our lives that we begin to realize our other relationships have changed.

Change is not inherently bad. In fact, it can be quite positive... if the changes are made from a place of love and from a place of heart-centered respect for those who are impacted. Some of the changes you may encounter after the death of a child are changes in your relationships, your chosen career path or job status, financial changes, changes in your living situation, changes in your religious or spiritual beliefs, or an overall change in your life path.

Relationship Changes

You have relationships with many different people throughout your life. Losing a child, especially a young child, is a tremendous stress on both parents: both individually and together. Every person they have a relationship with, both individually and together, has the potential to change after the death of that child.

Some relationship changes are immediate, but most develop over time. Some will be temporary and be able to be overcome and some will be long lasting or permanent changes. These can be one of the most surprising and difficult parts of the collateral losses losing a child can bring.

Spouses and significant others

One of the greatest concerns after the death of a child is your ability to connect with your spouse or significant other in the days, weeks, and months that follow. Your world has been torn apart. You both need time and space to process and grieve your own way, for yourselves, but also together. The strength and stability of your primary relationship is one that will be tested as it's probably never been tested before.

One of the questions often asked by spouses, especially those who grieve differently, is "Will our marriage survive?" The answer may well be, "It depends." It depends on a lot. It depends on how strong your relationship was before your child died. It depends how well you communicated then and communicate now. It depends how honest you are with yourself and each other and whether or not you are both able to recognize any problems in the relationship, either pre-existing or new. It depends if you are both willing to work on the problems, alone and/or together, with or without the help of a professional before it's too late, and irreparable damage to your relationship has occurred.

We know men and women often process grief very differently, and this can cause a temporary disconnect. This is not unusual and is fairly normal. With the help of professional counseling and an effort on the part of both partners to communicate how they feel and why they feel that way, this can be a hurdle that can not only be overcome, but result in a stronger relationship.

Some relationships are strengthened when they are brought together by the loss and when they can connect and support each other through it. These couples are often united in their grief and have similar coping strategies or are able to communicate their differences without judgment. They may also share a strong faith together and find comfort in that.

Some couples find themselves drifting apart after the death of their child. It may be temporary or it may deepen a rift that already existed and could, ultimately, lead to the demise of the relationship. This is not something that happens overnight. It's something that develops over time and in reality, may have begun long before the child died.

When parents separate or divorce after the loss of a child, it's not just because their child died. It's likely because their relationship was probably not healthy prior to the death of the child and the stress of losing a child proved to be too much for one or both of them to overcome and work through with regard to the relationship. Further misunderstandings about the different ways of coping and grieving and a perception that the other partner is not doing it right, can cause one of the partners to withdraw. There may be blame or anger directed to the other parent or about the situation that is not able to be overcome, be it fair or not.

One partner may seek the affection, compassion, and understanding they are not getting from the other outside of the primary relationship, leading to emotional and physical affairs. Or, one partner may simply practice escapism, making themselves busy with work, activities, or sports which can lead to resentment and anger if the other partner doesn't understand the sudden and persistent distancing, and communication is poor.

Sometimes, one parent recognizes the problem and reaches out to the other or seeks counseling but the other parent doesn't respond or participate. Sometimes, by the time the second parent is willing to come to the table to address issues, the parent who initially wanted to reconnect has moved on emotionally. Any of these behaviors or choices in isolation can strain a relationship. On top of the death of a child, they can just be too much to cope with for some.

Sometimes, it's just that parents grow apart over time. They were likely headed in that direction anyway, and both were aware of it. Those life changing gifts and awakenings we talked about at the beginning of this chapter might be apparent or chosen to be pursued by only one parent, or their paths might simply diverge as a natural evolution of their relationship. This can be a mutually agreed upon break up and for the greater good of everyone involved.

In reality, it might just be that the death of their child catalyzed the demise of their relationship that might have eventually happened anyway. Couples who realize this often part ways amicably and maintain a friendship and healthy relationship with each other and any other children.

Again, I stress, most professionals advise against making any major decisions, especially financial or life-changing ones like big purchases, choosing to have another child, separation, or divorce until after the first year has passed. Because the first year is so emotionally difficult and grief is a lifelong process, we are often not in a place emotionally where we can make rational life altering decisions and truly understand the consequences. Leaving a relationship should never be done lightly.

If communication breaks down between you and your spouse or significant other, seek support and professional counseling: both individually and as a couple. You don't need to go it alone. You are not the first or the last parent to feel this way or be in this situation. Take care of you and nurture yourself and your relationships.

If your partner refuses or won't participate in counseling or communicating with you or working on your relationship, you still need to do the work you need to do for yourself to heal and move forward. In the end, you can be responsible only for yourself.

People often ask me if my marriage survived. It did not. Most people assume it's because Meghan died. It is not. Our marriage was not healthy and strong before she died. I had tried to explain to my husband how in trouble I thought we were. We were not good communicators with each other. This was a long standing relationship issue for us. We had been emotional opposites all along and we coped very differently with her death.

After Meghan died, although initially brought closer together in our grief, we were unable to fix the cracks in our relationship that pre-existed her death. We grew apart. I grew in a completely opposite direction from my husband, her death literally sending me on a journey of the heart and soul. I changed. Eventually it became a chasm that was too big and too deep to cross. We tried to reconnect, but were never on the same page at the same time. Counseling ultimately did not help. The details beyond that are not important for anyone but us to know.

Meghan's death profoundly changed me, my priorities, and my outlook on life. We eventually separated and divorced. I initiated it. In the end, it was the best thing for our surviving children, for more than anything, I wanted them to see their parents in happy and healthy, communicative, and open-minded relationships, and that was not what we had. They deserved to see happiness and love, not negativity, resentment, and argumentativeness.

I was very mindful that the divorce of their parents would be yet another loss for them. However, I knew with all my heart it was the right thing for us and for them, even if my husband didn't see it at the time. I have always been honest with them. Both their father and I have since remarried. Our boys are amazing, sensitive, loving, and gifted boys. Their sister is, in many ways, at least in our home, as much as part of their lives as she would have been were she still walking on earth beside them or chasing them around being bossy. Their parents are now in healthy relationships and both boys are thriving.

Where your relationship with your significant other or spouse may end up is not an easy question to answer. It is especially difficult if it's soon after the death of your child. Please, be gentle with yourselves and each other. Talk. Be open. Be honest. Be respectful. Talk to someone. Seek professional counseling alone or together. There is absolutely nothing wrong with getting some help and guidance from a skilled counselor who can help you understand why and what you are feeling and provide tools to cope. It's the greatest gift you can give yourself and those you care about. Your child would want you to try your best. You owe them that.

Friends

Relationship changes often go far beyond your primary relationship with your child's other parent. Death has a way of showing you who your true friends are. You might actually be surprised who those people are. Over the years I've lost really good friends and found amazing and wonderful new ones. With others, the relationship just changed.

Surprisingly, some of those who I least expected to "get" my grief and support me in it were, in fact, the ones who still, to this day, say her name, remember the triggers and ask me how I'm doing with it all. I am so deeply grateful to have them in my life.

You also find new friends along the way. Some may be other bereaved parents, whom you connect with because of your shared bond and experience. Some might be former acquaintances who step up to support you because they care about you as a person, because they feel for you, perhaps, because they can relate on some level or, perhaps, because they are an earth angel. They might be members of the community, neighbors, or co-workers who reached out to you in your time of need and out of that grew a wonderful friendship. These new friends may be temporary people in your life or the relationship you form may last a lifetime.

Sadly, a few friends drifted away from me. However, much like the relationship with my husband, some of our relationships were changing before Meghan died. Others were friends who did not have children and just didn't "get" why we were behaving so differently. Still others did have children and simply couldn't deal with my grief or their own, and so they distanced themselves.

There were a handful of people who "broke up" with me because they couldn't understand why I was making the choices I was or the reason behind the personality and behavioral changes I was exhibiting. Neither of us at the time understood it was part of a larger grief reaction. Not being in a place where we were both willing and able to do the work of healing at the time, our relationship ended. It is my hope, that someday, we find our way to mending the relationship. Maybe this book will help them, too.

Not surprisingly, I also lost friends simply because of the divorce. This is unfortunately a common, and rather immature, consequence of any break up. Some would say they were not really friends in the first place, if they simply walked away from the relationship with no explanation.

Regardless of the reasons why, when these friendships deteriorate, even if it was for the greater good, it can be emotionally difficult and add to the pain of loss you already feel from your child's death. Subsequent losses of any kind add salt to the emotional wound of grief.

In the aftermath of the death of a child, it becomes really evident that some people, who haven't experienced it, just don't "get" it, or don't really want to be bothered with it, and simply drift away. Sometimes, they don't bother to find out the facts or to listen… not only to your words, but also to your pain. It's very difficult for others to put themselves in your very painful shoes. They cannot or do not want to relate or understand. Their own discomfort with death or their inability to even entertain the possibility that it could have happened to them, causes them to withdraw. We may interpret this as a lack of caring, which it may not be. They may care very much, and that is actually the very thing that is keeping them away.

Sometimes bereaved parents do things that are very uncharacteristic, causing others to distance themselves because they don't approve or understand the powerful catalyst for their change in behavior is grief. Some parents may adopt risky or inappropriate behavior. Others may not answer the phone, be snippy, abuse alcohol or drugs, or exhibit other concerning personality changes.

The bereaved parents may be unaware of their changed behavior or what is driving it and friends may not realize it's a symptom of overwhelming grief. It may feel uncomfortable for friends, and they don't like how their friend is behaving or how it makes them feel, so they back off.

Many of these relationship changes could be avoided, or, at least better understood if everyone followed the 3 C's discussed in Chapter six. Communication is so important and necessary to processing and understanding grief. Because of the tragic loss of their child and the process of grieving, personal and meaningful relationships the bereaved parents have with others may become more distanced for a while, or, perhaps, forever. Time will tell.

Because I had all I could do to function, I didn't pursue those people who drifted away. For the most part, there were no hard feelings. We just fell out of touch. It was hard at times, and I missed them, but I quickly moved on. I really had no other choice. No energy to give to trying to save the relationship, even if I wanted to. Now, all these years later, I find myself wanting to explain to them what I know now. I wonder if it would make a difference…

With others, particularly those I shared longer, deeper friendships with, we have reconnected after a time of being distanced. We've been able to re-kindle our relationship. The relationship is different, but tincture of time has allowed for conversations causing us both to see where we were back then and how it impacted our actions. We were able to talk about the situation, the reasons behind the distancing and behavior and personality changes, make apologies if needed, understand how the other person felt, and move forward. It serves no one to live in the past. Time and good communication can heal wounds. I do wish everyone had the ability to resolve relationships in this way, no matter what the reason for the demise of the relationship was.

The nice thing about the growth of social media is that we can often stay connected on a more superficial level through Facebook, Twitter, and other social media platforms. This does not replace heart-centered friendships and conversations, but it is an avenue for a relationship continuation that did not exist for me when Meghan died. I wonder if some of those relationships that ended after her death or my divorce might have continued differently were social media what it is today. It has allowed for a reconnecting with some people that were "lost," and it has been wonderfully therapeutic.

It all speaks to the reality that we rarely have the same friends throughout our entire lives. Friends come and go. As we grow and change, our interests grow and change. We meet new people along the way and hit it off, maybe just for a short time, maybe for a lifetime.

Relationships are all dynamic. Whether they are growing closer or growing apart, they are always evolving and changing. Everyone who we meet brings something to us and us, to them. Every relationship is an opportunity to learn something about ourselves and about life, no matter how brief. Adopting an attitude of gratitude for the gifts anyone brings into your life, no matter what the ultimate outcome of the relationship is, is what really matters. Friends are gifts.

Siblings and friends of the child
Siblings change, too. They have a unique and difficult grief. They have lost a sibling but they have also, in many cases, at least temporarily, lost a parent or both parents, as they knew them.

Parents are so consumed by their own grief that the family dynamic changes. Parents are often distant, lost in their own grief. Other relatives or friends, possibly people the child does not know or know well, suddenly start doing things their parents used to do such as taking them to school or activities, cooking, or cleaning. Strangers are in their house, sometimes a lot.

Kids are smart and sensitive. Even the very young can sense the emotional change in their parents and any change in the usual routine. They know their sibling is gone. They know their parents are not the same. You can't hide it from them no matter how hard you try. Some children may cling to their parents after a sibling dies, others may withdraw. Still others may act as if nothing has changed.

Children deserve the truth, no matter what their age, as long as the information is delivered in an age-appropriate way. Any adult who thinks they are doing a child a favor by sheltering them from the news, the rituals of death, or why those around them are sad, angry, distant emotionally, or not physically around as much, are really only stuffing their own grief. It's about the adult or parent, not about the sibling or friend of the deceased child and that is just not fair to that child.

Kids are resilient and wonderfully gifted to only take in what they can handle. They "get" it, on their level. Kids have their own coping strategies. They ask only what they are ready to know. They say what they feel, especially if they are encouraged to do so and feel safe in doing so.

I do think they deserve and need an age-appropriate understanding and explanation of what's happening and why. Otherwise, they may conjure up ideas in their head that are likely wrong and may last a lifetime. It could be a very real reason why so many of us, as adults, struggle with understanding and coping with death! Siblings and children need lots of love and TLC. Adults need to remember to ask how they are doing periodically, too.

When explaining death to children, don't use terms like the deceased is "sleeping" or has "gone away." This can confuse them and be misleading about the permanency of the deceased child's absence from their lives. Use concrete words like "died." Explain what that means. For more suggestions on explaining death to children and preparing them to attend a wake, funeral, or memorial service, Chapter four goes into this in more depth.

Kids often blame themselves, believe it or not. If you don't ask them what they are feeling or thinking, you may never know that! Imagine these children carrying that burden! They may not truly understand or process the loss of their sibling, or comprehend what their parents experienced and why they behaved the way they did until they are older or even until they have their own children. How well siblings and friends integrate the death depends at least in part, on how you model it to them, nurture them through it, and how well you integrate it. In many ways, it's monkey see, monkey do.

Children also tend to process through play, so if their stuffed animals or dolls are suddenly dying or going to a funeral, it's not morbid, it's normal! Pay close attention to their artwork and their play. It will give you insight into how they are making sense of and processing their sibling or friend's death. If you are concerned about them, or don't know what to say to them or how, speak to their pediatrician and ask for a referral to a counselor who specializes in grief counseling for children.

There is an amazing gift in losing a sibling. Like you, your children can learn about the capacity for love and that love transcends death. Children can learn how much their parent loves them by observing how their parents express and explain their love for your deceased brother or sister. They learn about coping strategies, grief, and rituals of death from a young age. Children can learn about relationships and communication, often through observation of their parents. When parents model open, honest, truthful, and heart-centered communication, the benefits to their children as they grow and enter their own relationships are tremendous!

Involving children in the rituals of death and being honest with them about the death of a loved one is not morbid or wrong. It is a tremendous gift. If only everyone learned at a young age the meaning of death and how to cope with it, instead of fearing and being uncomfortable with it, we'd all be emotionally healthier. We would all be able to understand, have the capacity to cope, and support others in their grief. Oh, how I dream of such a day.

Friends of the child that died also deserve to know where their friend went and why. The younger the child, the more simple the explanation can be. Remember, avoidance is about *your* issues, not your child's, no matter what you tell yourself. If the child is school aged, contact the child's pediatrician or school. They will often arrange for grief counselors to meet with parents and children to help them share the news and process it, especially if the deceased child was also school aged.

If your child was an adult when they died, their friends may want more detail about the circumstances of the death and a more prominent role in planning memorial events. This doesn't always sit well with all families. The grief of a mother or father is no different if their child is an adult with their own family than it is if they were born still. The grief of a parent is just that, the mourning of the loss of their child. It matters not how old they, or you, are; it hurts just as much.

Friends of your adult child may rally to support you or they may disappear and struggle. You may not even know who they are until they show up at a memorial service or funeral. It's important to involve them, but communication is important.

Kids, especially young children, are also pretty sensitive psychically. They don't have preconceived opinions on life after death or even a great understanding of the concept of death. They probably don't have an opinion about life after death, either. It is what it is to them. I will address this more in the next chapter about signs, but if your child says they saw a departed loved one, or talked to them, or you see them playing with them as if they are really present, don't try to correct them or tell them they are wrong. They might just be telling you the truth.

Although this may have you a little "wigged out," if it does not appear to be upsetting your child, let them be. Observe. Appreciate the joy they might be showing. Maybe, just maybe, they know something you don't. Maybe they are giving you a great gift and sign from your deceased child or other loved ones!

I have observed some amazing experiences through my boys after their sister died, and I have heard many, many more stories from others. I share many of them in Chapter ten. Death can make us more open-minded, and that is always a good thing.

The gift of life
One of the gifts of grief can be the gift of life to others. Some parents are able to and choose to donate their child's organs.

I was sad we couldn't do this. What a selfless and tremendous gift to another family whose child's life could be saved because your child lived and died. There is beauty in that pain, and I applaud all who have made that choice. A piece of your child lives on inside another child. The gratitude of that child's parents must be immense... such a beautiful, beautiful gift.

Other unexpected gifts

Perspective is often a gift we unwrap as we heal from the loss of a child. We often live our lives very differently because we have come to realize life really can be short. We really don't know what tomorrow will bring. Carpe Diem, meaning "Seize the day," suddenly makes a world of sense. We often learn to live for *today*. We have the opportunity to know that while we might want to dwell in the past because that's where our child was, we cannot make the assumption we can do "it," whatever it may be, later.

This shift in perspective can lead people to make significant, and often very positive, changes in their lives. They may quit an unsatisfying job or one that takes too much time away from their family. They may register for the class or book the vacation they always wanted to take. They may choose to spend more time with their spouse or surviving children and realize dirty dishes don't matter, people do. Family matters.

Courage is another gift we can unwrap as we move through the grieving process. Parents who lose children have no choice but to do the impossible. They have to say goodbye to their child. They had no choice. They did not want to be brave or strong. They do not want to be walking this path.

With time, when they realize they survived the most difficult experience ever, they find a confidence they might not have had before their child died. This confidence may help them to make positive changes in their lives, even if they are difficult ones.

Planning for our own mortality

Very few people are comfortable talking about, let alone planning for their eventual death. Discussing what is important to us when we are dying as well as after we die is a conversation most people avoid until they are forced to because death is imminent. All too often, these conversations never happen, and your loved ones are left trying to guess what would be important to you. Not to mention, potentially having to also base decisions on cost when grief and sometimes guilt may interfere. Not all, but some funeral directors may take financial advantage of families in this situation.

When a child dies, it's often the first time the parents are confronted with making funeral arrangements for anyone. Decisions need to be made that may include purchasing a burial plot for you as well as for your child so that eventually, so that eventually, you can be buried together. The names of the parents are typically etched on the headstone along with their child's with the parent's birth dates, but no death date. Seeing their own names on a headstone can really freak some parents out!

Being forced to confront death head on because of your own child's death gives you an opportunity; a really a wonderful opportunity to have a discussion with your spouse or significant other, parents, and other important family members about your wishes for when you die. This conversation should include not only the details of your wishes for services, burial or cremation, pre-payment, and details of your obituary, but also a health care proxy and durable power of attorney. These documents are really important should you not be able to make medical or financial decisions for yourself. Furthermore, they can release your loved ones from guilt and alleviate the burden of having to make difficult decisions at a time when your family may vastly disagree on who should be making decisions and what those decisions should be. These documents can be changed in writing at any time.

It's also a great wake up call to the importance of a will. Everyone should have a will, but it should definitely be prepared when parents have their first child. Even if you think you have nothing to pass on, important decisions like who will serve as executor of the estate or care for any minor children are critical to have in writing. Without a will, your family may have to incur the expense and added time of probate court before monies and property are released. They court also has to decide what is in the best interest of surviving children if there is no written will expressing your wishes. This can create an emotional and financial burden on your surviving family.

Any of these documents can be prepared fairly quickly and easily with the assistance of an attorney or with the help of some online services like Legal Zoom. They can all be changed at any time, some verbally, some in writing. Be sure to put it on your to do list.

Resilience

As we work our way through the fog of our grief and begin to integrate our child's loss into our lives, we realize that humans are tremendously resilient. We have a tremendous capacity to endure, grow, and change in the face of seemingly overwhelming adversity. Resiliency may be a super-power only the deeply bereaved discover.

Awareness of the amazing heart-centered loving work of first responders and the medical community

You may have heard great things about the local trauma hospital. Perhaps, you know nurses, doctors, EMT's, medical helicopter crews and hospital social workers are very good at what they do.

What you may not have realized is how much they care about you and your child. How after they cared for your child, they cried, too. They went to their church or synagogue and met with clergy. They, too, asked, "Why?" They needed counseling, too. They went home and hugged their children, told everyone they loved them, and in our case, secured their furniture.

They might anonymously come to your memorial, wake, or funeral service. They may donate to your family or the charity of your request or bring you food and you have no idea who they are or how they know.

Nothing brings people together like a tragedy. It's sad that is often what it takes, but it's not until you see it in motion that you really get a depth of appreciation for how fortunate you are to live in a place and time where such amazing medical care is available. How blessed we are to live in a time and place where people truly care about you and your child, not just as a patient, but as a member of the community. How they can relate to you and your experience. It breaks their heart, too.

We had a guest book on the original Meghan's Hope website page for awareness of the dangers of furniture tip-over. In reading it, one of the nurses who cared for Meghan at the hospital wrote that she wanted us to know that Meghan was very much loved and cared for by everyone in the emergency room that day. She was never alone, and they prayed for her and for us. She wanted us to know they cared and will never forget her and the gift she gave them. Needless to say, it brought me comfort and made me cry.

Gratitude

"We must be willing to let go of the life we planned so as to have the life that is waiting for us." — Joseph Campbell

It's hard to imagine being grateful after you have lost a child. What in the world could you possibly be grateful for? Your life, as you had planned it, is over. You need to start over. In a way you just don't want to. Yet you have no choice.

Gratitude is a gift. It takes practice. It begets peace. It helps us recognize our gifts, in spite of our hardships and pain.

After the death of a child, or any loved one, we can find much to be thankful for. You just need to look. It doesn't mean you are in any way belittling the death of your child or somehow diminishing their importance in your life. In fact, far from it.

309

As an example, I am grateful to Meghan for many things, most importantly, for the gift of her life. She taught me so much in her short three years with me. She taught me patience. She taught me the importance of play. She taught me how to mix pink paint in just the right shade of pink. She made me laugh. A lot! She brought out the best in her brothers and those she met. She was wise beyond her years. She taught me to let go and live in the moment.

After she died, she taught me what unconditional love really is. She gave me the gift of confidence. She opened my heart and my mind to spirit and led me down the path I was meant to walk. Had she not died, I'd not be the person I am today. I'd never have done the soul searching and dancing with my demons and shadow side that was necessary to become the person I am today. The person I was meant to be.

I might have never found my voice to speak out and advocate. The thousands upon thousands of lives that have been saved through the message of Meghan's Hope might not have been saved. Oh, my sweet baby girl, what an amazing gift you are!

How could I be anything but grateful?

Release of fear
As humans, we tend to make decisions from one of two places; either a place of fear or from a place of love. We often live our lives putting things off for another day or another time. Often, this is because we are afraid of something. We may be afraid of failing, being ridiculed, being wrong, being physically or emotionally hurt, of financial loss, of being rejected, or of something else. It's

fear that drives all of those things. Not in a fear of spiders kind of way. Rather, it's the fear that whatever it is that you are contemplating doing takes an awful lot of effort and there is no guarantee of a favorable outcome, so you are not willing to take the chance, at least not right now kind of fear.

I say choose from a place of love, not fear. It's not as hard as you think. Try it!

Perspective
When you are thrown into the hell that is losing a child your perspective changes. It has to. You simply cannot be the same person with the same life that you had five minutes before your child died.

As you begin to heal and incorporate your child's death into your life, you realize the worst possible thing you could ever imagine happening in your life already has. You've already lived through your greatest fear. You know all too well how short life can be. You are healing and you are coping. You are strong. You are resilient. Not because you are afraid. Because you love. Because what you learned the most from this entire experience is the power of love.

Often, the slap in the face realization that life is truly short, and that we really don't know if tomorrow will come for any of us, inspires us to do things we have been putting off or afraid to do. If we've already endured what most consider the most horrible thing that could ever happen to anyone, what is left to fear?

Thus, the gift we find is a way to let go of the fears that have been holding us back... the fears that keep us from fulfilling our true destiny. We feel called to follow our *heart*. For some, it may mean quitting or changing their job or career path. For others, it may mean going back to school. It may mean you finally find the strength and determination to get out of toxic relationships, kick addictions to the curb, or pursue a hobby or sport you have always wanted to try. It may mean you finally forgive yourself and others and forge new relationships and repair broken ones. The possibilities are truly limitless.

Choosing to act from a place of love is one of the most profound, liberating, and peaceful gifts you can give not only to others, but to yourself. Imagine a world where everyone chose from a place of love…

Your relationship with your child doesn't really end. It just changes.

The pain of the loss of our child's physical presence in our lives is almost impossible to describe. It's certainly impossible to imagine. Not seeing them, not hearing them, no longer feeling them... it's such a profound loss. We will never touch or hold them again. They are... gone.

Yet, they are not truly "gone." Yes, their physical presence is gone. Their body no longer functions. They are no longer a physical or tangible presence in our lives. That does not mean they do not exist for us on other levels. It does not mean our relationship with our child has to end. It just changes. As you begin to process, heal, and integrate your child's death into your life, you will begin to see the opportunities you have to continue a relationship on a different level… in a different way.

Throughout this book, I've made many references to the ways in which I connect with Meghan. The ways I remember her, honor her, and foster my relationship with her as a mommy. She is very much a part of our family and not a day goes by that I don't think of her, say or write her name in some way. Meghan's Hope is her legacy and another way I continue to mother her. She lives on in the lives that she's saved as a result of their parents hearing her story and making their homes safer. Her life and her death are revered and honored, and she is remembered in some way. Every. Single. Day. She is every bit my daughter today as she was the day she was born. It's just different.

How you continue your relationship will be as unique as your child was to you. There is no right or wrong way. Perhaps, you will write to or talk to your child. Perhaps, you will have a shrine or a ritual of remembrance that you incorporate into your day. Maybe you wear a locket with their photo or some other piece of jewelry to remember them. Perhaps, you visit with a medium or connect with your child in spirit yourself.

Our memories become our relationship. Through grief keeping activities, ceremonies, and tokens of remembrance, we maintain our relationship with our child through love. It's not the same, but it's real.

It can be difficult to allow yourself to see the good or the gifts that come out of the pain of losing a child. I still struggle with one of the greatest gifts Meghan gave me in an indirect, but profound way. Had she not died, I would not be where I am today. I am who I am because she lived **and** because she died. Her life and her death catalyzed a change in me that led me down a path to amazing experiences, gifts, and happiness. I doubt if I'd ever have had the courage to do the things I've done otherwise. It's a tough pill to swallow, but my gratitude to her for all she's taught me is difficult to convey.

"Love is a gift of one's inner most soul to another, so both can be whole." ~Buddha

Chapter Ten

Signs and Spirituality

How do I know if my child or loved one is sending me signs from "the other side?" Am I crazy? Are they real? Should I say anything to anyone?

There is much debate about signs from Heaven or the "other side." Some people refer to them as after life or after death communication. Signs like these often take the form of things you feel, see, or hear that remind you of your deceased child or loved one or, perhaps, are a direct communication from them.

Some people hear their voice, see their deceased loved one, see repetitive images or number sequences, hear songs, or have some other experience that makes them wonder if it's a sign. Often, when we think we're receiving signs from a departed loved one, we convince ourselves, or, someone else convinces us, that it is wishful thinking or a coincidence, not reality.

According to a PEW research study in 2010, 29% of the American public, more than one quarter of the population, say they have experienced after death communication. That same survey found 18% of Americans report having seen the ghost of someone who has died. The law of conservation of energy, from the brilliant mind of Albert Einstein, tells us matter and energy cannot be created or destroyed. WE are matter and energy!

A discussion about signs and after death communications often leads to a discussion about scientific theories and religion versus spirituality. If you pull psychology into the discussion, you would have scientific and medically based explanations as to why after death communication is highly unlikely or just plain impossible, and often treated a manifestation of depression, an acute grief reaction, or even psychosis.

While these could be very real conditions, I think society and the religious and medical communities must also *listen* to the bereaved with an open mind. The medical community must make an effort to understand their patient's experience, rather than assign a label, cause, or diagnosis, and treat it with a knee-jerk reaction. We all grieve differently. We all come to the bereavement table with a lifetime of our own, and with very personal, very real experiences and opinions. We deserve to be respected for who we are and how we cope.

I do not intend to delve into a discussion about religion versus spirituality, nor do I wish to debate the theories of psychologists and psychiatrists on why people seek or insist they have received signs from their deceased loved ones. Nor do I wish to discuss the scientific theories believed to disprove the possibility of after death communication. That is more than enough to fill another entire book!

Just as differing religions have differing beliefs, so do different spiritual practices. We are ultimately the product of our experiences, beliefs, and opinions. As I've said before many times in this book, the only opinion that matters is yours. If you wish to learn more about any of these topics, there is abundant information available for research.

Whether you believe in after death communication or not, I encourage you to have an open mind. Don't judge others based on *your* beliefs. You have not had their experiences. You may not share their beliefs, and that is okay. You have no right to tell them what they do and do not feel. Respect and understanding are basic values and are no less important here than they were in Chapter One.

What are signs and why do people look for them?

So what are signs? How do we recognize them? How do we know they really are signs?

Signs from our deceased loved ones are one of the greatest gifts we can receive. We all want to know our children and loved ones on the other side are safe. We long for validation of this. One of the most common and most controversial questions about the death of any loved one is can and do they send signs to us from the other side?

The answer really depends on who you ask and what you believe. Obviously, if you do not believe it is possible to communicate after death, the answer is, "No." If you do believe it's possible or are open to the possibility, then the answer is, "Yes." However, how you determine if you've received a sign can be very individual and subjective. It's also not always obvious at first.

I can tell you that signs are generally more accepted and understood by those who are spiritually open-minded. Interestingly, it seems that those who are bereaved are more open to spirituality and to signs than they may have previously been. This may be one of the gifts of that initial shock and numbness and of the depth of love a child shares with their parents. Our "thinking" brains are often turned off in those initial stages of grief and that can make us more open to receiving and recognizing signs without our logical mind trying to talk us out of it. It is a very different way of living for many of us.

Which psychic "camp" are you in?
There seems to be three distinct groups people fall into when discussing the possibility of after death communications.

1. The first group consists of people who absolutely and with conviction know that after death communication is possible because they believe in it, or they have experienced it.
2. The second group consists of people who absolutely and with conviction believe after death communication is not possible and attribute any report of receiving a sign as wishful thinking, because there is no mainstream science that can absolutely support it.
3. The remaining group consists of people who just don't know what to believe. It includes those who think they have received signs, many of whom may be afraid to discuss them because others around them may not believe or support them. Unfortunately, this includes a tremendous number of the newly bereaved.

Most people fall into the third group. They have heard stories or may have had experiences, but they are not sure if their experience is real or imagined. Furthermore, they are afraid to share their thoughts or admit to having had their own experiences for fear of ridicule or being diagnosed as crazy or mentally ill.

Discussing the arguments for and against after death communication is really beyond the scope of this book. There are many, many articles and books out there supporting both sides of the subject. I strongly encourage you to seek out that which resonates with you. What *you* believe is far more important than what anyone else believes. Your experiences are yours and yours alone. Trust them!

For the purposes of this book, I can really speak only to my own personal experiences and those other bereaved people and parents have shared with me. My disclaimer is this: I absolutely believe in signs. I do not believe in coincidence of any kind. I used to, but because of the spiritual experiences I've had, really my entire life, I no longer subscribe to coincidence as an explanation for anything.

I believe that everything does happen for a reason, and every situation and person we encounter offers us something we need on our human journey. What we choose to do with that information is entirely up to us. That's the beauty of being a human with free will.

I do believe in the psychic senses, the power of intuition, and the ability to connect with the energy of the Universe, by whatever name you use, whether it be God, Source, Allah, the Angels, Spirit Guides, Guardian Angels, or any and all spirit beings. I believe some people have the gift of being able to communicate with spirit and loved ones who have passed on with one or all of their psychic senses. Some may even see them or hear them.

Of course, not everyone shares this belief or has any or all of these gifts, and I absolutely respect and honor whatever anyone believes. Ultimately, what resonates with you and helps you process and heal is all that really matters. I encourage you to have the same sort of open mind.

Sometimes, the best way to explain something so abstract is by example. These are some of my personal psychic experiences and particularly, several of the things that transpired before and after Meghan died that made an absolute believer out of me.

I've always been intuitive, ever since I was a child. I knew things. I was empathetic. I felt energy. I could read situations and people and instinctively knew when they were lying or if they were energetically good or bad. I had lots of imaginary friends and often had conversations, out loud, with them, as if they were real. It was sort of confusing, because I didn't really see or hear them, yet it was as if they were real. I *felt* their presence and felt as if we communicated on a telepathic level. I often had vivid dreams although I've never been very good at remembering them or writing them down when I wake up. This makes interpretation harder!

Turns out I get it from my father's side of the family. I have many psychically gifted relatives. Sadly, most are "in the closet" or have yet to fully embrace their gifts. They do share their experiences with those who are likely to understand and will not judge them. It also turns out, I should have learned to embrace and listen to my intuition a lot earlier.

Along with my intuitive nature, came my strong sense of justice. I am a rule follower. I stand up for what I believe. I'm not afraid to state my opinion or fight for what I feel is right. I call people out. I was vocal as a child, often to adults who were not being nice to each other. It often got me into a world of trouble with my parents and adults in my family. In fact, I'm pretty sure I'm still grounded for speaking my child and adolescent mind!

My daughter's death catalyzed my awakening, or, perhaps, more accurately, my embrace of my psychic gifts. Looking back, it actually began to strengthen or, perhaps, I began to listen to it more when I was pregnant with my first child. Pregnancy can do that to you. It often stirs that maternal protective instinct that all mammals have. I found I had a heightened awareness about everything when I was pregnant. I embraced my intuition and my other psychic senses more readily at that time. It has only strengthened over the years since.

It is difficult for me to wrap my head and heart around the very loud and clear signs I received about my daughter's death before it happened. None of them were terribly specific: my guidance rarely is. That is so frustrating! Of course, none of them really made sense until after she died, which pissed me off. Could I have saved her life if I had just listened to my intuition? Yet, there have been many intuitive "hits" that have foretold some of the events that have since come to pass in my life.

The intuitive guidance I received prior to Meghan's death included:
- An absolute, seemingly irrational fear that something bad would happen to one of my kids. I had occasional dreams of a little white casket. This began when pregnant with my first. It was attributed to me

being an overprotective worrywart with a severe case of new mom-itis. All parents worry about their kids, I was told. I was normal to have this fear. That seemed logical to me, so I accepted the explanation.

- An increasing fear after I became pregnant with the twins. Despite carrying two babies, a boy and a girl, it was always my daughter that I worried about. Even when pregnant. I was told this is also not unusual, especially since I had suffered a miscarriage three months prior to conceiving the twins. As a childbirth educator and birth doula, I knew too much about what could go wrong. My anxiety was attributed to my level of knowledge. I knew something was not right, but I couldn't put my finger on it. It made my pregnancy, all 39 weeks of it, somewhat challenging emotionally due to the unexplainable dis-ease I felt about the health of my daughter.

- The continued and increasing fear that something bad would happen to one of my kids after the twins were born and especially after they became mobile. Ironically, I was even worried about furniture falling! I childproofed to excess. We secured large pieces of furniture, although in hindsight, not properly, because we didn't know any better. We didn't think smaller furniture, like the dresser that eventually fell on her and took her life, was a danger. I wanted to secure her dresser but my husband resisted. It was expensive and he didn't want to ruin it by putting holes in it. He was worried it would decrease the resale value. He convinced me it was too small to tip over. I allowed myself to believe this, even though I had a nagging bad feeling about it and other unsecured pieces. Adding to this fear, I had one child that was highly allergic, even anaphylactic to some foods, another that was behaviorally explosive and hyperactive, and a third one that was fast, fearless, and adventurous. They were all under five years of age! People continued to tell me I was neurotic and over-protective.

- An uncharacteristic wishy-washiness with regard to decisions impacting my professional life in the months prior to her death. Previously, I never had trouble making decisions. However I suddenly found that I could not commit to trainings I really wanted to take, decide if I should accept new doula clients, or determine if I wanted to schedule future classes. I couldn't even decide if I would attend a scrapbooking weekend with good friends. I even put off actively seeking an agent for a book proposal I had written about pregnancy and birth of twins even though I had it complete and was eager to get it moving. This was all just a few weeks before Meghan died.

- I had a vivid clairvoyant premonition of a little white casket surrounded by pink flowers when I heard the Celine Dion song "My Heart Will go On" on the radio as I was driving to that scrapbooking weekend. I remember feeling bewilderingly melancholy and sad when I started the drive, before I heard the song or had the premonition, despite the fact it was a much needed girls weekend. I could not shake my uncharacteristic sadness. I thought, at the time, the premonition was about my niece who was having open heart surgery that coming week. When her surgery was successful and she was fine, I forgot all about it until I walked into my daughter's wake, and saw that exact scene.

- A bad feeling about a photograph of Meghan. My husband had printed it in black and white. It was on our kitchen island just a day or two before she died. When I saw it, I literally shuddered. I had a strong negative and visceral reaction to it. That baffled me. It was as if she were... gone. She looked ghostly to me in the photo. I hated the lack of color. It was haunting. Perhaps, it was a premonition.

The profound signs that happened the day Meghan died

The day Meghan died was the most awful day of my life. Yet my own experiences before, during, and in the days, weeks, and months that followed have been nothing short of amazing. It does nothing to lessen the pain of her loss, but it did convince me, that without a doubt, our energy and our love, goes on and on and on.

- Having a "dream" the morning my daughter died that I was in our attic, floating. In front of me were two light beings. They communicated without words. I remember feeling panicked and being incredibly comforted at the same time as they reminded this was the way it was supposed to be. They were telling me Meghan had to go. That she had died. That it would be okay. That I and she knew this would happen. In retrospect, this had to be when she died. I was confused in the dream. I never woke at the time but remembered it vividly when I was woken by my husband's screams. I knew instantly she had died. I didn't know how or why, but I knew. Before I saw her, I knew. I held this experience in my heart and head for a long time, afraid to speak it. I thought I was nuts. I thought other people would think I was nuts. I finally told my grief counselor and a spiritual mentor who both reassured me. They didn't tell me I was right, wrong, or crazy. They just listened and validated my experience as being truth for me.

- As I did CPR, I knew she was gone. I begged her to come back, but only if she could return as my Meggie. As devastated and upset as I was, there was a very disturbing and nagging, yet odd realization that the puzzle was falling into place. That it made sense on a spiritual level. It made sense to my soul. That this was something on some level I knew would happen. I didn't process it then, but later realized THAT moment was the reason, that moment was the manifestation of all those signs and all my fears. Her death was the fear I'd carried with me for six years and the explanation for what I'd seen and felt. I had been right. I had known one of my children would die and die young. I had not known how... I had not known who or why... but I had known on a spiritual and energetic level. It was really, really difficult to wrap my heart and head around it, though.

- Her twin knelt at her feet as I performed CPR. He quietly and knowing said, "Meggie not wake up." Even her twin knew. He just... knew. He wasn't upset. To this day, he *gets* it. He continued to play with her, talk to her, and see her for a long time after she died. He never asked where she went. He didn't need to. He understood on a level none of us could.

- A retired police officer, who was also a neighbor, as well as psychically gifted himself, came to our home after hearing the 911 call. He later told me he saw that same black and white photo of Meghan on the island, the one I hated, except he saw a golden yellow light around her when he looked at the photo! It told him she was gone. This was before he had received confirmation of her death.

- The night she died, I couldn't sleep. As I lay in bed, her twin between my husband and I, two distinctly amazing things happened. I opened my eyes, and at the foot of my bed I saw a holographic image of my beloved grandmother Agnes with Meggie wrapped in her arms. They were both smiling. She was conveying to me without words she was safe, they were together, I needn't worry. I sat bolt upright in bed and stared. I shook my head. I was both a bit taken aback and tremendously comforted. I cried while smiling. I reached out, but then they were gone. I wondered if it was real. Yet I was completely awake when I saw them. My husband had also woken up although he didn't see the same image I did. As we lay back down, her twin reached up, eyes open but unfocused, as if in a trance, and touched his father's face, just like Meggie used to do, saying, "It's okay Daddy, It's okay." Meggie used to say that all the time while touching your face. Her brother never did that! It was as if he was channeling her to give a message in a way her father would understand.

Signs for other family and friends: The day the Angels fell down

"Mommy, when the angel fall down?"

This was the question posed by my three-year-old son, the evening before his twin sister's funeral. It was Christmas time, December 21st, and we of course had an angel atop our tree. That morning, she had fallen partially off the tree, so we fixed her up straight before we left the house for her wake. We didn't think anything else of it.

As we sat watching a TV show together that evening, he randomly asked about the angel. Assuming he was referring to the morning, my response, of course, was to say, "Honey, the angel is not going to fall down. We fixed it!" He said, "Yes, mommy, the angel fall down." He was pretty insistent. I figured he was tired. The poor kid had been through so much.

The next morning, the morning of her funeral, upon coming down stairs the very first thing I noticed was that the small angel on top of our mini tabletop Christmas tree in the kitchen was on the floor. I replaced her and blamed the cat for being mischievous. A short time later, when we walked into the playroom, we found the angel atop our Christmas tree was barely hanging on! Again! I could not blame that one on the cat. There was no reasonable explanation for it.

Then it hit me. *He was right! He knew the angel was going to fall again!* I got my Meg's twin and showed him the fallen angel. He smiled a bright, beautiful smile. I asked him how he knew. He just looked at me, smiling knowingly, as if to say "Why didn't YOU Know?" We set her straight on the tree once again and prepared for Meg's funeral.

Later that evening, we found another fallen angel! This one, a recent gift, had been held to my bedroom window by a suction cup. She had unexplainably fallen onto the windowsill. The suction cup still adhered to the window! By the time I found that one, I actually laughed out loud. I finally got it. The angels were falling down! My son had pre-existing knowledge the angels would fall. A sign? Coincidence? Think what you will. I don't for a minute believe it was only coincidence that nearly every angel in our house fell that day. Do you?

The next day Meg's twin gleefully played with his sister. Calling out to her, "Oh, Geggie, look!" and then looking at us quizzically, as if he realized we didn't see her and that he was the only one who could. He excitedly said he saw her many times in the months that followed, pointing her out with absolute certainty in his voice. I wish he remembered now what he saw and knew then...

On Christmas night, I remember talking to my older son about Meggie and Heaven and spirit. He asked if she could see us. I said, "Yes, I believe so." He asked if she could see the children in India. I explained if she could see us, she could probably see everyone, everywhere. I also wondered why a six-year-old child was asking about children in India, of all places. He was on a bit of a geography kick with a new Leapfrog toy, so it didn't seem all that bizarre, but still. As our conversation continued, he asked if she knew when bad things were going to happen or if she could stop them from happening. I tried to reassure him she was looking out for all of us as our own personal guardian angel.

The next day, December 26th, we woke to the news of the massive Indian Ocean earthquake and tsunami! Twice in one week, my boys seemed to predict the next day's events. How did they *know*? One in our own home, another on the other side of the world! I was a bit mind boggled. He again that night asked if Meggie would be able to be with the children who died in the tsunami. I responded, "Yes, yes she would.

I bet she is already there playing with them and their kitties in Heaven." He seemed to like that answer.

Earlier that week, on December 20th, two days after her death, her twin did his first finger painting. It was a landscape. He was sitting at the kitchen table with my father. He painted a sun and some clouds. Blue, brown and oranges dominated. He suddenly pointed to a spot in the sky of his picture and completely unprompted stated, "Meggie there. In the clouds." As if to tell us, "Duh, don't you get it? She's an angel now! She's in the sky!"

There were other signs that week. Some of which I've mentioned elsewhere in this book. There have been many more since.

So when people ask me about signs, I say yes. I've witnessed or received many signs, not only from Meghan, but from other deceased loved ones as well. I believe in them. Although I can't always explain them scientifically, I have no doubt we live on in spirit and can find ways to communicate. In that first week after she died, I received many signs. There were many, many more to come. They've taught me volumes. I no longer believe in coincidence.

Meghan's death was the start, or, perhaps, the rebirth of a spiritual journey that has opened my eyes to my own spiritual gifts and has led me to who and where I am today. That, however, is a story to tell another day. Maybe in another book.

Know this. Twinship transcends death. Love transcends all.

Signs Others Received

They say every person you meet has information for you. There is a purpose for them in your life, no matter how brief your interactions are. Perhaps, they bring a life lesson. Perhaps, it's simply information or insight. Perhaps, it's to help you fulfill your soul contract on this earthly journey. My life is certainly full of amazing evidence of this phenomenon, well beyond my experiences with regard to my daughter's life and death.

In the days, weeks, and months that followed Meggie's death, I had conversations with many people who shared with me their own spiritual experiences regarding her death. Some I asked about or sought out, but most people offered their own experience and guidance when they felt the time was right. Some of the ones that stand out most to me are the following:

- A neighbor, who was very psychic and spiritually oriented, later told me she had woken uncharacteristically early the morning Meg had died. She felt compelled to sit in her living room and meditate. Her house is situated such that her living room window provides a direct view of the back of my house. Meg's room was in the back of the house. She said while meditating, she became aware of a bright, bright light and an overwhelming feeling of love. It had moved her to tears. At first, she thought she was just having a wonderful meditative experience, but then she realized the light was not inside her home, but coming from outside. It was shining on my house and coming from my house, it was not the sun. It was probably about the time Meghan died.

- At Meghan's wake, that same neighbor said she felt so much light and energy around Meghan it was astounding. At her funeral, in the middle of the service, she saw, in her mind's eye, the belt of the constellation Orion. She didn't know what it meant but she felt it was a sign and a message for her and for me. When she got home, she looked it up. The constellation is associated with the Egyptian God Osiris, who was the God of the afterlife and of re-birth. There are many mythological associations with the night sky and many interpretations that could easily fill an entire book on their own! From a spiritual standpoint, Orion is associated with a gateway to Heaven, ascension, multi-dimensionality, or a portal or gateway to the Universe. I have always liked the constellation Orion. I find it stunning to look at the winter sky and view Orion with a sense of awe and peace. I definitely look at it a little differently now.

Other Signs through the Years

Hearts. Lots and lots of hearts. I see heart clouds, hearts of blue sky peeking through a cloud covered sky… some large, some small. In fact, sometimes I spot several in one day, particularly on days of significance or when I need them, not necessarily when I ask for them. Usually, I will, for some reason, just happen to look up, and there it is. I first noticed the heart clouds in the early days after Meghan died. I thought it was a fluke until I started to see them often. In fact when writing this book one day while outside, I glanced up and saw several heart clouds. I took that as a sign Meggie approved of my writing!

I also notice hearts in nature often in rocks or leaves, in food, in damp roadways, in photos, and random other places. Some would say I've attached an emotional significance to hearts and have become skilled at pattern identification, so I see them more often because I look for them and recognize them readily. However, I usually don't look for them actively. In fact if I ask for them or actively look for them, I'm much less likely to see one! I just happen to look up or down and there they are. So maybe, just maybe, they really are signs... I believe they are. Love is always welcome and always comforting. They always make me smile.

Whenever I receive bodywork in the form of Reiki, massage, reflexology, or some other experience where I can relax, meditate, and connect with spirit and my higher self, I often receive guidance or information that is validating and comforting. Sometimes I literally feel her presence or the presence of another loved one who has passed. I "hear" them communicating or conveying an energetic message to me. Connecting with spirit requires you get out of your thinking brain, which is why deep relaxation is often what facilitates messages or signs.

Sometimes, the message is passed on through another person via information they receive while providing the body or energy work. They may feel, see, or hear a message and pass it on to me. Often, these people are unaware that I have lost a child, yet the information they give about Meghan is spot on. I've also received reassuring messages during readings with Angel oracle or Tarot cards, from both others and myself. Let me tell you, the "Hello from Heaven" card or a similar one comes up every year on Meghan's birthday and Angelversary day, no matter who is doing the reading!

How Do I know if it's really a Sign?

There are as many possible signs as there are people looking for them. The beauty of signs is that they are meaningful and personal. Finding a rock in the shape of a heart while walking in the woods may mean nothing to you, but it's significant for me.

The following list is by no means all-inclusive, but it does include many of the common ways people receive signs from their loved ones on the other side. Be especially alert to repetitive signs, even if they don't seem to make much sense at the time. Remember, if you think or believe that it's a sign, it is! It does not matter what anyone else thinks, only what you do!

Some common signs people receive from the other side

- Feathers, especially white feathers are a common sign. Often they are found in places where you might not expect to find a feather like in your car, at a store, in a magazine or, perhaps, a friend posts a photo of one on social media. People who lose very young children or babies commonly report they frequently see small white feathers.
- A song on the radio that is meaningful to you and your loved one. Often, you'll hear it every time you are in the car or several times in one day while switching stations. It may even be the song playing when your alarm goes off in the morning.

- Smells that remind you of your deceased loved one with no other apparent cause. Perfumes, food aromas or cigarette smoke are common.
- Animal signs are very common. If your loved one really loved hawks, you may suddenly see hawks everywhere, perhaps even right outside your window. Cardinals are said to be a sign a loved one from Heaven is near. Butterflies and dragonflies are also common signs of communication from a deceased loved one. Both are symbolic of transformation. I do see butterflies often and frequently at significant times. In fact, as I was writing this chapter, a yellow butterfly literally knocked on my bay window, then hovered. Intuitively, I knew it was not just a message for me, but also for a fellow bereaved parent from her daughter, who loved butterflies herself, and has often sent yellow butterflies to her mother. I sent an email of my experience along to her. I kid you not. Ten minutes later, after writing that email, a yellow butterfly flew by again, as if to say, "Thank you." Coincidence? I think not. Sign? Absolutely.
- Electrical disturbances such as the lights or the TV's turning on and off on their own or flickering or smoke detectors beeping for no reason can be a way a loved one tries to communicate after death. This is especially true when it happens with no other explanation or on a day of personal significance.
- Feeling a loved one's presence is perhaps the strongest and most powerful sign... you just *know* they are there. You may feel their energy, feel as if someone walked by you or think you saw something or someone, but when you look more closely you don't see them. You are and were alone. Or were

you?   You may even find yourself having a conversation out loud with them spontaneously, as if to answer a question they posed, without consciously realizing it, as if they were right in front of you. Maybe because they are...

- You may see them. It may be in a dream that seems so very real... because it was, or you may see them while you are wide awake. They may seem to have a real physical presence and form, or appear more hologram-ish in nature. Perhaps, all you see is an area or a ball of light or a color or cloudiness. It's often brief, and most people think their eyes are playing "tricks" on them, but again, you *know* intuitively it was real, and you know it was your deceased loved one's energy.

- You may hear their voice as if they are right with you or hear from them telepathically through your thoughts.   Some people have entire conversations energetically or telepathically, where no words were spoken, but information was definitely exchanged.

- You may find yourself being guided by an inner voice or intuition to do something differently or spontaneously. Sometimes the guidance is strong, but you are not sure why you are feeling so strongly guided. That something different leads you to an unexpected sign. For example, perhaps your adult daughter loved horses. While driving one day and thinking about your daughter, you find yourself turning down a road you don't need or even want to go down, one you've never been on before, but you feel strongly guided to do so. As you drive down the road, still not knowing why, you happen upon a beautiful horse farm! You smile, and realize what a gift it was from your daughter! What a lovely sign.

- Repeatedly drawing the same or similar cards from a Tarot or Angel Card deck… even if it seems to make no sense, or is not the card you wanted or hoped to get. Your loved one is trying to tell you something you need to know.

- Money. Ever hear of the phrase "pennies from Heaven?" For some, it may be dimes or some other denomination that has meaning, but you may suddenly find them everywhere or are gifted them by people who have no idea of the significance they hold for you. This can happen with similar objects such as figurines.

- Finding or seeing small objects of significance. Maybe it's little hearts, or particular kinds of flowers, rocks of a certain color, hair ties, and bottle caps, the insignia of the branch of the armed forces your child served in, or some other small item that is of significance to or in relation to your deceased loved one. Perhaps, a favorite quote of theirs shows up on your Facebook page, or your child's favorite TV character suddenly appears everywhere.

- Number sequences of significance are a common sign. You may see them on license plates, building or mailbox numbers, clocks, or on your phone. You may look at the clock, and it will be the date or time of their birth or death or some other significance. You might pick up your phone and see the last phone call was from your deceased adult son, which seems impossible because he died weeks before and you know his was not the most recent call. You may look at the clock at 4:44 and feel comforted, because

Doreen Virtue tells us that 444 is a sign the Angels are with you.

The bottom line is if you think you have received a sign, you have! Don't doubt yourself. Thank your child or loved one for the visit or the message or the sign and let them know how much you appreciate it. Don't let anyone try to convince you that your experience was anything more or less than what you believe it was. It does not matter what anyone else thinks, only what you think.

Can we miss signs? Sure, we can. We may be preoccupied or self-doubting. We may think that unless we asked for a sign, we couldn't possibly receive one. It may not occur to us that we received a sign until much later, sometimes for days! I've probably seen six yellow butterflies, or maybe the same one, multiple times in my yard the past few days. It didn't just fly by; it looped, and appeared to try to get my attention. The first time I saw it, I thought, "Oh, a butterfly!" I saw it multiple times before I realized there was a message in it.

I do recommend writing down your experiences in a journal of some kind. It can make for a wonderful remembrance and when you are feeling as if communication is sparse or hard to come by, you can look back on all the signs you have received in the past, and remember the connections you have made with your deceased child or loved one.

Asking for a Sign

Is it wrong to ask for a sign? Some schools of thought would tell you that you should never ask for signs. Probably, because when you do, you either find a way to locate one, or you constantly second guess or doubt yourself. I'd say it's probably best not to ask for a specific sign. For example, I don't ask for hearts as a rule and rarely see them if I do. It may be wise to ask for a sign you will understand and recognize as being from or about your child or loved one, instead of asking for something very specific. They are energetic beings now; some signs are easier for them to send!

Other Ways to Communicate or Connect with Deceased Loved Ones

There are many ways you can try to connect or communicate with your child or other loved ones in spirit. It helps to be in a quiet space. If you can, clear the space energetically, by burning sage or using a sage room spray, open a window, or ring a bell. Set an intention for what you want for your experience. Try to do it at a time and in a place where you won't be disturbed. You might want to play some new age or soft relaxing music or perhaps a favorite song of your loved one.

Here are some ways to communicate:

1. Pray. Prayer is a way of communicating. It can be out loud or silently. Our deceased loved ones are energetic beings now. Thought is energy and therefore a wonderful way to communicate.
2. Meditate. Be still and open to receiving without expectations. Tune into your intuition and the energy around you. Pay attention to your thoughts, feelings, and physical sensations.
3. Write to your deceased child or loved one. Have an open conversation by writing a letter or keeping a journal. This can go on indefinitely whenever you feel like "talking" to them!

4. Have a conversation with them. Silently or out loud. Listen for their answer in the form of what you feel, see, hear, and think of within your own mind and body and around you. Write down your experience, so you remember all the details.

5. Seek out bodywork. The meditative state and deep relaxation that can happen with bodywork and energy work accompanied by an intention to heal or connect can be powerful. Have a massage, reflexology, or a Reiki or energy healing session. Keep an open mind and pay attention to sensations, feelings, memories and what you see and feel. Ask the person working with you to share any insight or message they receive as well. Know that sometimes with this kind of work, you may experience a range of physical and emotional feelings and remember things you've forgotten or blocked that are held in muscle memory, perhaps, even from previous lifetimes. It can be very powerful so you should make sure you have time to process afterwards.

6. Get a reading with an Angel Card Reader or Tarot Card reader or psychically gifted person. Or host an Angel Party and get card readings for all your guests!

7. Attend a gallery reading, which is a large group session, with a medium. Know that not everyone necessarily gets a reading at one of these events, but it can be a good introduction to mediumship and help you decide if you want to pursue an individual session.

8. Have a private session with a medium.

What is a Medium and Should You Trust Them?

Many people find themselves intrigued by mediums after a loved one has died. Are they real? How do you feel about those who claim to be able to talk to dead people? Did your feelings about mediums change after you lost a loved one close to you?

As professionals, those who are able to communicate with those who have died are referred to as mediums, they are people who are a bridge between this world and whatever lies beyond this world after we die. They are messengers. They bring messages to us from our departed loved ones.

It's not hard to find mediums. With the advent of the internet and social media, all you need to do is a web search and you'll find a plethora of them. There are famous mediums like John Holland and James Van Praagh. There are those who have written books, have radio shows, or are guests on radio shows and TV. Some even have their own TV shows, like the Long Island Medium.

They speak at conferences and metaphysical or spiritual expos and book stores. They assist law enforcement with unsolved crimes. They are sought out by world leaders and the rich and famous, as well as average everyday folk like you and me. Some lead workshops and trainings so that you, too, can learn to develop your psychic gifts and communicate with the spirit world.

The validity of mediumship is a controversial subject. As a point of illustration, I had a conversation about this with my husband about a year ago. He and I have differing views on most topics of spirituality and metaphysics. He is a self-proclaimed man of science, who thinks very concretely with a black or white perspective. He wants and needs solid, scientific proof before he will believe theories to be true.

I am much more open-minded to matters of spirituality. While strongly rooted in science, I am also strongly spiritual because of my own personal experiences. I have come to better understand and believe many things I once did not hold to be truth. I have come to accept a lot of gray areas as possible if not probable.

The following is an overview of the conversation my husband and I had about mediums and both of our arguments with regard to whether or not mediums were truly gifted or just lying to people to make them feel better. I think many people will find insight in our conversation, whether you believe in the ability to communicate with the dead or not.

I chose to go to a gallery reading with a well-known psychic medium at a local spiritual expo. The cost to attend the two hour session was $45. The venue held 400 people, and it was filled to capacity. A bargain, for a private reading with him is several hundred dollars. I'd never seen his presentation, but I had read some of his books. I've seen other mediums at similar gallery readings and individually for a private or small group reading. Not all of them resonated with me.

I did not go to see this famous medium because I expected or even wanted my loved ones to "come through." I went because I wanted to experience it first-hand. He is probably one of the most gifted and respected psychic mediums out there and certainly one of the best known. He was highly recommended to me. Fortunately, he was presenting nearby, so I took advantage of the opportunity to attend.

What struck me most about this medium was that he was very real. He was personal and conversational even though there were 400 people in his "living room." He has a fantastic sense of humor. Before proceeding with the readings, he explains the process describing how he receives information during a reading. In a gallery reading, he has no idea who he is reading for until he starts to share the information he is receiving and someone in the audience understands it and claims the information.

Mediums or anyone with psychic gifts, receive information in different ways. While some "hear" or have thoughts that are random and not their own, others "see" objects or symbols in their mind's eye. Still others literally feel sensations or emotions that are not theirs. Sometimes they just know something. They get a strong intuitive hit or read. Everyone has a psychic strength or gift, some more than one. It's learning to understand how you receive information, interpret it, and deliver the message with confidence that is the challenge.

I was quite impressed with this famous medium's readings. They were much more detailed and specific than I imagined they would be. He would begin by sharing information from a deceased person, and ask if anyone felt it was their loved one. Sometimes he received a name or letters. When more than one person claimed a reading, he was able to sort it out with increased detail from the deceased without asking the person who was claiming the reading for any additional information. In fact, he asked those claiming a reading not to give him more than what he might ask, usually just a quick, simple, yes or no to a very specific question, so as not to make it seem as if he was being "fed" additional information. Even when someone insisted the reading was for them, if he felt is was not, he did not give that person the message but got increasingly detailed information to figure out exactly who it was for.

I also happened to be sitting next to a good friend who is psychic and a medium in her own right. She was getting much of the same information and telling me about it before the famous medium himself revealed it. Before you ask, we were in the second to last row waaaaay in the back, so no, he didn't hear her. It was validating for her and fascinating to me.

Like many people, my husband was skeptical of the capabilities of mediums. There is a perception that those who attend these sessions "waste" their money to hear "lies that make them feel better." Actually, his (and many others who do not believe in mediumship) concerns are primarily twofold...

1. *Many mediums are no more than thieves, preying on the bereaved. They use techniques such as cold reading, verbal feedback, body language, and emotional cues/reactions from the bereaved to make their readings seem honest, accurate, and true. Readings are generic and general and could apply to anyone. Or, that the person seeking the reading tells the medium enough about their loved one or what they want to hear that they get the information they want or need. He feels these self-proclaimed*

mediums are collective liars behaving in a destructive and morally irresponsible way because they can't possibly be *really* communicating the deceased. He, like many, believes that mediums deceive people in order to make money... sometimes lots of money.

2. *There is no hard scientific data that proves mediums actually do have the abilities they claim to possess. That what they claim to be able to do flies in the face of science as we know it today.*

As a counter, I offered this:

- *To the point that it's either all made up, cold readings, or taking advantage of someone's grief and vulnerability I replied:*
  - o *The bereaved seek out mediums, it is not the other way around. I didn't have to go see a medium, or pay money to him or anyone else to get a reading. I freely chose to do that. That's the great thing about being human, free will.*
- *To his point that it's morally wrong:*
  - o *Who is he to judge? He is entitled to his opinion, as is everyone else.*
  - o *People have the right to choose. Someone is only going to choose to go to a medium if they want to. If they do, clearly they see nothing wrong with it.*
- *To his point that the ability to communicate with the dead is not scientifically proven:*
  - o *Maybe it's not, but there is a lot that science can't prove that we still hold to be true because we think the theory is right. Until it's disproved, often through the development of*

new technology. Look at all the things we thought were true scientifically that were later found to be incorrect.

o *Two words. Quantum physics. The more we learn, the more we realize maybe particles do exist in more than one place at a time. Maybe there is a multi-dimensional universe. If matter is energy and energy cannot be created or destroyed, then we cannot be destroyed either... WE are energy.*

o *How is communicating with the deceased different than praying to God or a higher power, or having faith or a belief in the afterlife?*

o *Who cares? People are looking for healing. If they find it this way, it's no one's business but theirs. It's not about us or what we believe; it's about them and what they believe.*

o *None of us know what we don't know. We are constantly changing and evolving as humans based on our experiences. Even scientists!*

o *Anything is possible. The ability to communicate with the deceased cannot be proven or disproven at this time. If there is even a glimmer of possibility to connect with a departed loved one, why shouldn't someone take that opportunity?*

Ultimately, my argument to him was that the bereaved often long to connect with their loved ones who have died. They want to know they are okay and safe in the next place. They want to know they are watched over by someone. Sometimes, they seek out a medium just because they need or want validation of their own experiences. Maybe they have psychic gifts that they are realizing and just want to learn more. Or, maybe, they are skeptical, but curious, and are looking to get proof one way or another about the possibility of an afterlife and the ability to communicate with a deceased loved one on the other side.

Some choose to actively pursue a connection with their deceased loved ones. They want and need it to heal. Mediums offer that connection. There is nothing inherently wrong with that. If it feels right to them, that's all that matters.

Are all mediums real, honest and good? Of course not. I am sure there are self-proclaimed mediums that do not actually have psychic gifts, who do cold read, who do very general and benign readings, who ask more questions than they provide answers and who charge high fees for their services. And, of course one needs to take care in making rash decisions that could cause themselves financial distress, especially when going through the vulnerable grieving process.

There are also those who are amazingly gifted and they all deserve, just like anyone else who works, to be paid for their time and appreciated for their talents and gifts. They deceased don't have human bodies or qualities anymore, they communicate with energy through the senses, thoughts, and feelings. They use their energy to forge a connection. The medium has to receive those communications and messages and simply deliver them. It is not their job to judge them or try to make sense of them. That's the job of the person receiving the reading. The medium must detach completely from their ego in order for a reading to be accurate.

So yes, it might be difficult to know if a medium is "good" or not. I've had several readings. Some have certainly been very accurate and validating, and given by people who knew nothing of my history. Other readings have felt too general or just way off base, or, I didn't trust them intuitively. Still others I didn't trust because the reader knew too much of my history and presented information that was too general, or, it did not resonate with me on a personal level. Some readings have been so-so, with parts of the reading really making sense and others not so much. I've been read live on the radio, one on one with several different mediums, and by others just sharing information they received psychically as part of energy work or bodywork I was receiving.

Certainly a one to one private reading offers the opportunity for a specific connection for you and validation for the medium of their skills. A large gallery reading, like the events held by famous mediums, is more random. Chances are high you will not get a reading at an event like that. For the medium, like any job, there is a learning curve.

Many mediums were psychic and highly intuitive as children. They may have seen colors and even spirit beings when they were very young. They may have been able to predict future events. It's easy to write it off as imagination or coincidence, especially as a child. That way, we don't have to embrace or admit the possibility exists that we were right. Mediums really do see and/or hear dead people. They are gifted. As children, the adults in their lives often scold them, tell them they are wrong or medicate them for hallucinating or psychosis. It's not until they are adults themselves and feel comfortable coming out of the closet and embrace their gifts, some even hanging out their shingle to help others. Mediums and all those who are psychically gifted often have a lot to overcome before they are able to embrace and share their gifts.

The take home message is that no one has the right to judge the decisions or actions of another person. This is true no matter what the subject matter is.

Perspective is everything. We may not agree with someone else's perspective, but we are not them. We are not living their lives. We have not had their experiences. Only they have. Only they know what will help them heal and find peace. It might be different than how we might choose to do it, but that doesn't mean it's wrong. They deserve and have the right to free choice.

We have no right to impose our opinions or beliefs on anyone else, for any reason. Regardless of whether or not mediums are real, if the person seeking validation, connection, or healing receives it, that is all that matters.

A very important life lesson for everyone that can be learned through the process of seeking emotional healing after a profound loss in our lives is that we never, ever, have the right to judge anyone. We need only worry about ourselves. There is no right or wrong way to do anything when on such a profound emotional journey... only our way.

There is so much more about spirituality, energetic anatomy, and signs that I could write about, but it would quite literally fill another book! Maybe that will be the next one I write!

If you find yourself intrigued by signs, spirituality and metaphysics find a local class or check a few books out of the library and begin to explore it. Anytime you feel as if you've connected with your child in spirit, trust it. Love is powerful and it will always find a way!

Chapter Eleven

The "New" You: Weaving Your Child's Memory into the Fabric of Your Life

"Life is eternal, and love is immortal, and death only a horizon; and a horizon is nothing save the limit of our sight."

~ Rossiter Worthington Raymond

If there is one thing we learn as we walk the path as bereaved parents, it's that death is not really an ending. It's a transition... a change.

We, the bereaved, are transformed, often in profound and powerful ways. As we emerge from the darkness of our pain and grief, we must decide how we are going to carry our child's memory with us. We must figure out how to weave their life, their death, their legacy, and our love for them into the very essence of who we are. Like a butterfly emerging from a chrysalis, the colors of our wings are a beautiful mingling of our child and ourselves... of our love. They enable us to be free and to fly. To be grounded on earth yet flirt with the heavens and the opportunity to be touched by spirit.

When we become parents, we suddenly understand unconditional love. We tap into that fiercely protective instinct all parents have. We want nothing more than for our children to be happy, healthy and safe... forever. We, of course, believe with all our heart they will have that, because they deserve it and we will do everything in our power to make it so.

When our child dies, no matter how old they are, or how old we are, we lose the hopes and dreams we had for them. We often feel like somehow we failed them in our parental responsibility to keep them healthy and safe.

It does not seem to matter if we had a pregnancy loss, lost a young child, or lost an adult child. It doesn't matter if our child died as a result of an illness like cancer or if they were killed in an accident. The age of the child doesn't matter. The circumstances of their death do not matter. All that matters is that they are now gone. Even if there was nothing at all that could have been done to prevent our child's death, we find a way to blame ourselves. We may never say it out loud, but it's a very common experience.

We, as bereaved parents, tend to feel completely out of control, especially in the early stages of grief. The rug has been ripped out from under us. Our hearts feel like they have been ripped right out of our chest. We lack trust. We lack impulse control. We tend to become protective, emotionally labile, and vulnerable. We are laughing one minute, pissed off at the world the next, then crying, and finally feeling more at peace, only to find the roller coaster never really stops for very long.

When people feel out of control, they tend to grasp onto whatever they can to feel more in control. They often do so without taking into account anyone else or how they feel.

They really just can't. Grief is like that. It's born of pain. Our brains just don't function the way they normally do. How could they? We are in a place of crisis and we tend to be very emotional and reactionary. Rational thought is not easy or sometimes even possible when grieving the loss of a child, especially in the early weeks of grief.

Inadvertently, things may or may not get said and feelings get hurt. The biggest problems come from a lack of understanding, a lack of communication... about feelings... about what to do... about what not to do... about how grief works... about the situation itself.

This is why understanding the stages of grief, the experiences of a bereaved parent, and knowing how to help them is so important. This is why it's so important to recognize that recovering from the death of a child is a life long journey. It is a transformation, not something to "get over", not a condition that can be cured. Those 3 C's we discussed in Chapter six really are vital to any relationship, and are more than just tools for coping with the death of a loved one, they are life skills.

Parenthood also offers us the opportunity to see things from a different perspective. One of the joys of parenting is the chance to rediscover and see the world through the eyes of your child. Kids have a way of showing us how important the little things are. They notice the details. They ask questions... over and over and over again. They love unconditionally. Play is their work. They have no pre-conceived ideas or opinions. They have no bias. They don't judge. They express themselves freely and often. They are creative. They are fearless explorers. They are very good at simply being themselves. We can learn a lot from them, in their living and in their death.

How can we learn anything from our child's death? Just as in the gifts we received of their birth and their lives, there is a tremendous opportunity for growth, change, and goodness that can come of the death of any loved one, especially a child. Children are, in many ways, our greatest teachers. We just have to be open and willing to receive the lessons, and then apply them in our lives.

Death has a way of putting things in perspective. I remember promising Meggie after she died her death would not be in vain. I would forever remember all of her Meggie-isms, the nuances of her personality, what she taught me about living life, and apply it to my life. I wanted to live my life the way she did... like a child does.

Life is clearly all too short for some of us. Losing a child tragically and unexpectedly rocks your world and turns it upside-down and inside out. It often catalyzes us to change the way we live our lives. A change in the way we parent our other children. It impacts all the choices we make going forward.

I promised myself and Meggie the day she died; my kids would always come first...including her. Every job I've had since I've made it clear to my boss that my kids come first and if I could not have the time off and flexibility I needed to stay home with them when they were sick, on vacation, had after school sports and activities, and be there whenever they needed me, then I wasn't the girl for the job. I tell them the truth; December sucks for me, and that I always take her anniversary day off. Getting time off around Christmas is never easy, especially in health care. I'd literally quit my job if I wasn't able to get this time for my family. It all amounts to more than what I'm allowed in paid time off every year. I will take it unpaid, but I need to have the time off when I need it. Fortunately, I've been blessed to work for amazing women who get it. My current boss is a bereaved mother herself.

This was especially important during their early school years... they came first. I'm certain that has made a difference in their lives. Work, while necessary, is not the most important thing. No job is worth missing that end of the year concert or play, the big project presentation, the special awards, or seeing that goal scored or stopped. Nothing is. I'm not sure I'd have had that same perspective had I not lost Meghan.

While it's true I can't see everything now because they are older and often in direct conflict with each other in their sports and activities, I make sure it's balanced. I work less than 40 hours so that I can be there to take them to/from their activities and help them with their homework and cook them dinner. Things are financially tighter, but our family is also emotionally tighter, closer, happier, and healthier.

We talked about some of the gifts of grief in Chapter Nine. The gifts your child has left for you may be as unique as they were. They may be tangible or perhaps simply a heightened awareness or a new outlook on life.

So what can we learn from the death of our children? More than you think! I like to think about the gifts that are born out of love, life, and death as different yarns that make up the fabric of our lives. As they get woven together, we create, together, a one of a kind blanket of memories, love, compassion, and understanding. A blanket we can wrap around our heart, anytime, and anywhere.

Ways to weave memories and love into your life through life lessons, as taught by our children:

- Life is short. Seize today!
- Say I love you every day.
- Be yourself, as the saying goes, everyone else is already taken.
- Use your imagination.
- Be creative.
- Trust your instincts.
- Play hard.
- Read out loud.
- Ask questions… lots and lots of questions.
- Question the answers to the questions!
- Accept others for who they are, as they are. Not for what they look like, what they do, what they wear, or what they believe in or not.
- When you're at your wit's end or angry with someone, stop and think, how would I feel if they were gone? It is powerful. Try it.
- Play dress up!
- Be honest. Speak from your heart.
- Follow and speak your truth.
- It's okay to ask for help.
- Laugher really is good medicine.
- Be silly.
- Love and accept yourself for who you are.
- The power of forgiveness.

- The power of prayer, your faith or religion or spirituality.
- The goodness and kindness that exists in others.
- How to prioritize what's really important in your life.
- Advocacy.
- Confidence.
- Resilience.
- Humility.
- Grace.
- How much you and your child mean to those around you. Family, friends, neighbors, members of your community, and strangers in need.
- Empowerment.
- Charity - the desire to give to others.
- Community - connecting with those who can relate to your situation.
- The talent and limits of medicine.
- Doctors and nurses are human, too.
- Pets and young children sense and see things we do not.
- Innocence.
- Get on touch with your inner child.
- Joy, pure joy.
- Death is not the end, just a transition.
- How to cope with death.
- The strength of spirit. If we can do this, we can do anything.
- Have fun!
- Did I mention love? Yes. Love. Love. Love. Love. Love. LOVE.

Meggie taught me many things, one of them was the way she lived her life with joyfulness and abandon. She was often naked and gleeful about it! She was the loudest, the clingiest, the one who never slept, and the one who cried the most of all my children. She was demanding, but simply because she asked for what she wanted.

She was also the one who said it like it was, wore her emotions on her sleeve, and let you know exactly how she felt. She found wonder and joy in everything. She would giggle as she ran in the opposite direction of her brother, of course. When they would do something wrong, she'd smile sheepishly and say, "Ry-Ry did it!" throwing her twin under the bus! She thought "Happy Birthday" was "Happy Bird Day." She thought the Jingle Bells song was the Tinker Bell song. Chipmunks were "monk chicks," Caterpillars were "paterpillars," and every time she saw one she'd poke it and it would curl up. Then she'd ask me a zillion times, "Mommy, why the patterpillar a circle?" Every cat, including her stuffed ones, were all named "Duncan" after our family cat. There was no telling her anything different. In fact, if she really wanted your attention, she'd clamor into your lap, take your face in her tiny little hands so she had your full attention and say, "You listen (or talk) to Meggie!" She lived every moment for the moment. What a gift for her, and for us.

While we loved these things about Meg and miss them terribly, we incorporate them into our everyday lives, even now. We still say, "Oh, look! A monkchick!" On birthdays, we sing "Happy Bird Day to you…" On her birthday, we run around the cemetery singing "Tinker Bell all the way," since that was the way she taught us to do it. We look awfully silly but we all giggle and are silly when we do it. I like to believe she is right there running with us. It is a way to celebrate her and the joy she brought to our lives.

As you walk the path out of the darkness and into the light of healing, you will integrate your child's life and their death into your life now. It will be different and new, but it will still include the love you have always had for your child.

You will learn to weave memories, new traditions, what you've learned throughout the grieving process, and your new perspective into the fabric of your life. The happiness and the sadness, the laughter and the tears, the joy of their life and the pain of their death, it all becomes a part of you. It changes you. It is how you become the "new" you.

You, in turn, may choose to change the world! Perhaps, it's simply by example or by sharing your experience with others, so they can gain greater insight, understanding, and perspective. Maybe, you become a grief mentor or a facilitator of a local bereavement support group. Perhaps, you volunteer at the hospice where your child was cared for, or fundraise for the organization working for a cure for the disease that took your child's life. You may get involved with advocacy groups or lobby for legislative changes to make the world a safer place for kids. You may start your own awareness campaign. Those around you will see the change in you and understand what a profound catalyst life, death and love are. They will see how powerful a parent-child relationship can be! How powerful love is.

Throughout this book you have walked the path to healing. You have learned about grief. You have learned how it feels and why. You have learned what you can do for yourself and for others to support them on their journey. You have learned you are not alone, but now a part of an amazing community of fellow bereaved parents who "get" it and are there for you. You will never have to walk alone if you do not want to.

You have learned you can and will find your way out of the darkness and to a place of healing… a place where you are able to integrate your child's life and their death into your life, and move forward… together.

You will always have your memories. You will always have love. No one can ever take that away from you! It is woven into your heart and into your soul. You have learned the amazing power of unconditional love… it transcends death. No one and nothing can ever take that away from you.

It is my profound hope that you have found this book to be helpful to you in your journey. You now know that it is a journey… along an ever changing path. It's one you will continue on for the rest of your life.

You will continue to walk this path out of the darkness and you will begin to see the world in color again. It's kind of like Dorothy in the Wizard of Oz. You have landed in a new land… unexpectedly uprooted from life as you knew it and dropped by a twister of emotional upheaval, the result of the death of your precious child.

As you emerge from that house of despair, a new path is before you. There are scary and unexpected things on the path, but there are also wonderful gifts and new friends on this path. Over time, you learn what they are and how to cope with them. You will learn to integrate them all and move forward in your own life. And while there is nowhere like home, home is forever changed.

You can't click your heels and go back to the way it used to be. But you have wonderful new gifts. You have new friends who understand you in a way no one else can. You have a bigger heart. You have courage. You have confidence. You have a knowing about life that others around you just don't have. You have perspective and insight you did not have before you began this journey. You have love. You will always have love. You will always carry the love for your child in your heart and in your soul. Always.

"Just when the caterpillar thought the world was over... it became a butterfly"
~English Proverb

I wish for you love, light, and peace as you continue to walk this path out of the darkness and toward healing. May your child's spirit live on in your memories, through your words, in how you live your life, and forever in your heart. Know that your child will never be forgotten.

Remember... love never dies.

Namaste (the Divine in me honors the Divine in you).

A Letter to Meggie

My Meggie Moo,

Mommy wants to thank you, my sweet, beautiful daughter. Thank you for being you and for coming into my life. The three short years I had you were amazing. You brought so much love, so much light, so much silliness, fun, and zest for life into my life and to the lives of all you touched. You, along with your twin brother and soul mate of an older brother, brought me more joy than I could have ever imagined.

Thank you for the challenges you presented to me that helped me grow as a mama. It sure seemed like there were a lot of them! I learned to prioritize. I learned to see the simple joys in everything. I learned to savor the moment and just live in it. I learned planning is for those without twins! You made me laugh. You made me cry. You made everyone fall in love with you. Your personality was so much bigger than your teensy and delicate frame. You were wise beyond your years.

I want to thank you for choosing me as your mommy. I am so grateful for the honor and the privilege. I want to thank you for escorting your twin brother Ry to this earthly journey. I know he didn't want to come alone and needed your guidance to find the courage to fulfill his own mission with us.

363

I want to thank you for the depth of your love and admiration of your big brother, Kyle. I wish he could remember how much you adored him. You brought out the best in him. It was almost as if HE was your twin! They miss you terribly… even though you always bossed them around. You were the ringleader. The smallest and the youngest, you were always in charge and they followed your lead dutifully. Even when you blamed them for everything! They were lost without you for a long time.

I want to thank you for the gift not only of your life, but of your death. I know that seems odd. Please don't misunderstand. I'd give anything to have you back in my arms. *Anything.* To stroke your silky hair. To kiss, hug, and snuggle again. To mix pink paint for you, have dance parties, play with the kitties, chase the "flutterbies", and poke "paterpillars" to see them curl up. I miss you so much, it still hurts. My heart is forever broken and aches to have you back.

Despite the pain of your loss, you have inadvertently given me a tremendous gift. Your death awakened me to my own path in life. It became clear to me the path I needed to follow. It led to tremendous changes, emotional and painful on many levels, but also so very necessary and right. It catalyzed a spiritual journey and the realization I needed to be true to myself and my soul's purpose.

Perhaps the biggest debt of gratitude, my sweet, precious little Meggie, is what you have given to thousands of families around the world. You, my amazing daughter, are quite literally, a life saver. I am so fiercely proud that your gorgeous little face and your heartbreaking story has compelled so many others to take action to save their children from dying the way you did. You... are my heroine.

I love you, Meggie-moo.

Kiss. Hug. Snuggle.
Love, Mommy

Resources for Bereaved Parents and Those Who Support Them

This list is by no means all-inclusive. I've included many of the go-to resources that bereaved parents and those supporting them might find most helpful. For additional and the most up to date resources, please visit the Out of the Darkness website at

http://www.outofthedarknessgriefsupport.com/

General Resources for Coping with Grief and Loss

What's Your Grief?
Information and Support on the grieving process
http://www.whatsyourgrief.com/

Grief Watch
Resources for bereaved family and professional caregivers, also a store to purchase remembrance items, birth announcements, etc.
http://griefwatch.com/

Centering Corporation – A Grief Resource center
Books and information
http://www.centering.org/

The Grief Recovery Institute
General information about recovery from grief be it for the professional or the grieving individual
http://www.grief-recovery.com/

Wintergreen Press
Materials and resources for grieving families, from the author of Empty Arms
http://www.wintergreenpress.com

Elizabeth Kubler Ross's website
The author of On Death and Dying and On Children and Death a wonderful site with many resources and tips for those touched by grief and loss
http://www.elisabethkublerross.com/index.html

Hospice
Hospice.net a website dedicated to end of life issues including explaining death to children and general information on bereavement
http://www.hospicenet.org/

Suicide Prevention Hotline
1-800-273-8255

Support Groups and Organizations for the Coping with the Death of a Child

The Compassionate Friends
http://www.compassionatefriends.org/home.aspx

The MISS Foundation
http://www.missfoundation.org/

Bereaved parents of the USA
http://bereavedparentsusa.org/

Now I Lay Me Down To Sleep Bereavement Photography (NILMDTS)
https://www.nowilaymedowntosleep.org/

SHARE
Pregnancy and Infant loss support and resources for parents and caregivers
http://www.nationalshare.org/

Remembering Our Babies
Keepsake items, jewelry, and much more
http://www.rememberingourbabies.net/store/Default.asp

Places and Events to Honor and Remember Your Child

Angel of Hope
A listing of the locations of Angel of Hope Memorial Statues as based on the book The Christmas Box written by Richard Paul Evans
http://www.richardpaulevans.com/angel-statues/locations

Children's Lighthouse Memorial, Edgartown, Martha's Vineyard, MA
http://www.marthasvineyardhistory.org/childrenmemorial.php

Compassionate Friends Worldwide Candle Lighting (2nd Sunday in December)
http://www.compassionatefriends.org/News_Events/Special-Events/Worldwide_Candle_Lighting.aspx

Compassionate Friends Walk to Remember
http://www.compassionatefriends.org/News_Events/Special-Events/Walk_to_Remember.aspx

Grandparent Support

AGAST – Alliance of Grandparents, A Support in Tragedy International – support for grandparents who have lost a grandchild and information on how to help their children (the parents of the child)
http://www.agast.org/

Perinatal Loss

A Place to Remember
For those who have been touched by a crisis in pregnancy or death of a baby
http://www.aplacetoremember.com/aptrfront.html

Aiding Mothers and Fathers Experiencing Neonatal Death
http://www.amendgroup.com/

March of Dimes Pregnancy and Newborn Loss Resources
http://www.marchofdimes.com/printableArticles/572.asp

March of Dimes Bereavement Kit
Free to those who have had a loss
http://www.marchofdimes.com/printableArticles/572_3997.a
sp

Waiting With Love
For those who choose to continue a pregnancy knowing their
baby will die before or shortly after birth or who learn their
newborns will die
http://www.erichad.com/wwl/

Angel Babies Forever Loved
http://www.angels4ever.com/

A Heartbreaking Choice
For families who choose to end their pregnancies after
prenatal diagnosis
http://www.aheartbreakingchoice.com/

Hannah's Prayer
Christian support group for loss from conception through
early infancy
http://www.hannah.org/

*Bereavement Services Gunderson Lutheran Medical
Foundation*
Resources for parents and health care providers, information,
sales of remembrance rings, memory boxes, and caregiver
training
http://www.bereavementprograms.com/index2.html?default=
courses

Hygeia
A global community for perinatal health, loss, and bereavement
http://www.hygeia.org/

MEND Mommies Enduring Neonatal Death
A Christian support group
http://www.mend.org/about_our_purpose.asp

Pregnancy loss and support program National Council of Jewish Women New York Section
A nationwide support group that coordinates telephone counseling and support groups
http://www.ncjwny.org/services_plsp.htm

Remembering our Babies
http://www.rememberingourbabies.com/

SHARE Pregnancy and Infant Loss Support
National organization with resources for loss for parents, friends/family, and professionals, free information packet, support groups and chats, and more
http://www.nationalshareoffice.com/

WISSP Wisconsin Stillbirth Service Program
For any family who has experienced stillbirth
http://www.wisc.edu/wissp/

A TIME - A Torah Infertility Medium of Exchange
A group that helps with infertility and loss from a Jewish perspective
www.atime.org

Carrying to Term – a website for parents who choose to carry their pregnancies following devastating prenatal diagnosis
http://www.geocities.com/tabris02/

The Stillbirth Alliance
http://www.stillbirthalliance.org/

The Center for Loss in Multiple Birth (CLIMB)
http://www.climb-support.org/enabled/index.html

Multiplicity
Loss, prematurity, and special needs in multiple pregnancy with links to other multiple resources
http://www.synspectrum.com/multiplicity.html

Infertility

The National Infertility Organization
http://www.resolve.org/main/national/index.jsp?name=home

SIDS

The National SIDS/infant death resource center
http://www.sidscenter.org/

The American SIDS Institute
www.sids.org

Down Syndrome

Diagnosis Down Syndrome – Information about Down Syndrome and Grieving the loss of the ideal and perfect baby
http://leeworks.net/DDS/speech.html

For relatives and friends of a baby with Down Syndrome –
what to say and not to say
http://www.downsyn.com/relatives.html

National Down Syndrome Society
http://www.ndss.org/

Subsequent Pregnancies following a loss
SPALS Subsequent Pregnancy after a Loss Support
http://www.spals.com/

For Siblings:

The Sibling Connection
http://www.counselingstlouis.net/

Books for Siblings

Water Bugs and Dragonflies by Doris Stickney
What's Heaven? Maria Shriver
Where do People go When They Die? Mindy Arva Portnoy
The Fall of Freddie the Leaf by Leo Buscaglia
Sad Isn't Bad – A Good Grief Guidebook for Kids Dealing
with Loss by Michaelene Mundy
Tear Soup by Pat Schweibert and Chuck DeKylen
The Next Place by Warren Hanson
Thumpy's Story by Nancy Dodge
We Were Gonna Have a Baby, But we had an Angel Instead
by Pat Shweibert
Where's Jess? Ray and Jody Goldstein

Healing Instruments

International Harp Therapy Program
http://www.harprealm.com/

The Gentle Wind Project – Healing Instruments
http://www.gentlewindproject.org/

Helping Hands

Lotsa Helping Hands
http://www.lotsahelpinghands.com/

Meal Train
http://www.mealtrain.com/

Memorial Websites

Much Loved
http://www.muchloved.com/g_home.aspx

Legacy.com
http://www.legacy.com/ns/
http://memorialwebsites.legacy.com/

Virtual Memorials
http://www.virtual-memorials.com/

Memory Of
http://www.memory-of.com/Public/

Remembered Forever
http://www.remembered-forever.org/

Qeepr - Create and share a free online memorial
http://www.qeepr.com/

Funeral Planning

Funeral Planning
http://www.meaningfulfunerals.com/
http://www.missfoundation.org/professionals/toolbox/funeral
s

Cremation information "everything you wanted to know... but were afraid to ask"
http://www.cremationinfo.com/cremationinfo/index.htm

Do it yourself Funeral Planning
http://www.naturaldeath.org.uk/index.php?page=diy-funerals

Biodegradable Urn
https://urnabios.com/

Beautiful urns for babies, children, and adults
http://www.inthelighturns.com/youthful.html
http://www.stardust-memorials.com/
http://www.urngarden.com/infant-and-child-urns
http://www.perfectmemorials.com/

Fundraising for Funeral Expenses
Go Fund Me
http://www.gofundme.com/

Customized Caskets for Children and Adults
http://www.treyganemdesigns.com/

Memorial Gifts and Keepsakes

International Star Registry
http://www.starregistry.com/

Fly a Flag over the U.S. Capitol Building in honor or memory of someone
http://www.aoc.gov/trades-and-areas-practice/capitol-flag-program

Totally Out of Hand (custom jewelry from art work)
http://www.totallyoutofhand.com/

With Sympathy Gifts
https://withsympathygifts.com/

The Grief Tool Box
http://thegrieftoolbox.com/

Substance Abuse support

Alcoholics Anonymous
http://www.alcoholics-anonymous.org

Narcotics Anonymous
http://www.na.org

Alanon: For family and friends affected by someone's drinking/ drug use
http://www.al-anon.alateen.org

Gamblers Anonymous
http://www.gamblersanonymous.org

Overeaters Anonymous
http://www.oa.org

Food Addicts in Recovery Anonymous
http://www.foodaddicts.org

About the Author

Kimberly Amato is an insightful, compassionate, and heart-centered educator whose professional life has been dedicated to helping others overcome adversity and reach their highest potential. She does this through her work as a Physical Therapist, Childbirth Educator, Birth Doula, Reiki Master, and CPR, First Aid, and Child and Home Safety instructor and advocate. Kimberly often says she doesn't know what she wants to be when she grows up! It's clear from all that she does; her life's purpose is to help and support others in their journey.

As a Reiki Master, grief mentor, and bereavement doula, Kimberly provides insight, non-judgmental support, and facilitation of healing of the mind, body, and soul. She is passionate about nurturing others and supporting them on their journey with love, light, and a peaceful and reassuring presence. She has had the honor of supporting others through their greatest joys and their deepest sorrows, providing comfort, insight, and unwavering support.

Kimberly doesn't just talk the talk, she walks the walk; on a path no one ever wants to go down. The same one you are on now. She is also a bereaved parent, losing her 3-year old daughter Meggie to a furniture tip-over accident in 2004.

Kimberly has turned the tragic loss of her own daughter into a passionate and successful world-wide advocacy campaign dedicated to child safety. Her goal is simple; to keep kids safe and spare other parents her pain. Meghan's Hope was born the evening Meghan died, in the form of a one page email warning friends and family of the dangers of furniture tip-over.

It has grown from a website first published just two weeks after Meghan's death, to an organization and Facebook page known around the world as a go-to resource for tip-over prevention and child safety. Her blog post, *Be with Me. Just for Today,* went viral and opened the eyes of millions of people around the world to the pain of losing a child, and compelling them to take action to make their own homes safer. Meghan's Hope is how Kimberly continues to mother Meggie. Knowing Meggie's story has saved literally thousands of lives helps her heart to heal.

A life-long sensitive and intuitive helper, Kimberly has found that her calling also includes supporting others through their losses, as a bereavement doula and a grief mentor. Her compassionate, insightful, knowledgeable, and nurturing support is a gift to anyone struggling with the roller coaster of emotions associated with loss and grief. She has mentored and supported many others on their journey out of the darkness toward healing after a profound loss in their lives. It is an honor to help you with yours.

Kimberly is also a dynamic and gifted educator, workshop leader, blogger, and author on a mission to help and support others in their journey to be their best selves. She incorporates her educational background, sense of humor, spirituality, and life experience into creating a safe, loving, and nurturing environment, striving to empower those she works with to embrace and utilize their inner gifts with confidence.

Her work has been published in several trade magazines and she also blogs for a local newspaper on home and child safety. Kimberly has presented at both local and national conferences and has been interviewed by numerous local and national print and TV media outlets about Meghan's Hope, furniture and TV tip-over prevention, and child and home safety.

Kimberly lives in Massachusetts with her two sons, her husband, and their long haired fur babies; cats Lainey and Rusty. Meggie is still very much a part of their lives and she is honored and included in family events in unique and special ways. A table to honor her memory shares a place in the heart of their home, the dining area of the kitchen. Her bedroom is now a sanctuary for creativity and quiet reflection.

When she is not working as a physical therapist, teaching, writing, or taking her boys to a soccer practice or game, she enjoys running 5K's with her family, playing games with friends and family, sitting quietly with a cup of tea and watching the birds, and ballroom dancing with the love of her life, her husband, Joe.

She's only half-crazy though! Kimberly enjoys running 5K, 10K, and half marathon races, preferably in costume, because it's more fun that way! She will be running the 2015 Disneyland Tinker Bell Half Marathon and Pixie Dust Challenge in honor and in memory of Meggie, who happened to love Tinker Bell.

It's rumored she also has a not-so-secret love of chocolate and especially chocolate cake!

If you wish to contact Kimberly, you may do so at info@meghanshope.org

You can also contact Kimberly through the Out of the Darkness website at
http://www.outofthedarknessgriefsupport.com/contact.html

Find us on Facebook!

Like *Out of the Darkness* on Facebook for updates and helpful resources and links for the bereaved and those who love and support them.

For information on child safety and prevention of furniture and TV tip-overs, like and follow *Meghan's Hope* on Facebook and Twitter. You can also find us on Pinterest!

If you'd like more information on matters of spirituality, like and follow *Pathways to Love and Light* on Facebook.

38008464R00220

Made in the USA
Lexington, KY
19 December 2014